Paint Your Own
Illuminated Letters

Paint Your Own Illuminated Letters

Stefan Oliver

CHARTWELL
BOOKS, INC.

Published by Chartwell Books
A Division of Book Sales Inc.
114 Northfield Avenue
Edison, New Jersey 08837
USA

Copyright ©1998 Quantum Books Ltd
This edition printed 1999

ISBN 0-7858-1064-1
OCELYT

This book is produced by
Oceana Books
6 Blundell Street
London N7 9BH

Project Manager: Rebecca Kingsley
Project Editor: Sally MacEachern
Designer: Wayne Humphries
Editor: Clare Haworth-Maden

Typeset in Weiss
Manufactured in Singapore by Eray Scan Pte. Ltd
Printed in Singapore by Star Standard Industries Pte. Ltd

Contents

◆ ◆ ◆

Introduction

◆ ◆ ◆

Writing is an essential part of our culture. We need to be able to communicate with others by writing, to keep records of our own thoughts, and to preserve calculations and information of all kinds. Perhaps more importantly, we need to be able to read what others have written, so that we can absorb their wisdom and knowledge, profit from their experiences, and learn from their discoveries. We can take a book on any subject and glean information from it. We can take a work of fiction and be transported by the skill of the author into realms beyond our own imagining. We can read of thoughts and deeds committed to writing thousands of years ago.

All this is available to us because humans both learned language and devised ways in which to set this language down in a form that could be understood by others. It is true that there are many different languages spoken in the world, and that there is a variety of ways in which to set them down, but scholars can learn these different scripts and languages and then translate them so that ordinary people, who only need to know a language for everyday use, can read translations of anything that has ever been written, anywhere in the world. No doubt, computers will soon be readily available that will not only be able to transcribe spoken words, but will also simultaneously translate these words into any number of languages, so that all human knowledge and information will become universal.

Humans alone, of all creatures, starting from the first, primitive beings, had the intelligence to develop the most amazing ability to speak to each other, not only of the basic necessities of life, but also to express feelings and emotions and construct beautiful poetry. Not only did humans learn to vocalize these things, but they furthermore learned to write them down so that others could share their innermost thoughts and ideals. What is also astonishing is that people in various parts of the world independently but simultaneously developed their own different systems of speaking and writing.

THE POWER OF LANGUAGE

We probably all have an image in our minds of our early ancestors, their daily rounds of work done, seated around the fire in the dark of night, listening to tales of brave deeds, fierce battles, or of ancient myths and legends. Although listening, they had probably heard it all before. However, the words would be reinforced in their memories, and when they became too old to follow an active life they in turn would tell the stories to their families, thus playing their part in confirming the verbal traditions.

It would be good to think that, as humans learned to write, these ancient tales and legends were written down, but this does not seem to have been the case, for it appears that the first efforts at writing were made to record transactions, and that writing was thus first used for the mundane ends of trade.

THE FIRST TYPES OF WRITING WERE:

• Picturegrams: these were the earliest symbols used as a form of writing to convey a meaning, and each stylized symbol represented a meaning by its image. By combining several together, it became possible to express an idea.

i) A bird and an egg may have meant "fertility."
ii) Strokes descending from heaven may have meant "rain."

• Ideograms: these evolved from picturegrams, and their symbols were used to represent ideas.
i) Crossed lines may have meant "enemy."
ii) Parallel lines may have meant "friend."

• Rebus: this further development came about when one or more symbols were employed to represent something with a similar sound. (This device later became popular in the Middle Ages for use as personal badges or emblems. Abbot Ramrydge at St. Albans, for example, used a ram's head with "rydge" written on its collar; Ashton had an ash tree growing from a ton; and Sir John Peché adopted a peach with an "é" written on it.)

• Phonograms: once it was accepted that symbols could represent sounds, they became more stylized and their numbers were reduced. An alphabet began to emerge.

abc

The History of Writing

◆ ◆ ◆

THE ORIGINS OF WRITING

As far as we know, the earliest forms of writing (which used some 600 symbols) are those that were discovered in the Middle Eastern region known as Mesopotamia, which stretched from what is today the Persian Gulf to Iraq. The examples that have been recovered appear to be accounts and tallies. The writings were made on clay tablets (when they were still soft) with a stylus that was probably made from wood, bone, or dried reed. The stylus was pointed at one end and wedge-shaped at the other, and was used to make lines and wedge-shaped depressions in the soft clay.

By 2000 B.C. the Akkadians – the early ancestors of the Arabs and the Hebrews – by then the dominant power

DRAWING OF A CLAY TABLET, WITH A WOODEN SCRIBER, ONE END POINTED, THE OTHER WEDGE-SHAPED, SUCH AS WOULD HAVE BEEN USED TO MAKE THE CHARACTERISTIC MARKS.

DETAIL SHOWING THE WEDGE-SHAPED MARK MADE BY THE BROAD END OF THE SCRIBER.

in the area, were using and developing a cuneiform script. When they were conquered by the Babylonians in around 1800 B.C., cuneiform became the official writing system. The ability to write was not widespread, however, and a cast of scribes evolved which devoted its efforts to learning and writing the cuneiform system. The scribes became very powerful, for their literary skills meant that they wielded more power than their often illiterate masters. This form of writing came to be widely used in the Middle East, and was adopted by other peoples, even if they spoke different languages.

EGYPTIAN WRITING

Over the same period, a different system of writing was evolving in Egypt. The Egyptian civilization was highly advanced, and its system of writing was well in place by 3000 B.C. The Egyptians regarded writing as a gift from their ibis- or baboon-headed god, Thoth. Their system of hieroglyphics comprised around 5000 different symbols, and Egyptian scribes were very powerful and important people, because few would undertake the long training needed to master the complicated script.

HIEROGLYPHS

The word "hieroglyph" means "writing of the gods," and is derived from the Greek words *hieros* ("holy") and *gulphine* ("to engrave"). The system of hieroglyphs was mostly made up of three kinds of symbols: picturegrams, which are stylized drawings representing objects, with combinations of symbols expressing ideas; phonograms, which represent sounds; and determinatives, which are used to indicate what is in discussion. The names of gods and pharaohs were written in red pigment, or placed in cartouches (oblong shapes).

Hieroglyphs were mostly read from right to left, and this was indicated by the direction in which the heads of the creatures used as symbols were pointing. Because writing was considered to be the gift of the gods, the symbols were always drawn with great

PAPYRUS REED.

care and treated as if they were almost sacred in themselves. They were carved on monuments in stone and written with reed pens on scrolls of specially prepared papyrus.

PAPYRUS

The papyrus reed grows to about 8 feet tall, and the plant floats in great matted clumps, forming islands on the Nile. In ancient times the reeds were harvested, and those destined for the production of scrolls were split into strips. These were laid carefully beside each other and another layer was placed crossways over the top. These were then pressed, and because the natural gum in the plant would make all the strips stick together large sheets of flattened papyrus could be built up. These were stuck together to form long rolls, which were cut as needed to make up scrolls – some as long as 35 feet – for the scribes.

BOAT MADE FROM PAPYRUS REED.

When writing, the scribe sat cross-legged, resting the papyrus scroll on a board over his knees. Unwinding and rewinding it as he worked, he wrote with a reed pen, dipping it in black and red ink contained in pots at his side. The black ink was made from water and soot, with gum arabic acting as a fixative, and the red from minium (red lead oxide) and water, as well as gum arabic.

SCRIBE SITTING CROSS-LEGGED, ROLLING UP HIS SCROLL AS HE WRITES, HIS INKS BESIDE HIS KNEE.

The Egyptian state had a monopoly over the production of papyrus and exported it all over the Mediterranean region, thus deriving a significant revenue from the reed.

THE HIERATIC SCRIPT

The drawing of hieroglyphs required great skill and was very time-consuming, and so a more cursive and flowing script gradually evolved. This was called "hieratic" (from the Greek word *hieros*, meaning "sacred') because it was originally used by the priests. In the first century B.C. a quicker system was developed, known as the "demotic script" ("the writing of the people"), which subsequently became the prevalent script in use in Egypt.

THE CHINESE SYSTEM

Meanwhile, in China, another writing system was evolving – a system that has continued to be used up to the present day. It developed from pictograms and combinations, a stylized form of writing combined with phonetic signs which indicated the correct pronunciation of each group of symbols. The characters were originally written with a brush, which made thick, downward strokes and thin, upward strokes. It thus became necessary to write the strokes of the character groups in the correct order to avoid confusion. Such was the precision, and the degree of skill and care, needed, that beautiful Chinese writing became an art form in itself, one that was accorded the highest recognition. Even though the characters have hardly changed since they were first used 4000 years ago, and can now be written with a pen or even a ballpoint, the art of the scribe is still esteemed as highly as that of any other decorative artist.

THE INDIAN WRITING SYSTEM

In the fourth century B.C., a written language was already well established in India. Sanskrit – the language of the Indian gods – and Brahmi, which is the root of Hindi, were both in widespread use.

CHINESE WRITING

PICTOGRAMS USED IN THE FIRST EXAMPLES OF CHINESE WRITING HAVE SURVIVED 30 CENTURIES.

FROM TOP TO BOTTOM:

1 SUN
2 MOUNTAIN
3 TREE
4 MIDDLE
5 FIELD
6 FRONTIER
7 DOOR

CHARACTERS FROM A CHINESE POEM.

THE FIRST ALPHABETS

The writing systems that we have looked at so far relied on their ability to depict items, words, and ideals by means of a symbol, and it was thus necessary to master a huge range of separate symbols in order to compose a sentence. It was not until around 1000 B.C. that the first rudimentary alphabet was evolved by the Phoenicians. These were a merchant people who had gradually spread across the shores of the western Mediterranean. They were a tough, adventurous race of traders, and it is thought by some scholars that they even traveled as far as England and India. Their alphabet spread with them, and it was from this that the Aramaic and Hebrew alphabets are believed to have developed. Both of these languages were used to write down the Old Testament, the ancient religious books of the Hebrew, and subsequently also Christian, religion.

By about 3000 B.C. the Greeks, also a trading people, had evolved their own alphabet, from which developed the Latin alphabet. Both of these included capital- and small-letter forms; the former was used for carving on stone, and the latter for writing on papyrus scrolls or wax tablets.

FROM THE THIRD CENTURY B.C., LAPIDARY SCRIPT FLOURISHED ON THE MONUMENTS OF THE ROMAN EMPIRE.

THE SPREAD OF LATIN

As the people of Latium (the western-central Italian homeland of the Latin people) became the dominant power in the Mediterranean area and spread into western Europe, their language and alphabet went with them. They had a high proportion of literate people and writing was an important means of communication, and also of erudition and learning (from their own, as well as Greek and other civilizations' ancient classics).

The square, widely spaced capital letters that we can still see today carved on their monuments remain the largely unchanged basis of the modern English script. They evolved in that form because of the constraints imposed by the tools that were needed to carve them. However, when they were written with a reed pen on papyrus, it was possible to inscribe them in a more relaxed, and less widely spaced, form. So developed the style later known as "rustic" (a term applied to any artifact or artistic endeavor that displays a more relaxed and cruder execution than evidenced on its original exemplar).

THE INFLUENCE OF CHRISTIANITY

By the time of Christ, there were thought to be some 3000 different languages in use in the world, only about 100 of which were written down. The life, teachings, and death of Jesus Christ instigated a new religion – Christianity – one that would have a profound influence on the world and, indirectly, also on the history of writing.

Christ had instructed his followers to teach the Christian creed to all nations and peoples, so they accordingly set out to spread Christ's Gospel all over the world. The Christian missionaries were seen as a direct threat to the power of the Roman Empire and its gods, and they were therefore rigorously persecuted and suppressed, particularly by the Emperor Diocletian (215–313 A.D.). However, in 313 A.D., the Roman emperor Constantine I accepted Christianity and was baptised. From then on Christianity was the official faith of the Roman Empire. Missionaries were now able to travel to the subjugated countries of the empire, taking with them the written accounts of the life of Christ, the Gospels, and copies of letters (the Epistles) from prominent Christian leaders. They ventured far and wide, as far as Africa and India, and possibly even America.

WRITING INSTRUMENTS

The Romans developed the use of parchment, folding and cutting it into the form that we would recognize today as a book. These volumes were much easier to handle than long rolls of papyrus: they were less bulky, far more durable, and it was much quicker to find a particular part of the text by referring to a page number than it was to hunt through a long scroll. Papyrus was too brittle to be used in book form, and could only be successfully employed as a scroll.

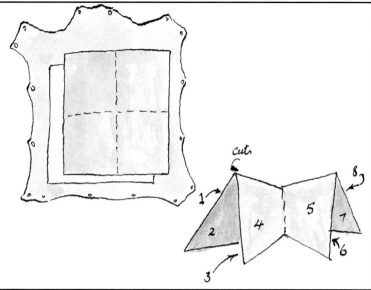

THE FIRST BOOK

THE SHEET OF PARCHMENT WAS CUT OUT OF THE WHOLE CURED SKIN AND FOLDED IN FOUR, EIGHT, OR SIXTEEN ACCORDING TO THE SIZE OF THE BOOK TO BE PRODUCED. THE REMNANTS WERE USED FOR BINDINGS AND ALL KINDS OF OTHER USES. NOTHING WAS WASTED. THE SKINS WERE FOLDED AND SEWN TOGETHER IN THE MIDDLE TO FORM THE BOOK. THE TOPS WERE SLIT WITH A SHARP KNIFE, TO SEPARATE THE PAGES. AS MANY OF THESE AS WERE NEEDED TO MAKE THE BOOK WERE MOUNTED AND BOUND WITH THICK PARTS OF THE SKIN AND GIVEN COVERS MADE FROM WOODEN BOARDS.

PARCHMENT

Parchment was made from animal skins – usually goat- or sheepskins. (High-quality vellum – its name derived from the Old French word *velin*, "a calf" – was made from the skin of a calf.) The skins were soaked in lime and then stretched on a frame. As they dried out, they were vigorously scraped to remove the hair and fatty tissues. The skins had to be correctly cured so that they were both pliable and odorless. They also had to be carefully stored so that they did not go moldy or curl.

When the scribe received his skins, he had to sort through them carefully in order to match them for color and thickness. Before use, they had to be well rubbed with pumice or a cuttlefish shell in order to remove the animal grease. The outer side, on which the animal's fur had grown, was the tougher; though both sides could be used, care had to be taken to match the pieces cut for the pages so that the same side was used. The toughest, thickest part – from the center of the animal's back – was often favored to cover the boards that made up the binding.

QUILL PENS

Quill pens were found to be far superior to pens made from reed. They were more universally available, easier to prepare, capable of finer cutting, and so offered cleaner results, and were also more durable. They did, however, dictate the styles of lettering that could be produced. Because they were cut into a chisel shape and thus had sharp corners that were liable to catch in the

writing surface and splatter ink in all directions, in the main they could only be used successfully when forming a downward stroke. This drawing of the pen downward, or to the side, gave the characteristic thick-and-thin ink line that, when carefully controlled and skillfully executed, produced letters of distinction.

UNCIALS

The Christian missionaries, spreading their creed northward as they went, had to spend much time making copies of their sacred writings. The pressures of speed, and the limitations of their tools, caused the development of a new style of lettering: the "uncial." Uncials still comprised capital letters, but they were much rounder in form. There soon developed from these the "half uncial," which was a small-letter form.

In order to write the letters properly, it was necesary to use a chisel-pointed pen, with the tip of the nib touching the writing surface parallel to the horizontal line formed by the bottom of the page. (Most people find this quite difficult, as the natural inclination with a chisel-ended nib is for it to touch the paper at an angle of 45° to the horizontal.) It meant that the scribe either had to master the art of twisting his wrist at an acute angle or that he had to tilt the page, with the attendant difficulty of keeping his lines straight and his letters upright, or else that he had to use a pen with the nib cut at a special angle.

THE DARK AGES

With the fall of the Roman Empire, its civilization, laws, culture, and arts were overrun and destroyed by a succession of invading barbarians who had no knowledge of, or interest in, such things. A tide of ignorance and destruction swept across Europe, and much that was learned was pillaged or forgotten.

THE INSULAR STYLE

In the furthermost corners of the former Roman Empire, however, which were remote from the ravaging hordes, religious works of great beauty were being produced in monasteries in isolated spots, notably in Ireland and the north of Scotland.

Removed as they were from outside influence, these monasteries evolved a style of lettering which later became known as the "insular style." This originally developed from uncials, but subsequently flowered into a script of angular complexity, embellished with intricate lacework and convoluted, swirling curves, incorporating strange creatures in its letter forms and decoration. Whole pages were covered with the most complicated and carefully worked interlacing patterns of ribands and creatures in a "carpet" design. The initial page of the Gospels was formed and filled so that only the great capital letter and a short phrase were used. In the body of the text that followed, capital letters, picked out in green, yellow, black, and red, often incorporating a weird and twisted creature, marked the start of paragraphs and verses.

THE DARKNESS RECEDES

As the ferocity of the barbarian invasions subsided, Pope Gregory the Great sent missionaries out from Rome into the rest of Europe again. These, too, took their sacred writings with them, which were still written in Roman capitals, large and small, though the rustic form was also used. In the seventh century, when missionaries from Ireland and Scotland moved back into England and then on to the continent, uncials, half uncials and Roman letters were all being used together.

With the crowning of Charlemagne as the Holy Roman Emperor in 800 A.D., a new era of enlightenment dawned in Europe. Charlemagne understood the importance of reading and writing as a way of communicating,

UNCIAL LETTERS, ALWAYS WRITTEN AS CAPITALS.

HALF UNCIALS, OR SMALL LETTERS, WERE A LATER DEVELOPMENT.

recording, and learning, and set about doing all that he could to establish literacy in his dominions.

He appointed the English abbot of York, Alcuin, to run the court school at his capital, Aachen, and also made him abbot of the monastery of St. Martin in Tours. Alcuin was given the task of revising the different styles of script that had variously evolved and of producing a standard hand to be used for the production of books. At the same time he was charged with reviewing all the texts then available and, with recourse to their original forms, removing any corruptions that had crept in over the years.

THE CAROLINGIAN STYLE

The style of writing that Alcuin developed became known as "Carolingian miniscules," after its patron. This was a small-letter, or lower-case, form, using Roman capitals. It was a much rounder and more flowing hand, for use in the body of the text. Major capitals and those in the text were written in Roman capitals, and opening lines were inscribed in uncials, as were the capitals that began verses in the text. This Carolingian style became the standard hand used in Europe until the twelfth century.

GOTHIC LETTERING

In the tenth century there began to evolve a form of writing that was more compressed and angular than the Carolingian style. It was quicker to write and took up less room on the page, so enabling economies in time and materials to be made. (In an age when there was an increasing demand for books that had to be painstakingly produced by hand this was a major consideration.) As the forms became more compressed and dense, the hand became known as "black letter," but because it developed during the period that historians call the Gothic, it subsequently assumed that name.

The Gothic script evolved in several different forms, but the two main groups are "Gothic textura quadrata" and "Gothic textus pressius." The former has diamond-shaped "feet" on the straight letters and forked ascenders on the tall letters. This style could be written with the nib's tip at the more relaxed angle of 45° to the horizontal line. "Gothic textus pressius" has no feet or serifs (lines at the extremities of the letter) at the bottom of the straight letters and is written with the nib parallel to the horizontal line of the page. Both relied for their beauty on discipline to keep the tops of the letters perfectly level and all the upright, straight strokes exactly parallel to each other and the vertical line of the page.

CHANCERY SCRIPT AND ITALIC

In Italy there evolved two scripts: chancery and italic. The papal court, with its constant need to communicate across western Europe, developed its own style from the Carolingian miniscules, which subsequently became known as "chancery script."

As the demand for books of all kinds grew with the advance in learning, there evolved a humanist script that was even quicker to write, which we now call "italic." Book production had been almost entirely confined to the monasteries before then, but by the fifteenth century the clamor for books was so great that secular *scriptoria* ("writing rooms") were set up around the universities situated in the main cathedral towns to produce the wide variety of material required.

THE ADVENT OF PRINTING

The advent of printing – the invention of the German pioneer Johann Gutenberg (1398?–1468) – heralded the death knell of handwritten and hand-decorated books. Type was made of wood, and later metal, and illustrations were cut into wooden blocks and then engraved onto copper plates (in our own time, photography has taken over this illustrative role). The manufacture of paper was developed at the same time to provide a suitable and cheap material upon which to exploit the new technology.

WOOD ENGRAVING

A block was prepared from specially selected and seasoned wood. Boxwood was found to be the best, and a carefully treated selection of wood of the same thickness as the type was chosen, cut across the grain, so that the artist worked on the end grain. The outline of the design was drawn onto the wood and the artist-engraver cut away the wood so that only those parts were left that were to be used to print in black. In doing this, a small tool called a burin was used, held in the palm of the hand so that the "tooth" projected between the thumb and forefinger. Burins were made in a variety of shapes, and by careful manipulation the engraver could produce the finest of lines and the most skillfully executed blocks.

COPPER-PLATE ENGRAVING

Copper-plate engraving was executed with the same tools as used in wood engraving, but it was possible to produce much finer work through the application of half-tone shading created by the controlled use of fine dots struck into the copper. The whole text could be engraved onto the plate, allowing for a much more decorative style of treatment and saving the trouble of resetting the item in type.

A round and flowing script of great beauty was developed by engravers, which was assiduously copied throughout Europe, as it naturally evolved from the italic hand that had become universally popular. With a quill pen cut to a point, it was possible to imitate this lettering and, by increasing the pressure on the downward strokes, the points of the nib could be spread and thus a thicker line inscribed. By relaxing the pressure a thin line was drawn, and by careful application the most beautiful and convoluted swirls and curves, with elegant, thick-and-thin letter forms, could be produced. With the introduction of metal nibs, this style of writing became

ABOVE: GUTENBERG PRESS, SHOWING CONE-SHAPED STAMPS FOR INKING THE PRINTING BLOCKS.

LEFT: A PAGE OF THE "FORTY-TWO LINE" BIBLE, C.1455, TRADITIONALLY ASCRIBED TO JOHANN GUTENBERG.

the norm, and earlier techniques were forgotten and lost.

THE REVIVALIST STYLE

At the end of the nineteenth century a movement emerged, led by William Morris, intent on rediscovering the arts and techniques of earlier days. He was repelled by the sterility and artlessness of the prevailing products of the time and therefore sought to revive the skill, expressiveness, and elegance of earlier eras.

Influenced by the stimulus provided by William Morris, Edward Johnston, after much study, discovered how the artists of the medieval *scriptoria* produced their stunning works. He developed the "book-hand" style, modeled on Carolingian script, from his research, and this has become the basic script used by modern calligraphers. Following his example, and learning from his published works, a new school of calligraphers in Europe and the United States has today elevated the art to the heights of loveliness.

ILLUMINATED LETTERS

If you walk into the manuscript room of a museum, you will be stunned by the sumptuous richness of the volumes that are set out on display. Only when you have got over the initial shock of the first, dazzling encounter, will you start to take in the extraordinary detail, the convoluted strapwork, the intricate miniatures, and the astonishing and fantastic depictions of creatures of a bygone culture, displaying richness of imagination, strength, and boldness of execution, confidence in faith, and pride in a mastered skill.

ANONYMOUS MASTERS

Many of the earlier craftsmen remained anonymous, as they were usually monks who were working for the greater glory of God. With the establishment of universities, secular

scriptoria were set up to supply the books for an increasingly hungry clientele. Of these, more information survives, and some names have endured through the mists of history to be acknowledged as brilliant artists. Some artists, however, are only known by the place where they worked, like the "Master of Egerton" or the "Baucicout Master."

AN EVOLVING STYLE

The use of color with which to enhance capital letters and to draw attention to, and mark, different passages in the text was first practiced by the ancient Egyptians, and later the Greeks and Romans. This convention continued for some ten centuries, the decoration becoming increasingly complicated, spreading from the capital letter to the margins and borders of the text, and filling every space with complex, linear decoration.

In this book I will explore a wide variety of capital letters taken from a selection of manuscripts that span the whole range of styles, from the earliest, simple, pen-drawn capitals, through the periods of flamboyant artistry, to the capitals carved on wooden blocks used in the first printing presses.

INITIAL LETTER "V" – VISIO ABDIE – THE VISION OF OBADIAH. THE ILLUSTRATION SHOWS OBADIAH OF I KINGS 18, WINCHESTER BIBLE.

Symbolism

◆ ◆ ◆

Flowers

Flowers and foliage are the most commonly used decorative subjects in humanity's attempts to render the utilitarian, decorative. Their diverse forms have been depicted both realistically and in formal stylization.

When you consider the amazing abundance and variety of flowers, as well as their beauty, color, and construction, it is small wonder that they have been used in this way. The amazing variety of leaf shapes, too, in their cool shades of green, have such elegance and symmetry that it is not surprising that they represent some of the oldest decorative forms known.

Flowers and foliage are thus a very common element in the decoration of capital letters and page borders. In earlier works it was common to find them represented in stylized form, but by the end of the fourteenth century they were being rendered with greater realism. By the sixteenth century botanical illustrations were appearing, complete with dew drops and realistically drawn fruits, berries, and insects.

CHOICE OF FLOWERS

What influenced earlier artists in their choice of flowers is not known, but there are many possiblities. The most obvious is simple preference. Another is symbolism: it may be that the flower was a badge of the household or even featured on the heraldic achievement of the recipient. It could also have been the emblem of a patron saint or have had some other personal meaning.

THE MEANINGS OF FLOWERS

Over the centuries individuals flowers have come to symbolize specific meanings. To the medieval mind the message conveyed by the flower would have been as real as a written one and, to the illiterate, more intelligible. But note that even if we think we can discern a message symbolized by the floral decoration of a manuscript we may be making an enormous assumption in believing that this was intended. However, it is worth noting some of the better-known flowers and their symbolic meanings for future use when planning your own projects.

THE MEANING OF FLOWERS...

EMOTIONS

Agrimony – thankfulness.

Aloe – grief.

Anemone – forsaken.

Balm – sympathy.

Basil – hatred.

Bird's foot trefoil – revenge.

Carnation, pink – a woman's love.

Carnation, striped – refusal.

Carnation, white – disdain.

Campanula – gratitude.

Chrysanthemum, red – I love.

Chrysanthemum, yellow – slighted love.

Elderflower – compassion.

Forget-me-not – true love.

Gorse – love in all seasons.

Lavender – mistrust.

Lime blossom – conjugal love.

Myrtle – wedded love.

Orange blossom – marital love.

Lobelia – malevolence.

Love lies bleeding – hopelessness.

Marigold – pain and grief.

Mint – suspicion.

Pear blossom – lasting friendship.

Periwinkle – remembrance and lasting happiness.

Moss rose – confession of love.

COLUMBINE

Rose, red – love.

Rose, yellow – jealousy.

Rosemary – remembrance.

Rue – regret.

Snowdrop – hope.

Tulip, red – declaration of love.

Tulip, yellow – hopeless love.

STYLIZED ROSE

PIETY

Acacia – immortality of the soul.

Almond – divine approval, favor, and also hope. (The Virgin Mary is sometimes shown with an almond.)

Bull rush – hope, by the faith of salvation.

Carnation, red – pure love. (Ancient varieties had long yellow stamens which were said to look like nails, so red carnations with these stamens were used to represent the passion and crucifixion of Christ.)

Christmas rose – the nativity.

Clover leaf or trefoil – the Trinity. (St. Patrick is said to have used the shamrock's trifoliate leaf to explain the doctrine of the Trinity in the fifth century.)

Columbine – the Holy Spirit. (The flower looks like a group of doves drinking at a fountain, and its name is derived from columba, the Latin for dove. It also represents God's seven great gifts and the works of the Holy Spirit.) Conversely, the columbine also represents folly and anxiety.

Cowslip – divine beauty.

Dandelion – the passion of Christ (because the leaf resembles a thorn).

Glastonbury thorn – the nativity when shown as a single rose with bud and leaves. (Joseph of Aramathea was said to have made a visit to England and to have stuck his staff into the ground at Glastonbury. This apparently took root and grew into a wild rose bush.)

FORGET-ME-NOT

CARNATION

TREFOIL

Grapes – an emblem of Christ, who said: "I am the true vine. My father is the vine dresser." Grapes shown with wheat symbolize the Eucharist, the body and blood of Christ.

Holly – the passion of Christ. (The prickly leaves are reminiscent of the crown of thorns, and the red berries represent Christ's blood.)

Iris (the sword lily) – sorrow and suffering. (Particularly associated with the Virgin Mary. When Joseph and Mary took the infant Jesus to be presented in the temple, Simeon took the child in his arms and said "now your servant can depart in peace, for my eyes have seen the salvation that is promised." He turned to Mary and said "a sword will pierce your soul, too." The sufferings of Mary were said to be as swords that pierced her soul).

Lily – purity; the Virgin Mary. (The angel Gabriel is depicted handing a lily to Mary in paintings of the annunciation.)

Lily, Madonna – Easter and purity.

Narcissus – triumph of divine love.

Palm – spiritual victory. (Often shown in association with martyrs.)

Pomegranate – the Church in unity; fertility. (Also the heraldic emblem of the Church of Granada).

Rose, red – emblem of the sorrowful mysteries of the Rosary.

Rose, yellow – emblem of the glorious mysteries of the Rosary.

Rose, white – emblem of the joyful mysteries of the Rosary.

Strawberry – the fruitfulness of God's spirit.

GRAPES

BROOM

PERSONAL QUALITIES

Alyssum – worth beyond beauty.

Azalea – temperance.

Bachelor's button – celibacy.

Bee orchid – industry.

Bluebell – constancy.

Broom – neatness, humility. (A sprig of broom was also the badge of the Plantagenet dynasty of English kings.)

Canterbury bell – constancy.

Carnation, clove – dignity.

Cherry – good works.

Daisy – innocence.

Dock – patience.

Fennel – praiseworthy strength.

Fuchsia, scarlet – taste and gracefulness.

Geranium, red – comforting.

Hyacinth, blue – constancy.

Jasmine, white – amiability.

Iris, rainbow colored – the bearer of good tidings.

Ivy – eternal life (because it is evergreen). Fidelity (because of the way it clings) and also lasting friendship.

Laurel – victory and triumph.

Larkspur, pink – fickleness.

Lemon blossom – fidelity in love.

Lilac, white – purity, modesty.

Lily of the valley – humility, happiness.

Marshmallow – mildness.

Mullein – good nature.

Oak – faith and endurance.

Olive branch – peace.

Peach – unequaled.

Pink, variegated – refusal.

Poppy – consolation. Head showing all its seeds: fertility in our times, remembrance.

Rose, full open with two buds – secrecy.

Rose, red and white together – together in unity.

Sage – long life and esteem; wisdom.

Salvia, red – energy.

Speedwell – feminine fidelity.

Star of Bethlehem – purity.

Strawberry – righteousness.

Sweet William – gallantry.

Thistle – earthly sorrow and sin.

Valerian, pink – unity.

LAUREL

OLIVE BRANCH

POPPY HEAD

Veronica – fidelity.

Violet – faithfulness; innocence; modesty.

Wallflower – fidelity in misfortune.

Waterlily – purity of heart.

Wheat, a sheaf – riches; thanksgiving.

Wheat, a single straw – agreement broken, quarrel.
  Also bountifulness.

DIRECT MESSAGES

Burr – "you weary me."

Burdock – "touch me not."

Pansy – "I think of you always."

Pansy, blue and brown – "think of me."

Salvia, blue – "you are wise."

Tansy – "I am your enemy."

INANIMATE OBJECTS

Hawthorn – bread and cheese (staple foods).

PERSONAL AND NATIONAL EMBLEMS

Iris (sword lily), yellow – the emblem of St. Denis,
  the patron saint of France and, as the heraldic
  fleur-de-lys, the French national emblem.

HERALDIC FLOWERS

I FLEUR-DE-LYS

II RED ROSE

III WHITE ROSE

IV TUDOR ROSE

V LILIES

VI QUATREFOIL

VII TREFOILS

VIII CINQUEFOIL

IX POMEGRANATE

Colors

◆　◆　◆

Everyone has their own ideas about color, and people tend to choose and use those colors that they like. Colors can make a statement or can harmonize with their surroundings to such an extent that they fade into insignificance.

While you may choose to copy the color schemes that I have used in the projects in this book, it is important to remember that I have chosen them because they harmonize with other projects, because they introduce a new element, or simply because I like them. Do not be afraid to change the colors that I have chosen if you would rather use different ones. Unless you want to create an accurate copy, you should regard the projects, or other exemplars, as models and guides.

MIXING COLORS

It is very tempting to buy a selection of colors to save yourself time and trouble. (You will see that I have used a selection of ready-mixed colors in the projects.) If you can, however, try to avoid buying greens, for if you do so your work will always have the same look.

There are only three basic colors – red, yellow, and blue – all the others are derived from mixing them. You should attempt to undertake your work using only these three colors, experimenting with mixing them so that you learn to produce all the colors that you need. For example:

RED AND YELLOW = ORANGE

YELLOW AND BLUE = GREEN

BLUE AND RED = PURPLE

Try mixing the yellow and blue first, as this gives the most obvious effect. Mix a dish of strong yellow (you do not need a lot). Add two or three brushfuls of clean water so that you produce a modest puddle of color. Add one dab of blue, mix the colors, and then paint a small dab on a clean sheet of white paper. Repeat with a second brushful of blue, mix the colors again, and paint a second dab neatly beside the first. Repeat this process over and again. You will thus gradually produce a range of greens, from the original yellow-green through to blue-green. Do the same with the red and yellow colors to produce a range of oranges and then, using the red and blue, to produce a range of purples.

SHADES

By mixing any color with black, a darker tone is produced.

TONES

To produce in-between shades, add gray to your chosen color.

TINTS

To produce lighter shades, add white (but take care if you are using watercolor, for white introduces an opacity to an otherwise clear color, which may look out of place).

COLOR CHOICE

In theory, if you draw a color plan like the color wheel illustrated, the colors that go together are those opposite each other and those next to each other. Colors also have a heat rating. Reds and oranges are "hot," and blues and greens are "cool."

The subject of your project will have a great bearing on the color that you use to decorate it. This may seem obvious, but you do need to plan your work so that when it is finished it conveys the right impression. You will soon discover that the most striking effects are produced with the fewest colors, so keep your choice of colors strictly limited. If you look at early medieval works, you will see that they employ the basic primary colors in many small, fragmented areas. When highlighted with burnished gold, a brilliant, jewellike effect is produced.

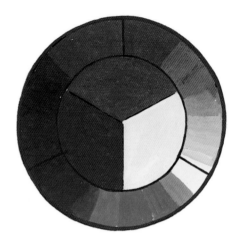

HERALDIC COLORS

Heradic colors are traditionally described by the names of gemstones and planets, as outlined in the box below.

COLOR		STONE	PLANET	METAL	SIGN
	Gold –	Topaz	Sun	Gold	Leo
	Silver –	Pearl	Moon	Silver	Cancer
	Red –	Ruby	Mars	Iron	Aries
	Blue –	Sapphire	Jupiter	Tin	Taurus
	Green –	Emerald	Venus	Copper	Gemini
	Purple –	Amethyst	Mercury	Quicksilver	Sagittarius
	Black –	Diamond	Saturn	Lead	Capricorn

THE SIXTEENTH-CENTURY ARMORIAL FAMILY TREE OF ANNE HALE;
NOTE THE USE OF THE COLORS YELLOW AND WHITE IN PLACE
OF GOLD AND SILVER.

Heraldry

◆　◆　◆

No work dealing with art up to the advent of printing in the fifteenth and sixteenth centuries can fail to take note of heraldry. In an age when the majority of the population was illiterate, easily recognized heraldic devices were used to signify ownership, patronage, possession, authority, and corporate identity. Heraldic forms and devices were so important that they appeared on manuscripts and documents, on churches, colleges, and buildings, as well as on personal possessions and everyday items. The art form has since developed over the centuries, and although nowadays due regard is paid to historical precedent, it is still evolving and will no doubt continue to do so.

The origins of heraldry lie in the painting of devices on warriors' shields that were intended both to terrify the foe and to invoke the supernatural powers of a protective deity. With the advent of metal weapons, a protective garment of chain mail was adopted, over which was worn a long, loose-fitting surcoat made of stout material. This "war coat," or "coat of arms," would be painted with the same device displayed on the shield. (The heraldic coat of arms is more properly called an "achievement.") With the advent of metal helmets covering the face, heraldic devices were necessary to identify people in the heat of battle, and so they became personal emblems of identification. At first people would often use different emblems for different occasions, but later these became both personal and hereditary, when personal emblems, in the form of seals bearing the device displayed on the shield, were used to mark possessions and authenticate documents. An absent lord who needed to communicate with his distant and often illiterate servants would send a messenger wearing a tabard (a garment decorated wth his master's arms) to prove his identity. The messenger would then display the master's seal attached to the message that he was carrying to prove its veracity. When a son inherited his father's estates, he would display the family arms as a sign of his right of possession.

Thus it was that heraldic devices became both hereditary and associated with the titles that were being claimed. Later the achievements became associated with land, and so it became common to see several different devices displayed on one shield as its bearer became more powerful and acquired more land. Each component of such a device is known as a quartering. A shield can have any number of quarterings (sometimes even more than 200).

Sometimes disputes arose over the use of arms, for it was not uncommon for completely unrelated people to adopt the same designs. Eventually the monarch's messengers, the heralds (from whom the word "heraldry" is derived), adjudicated in disputes and issued new coats of arms to aspirant "armigers," as one who has the right to bear a coat of arms is called. They also were charged with keeping records and making themselves familiar with the devices of armigerous people. When the monarch

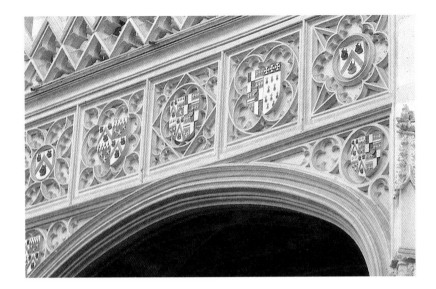

went to war, the heralds were able to recognize members of the opposition by their heraldic devices and thus advise the king of the strength of their forces. After a battle, they identified the slain.

Heraldry is still in use today, for many successful individuals continue to be granted the right to bear arms. Modern heraldic devices are devised to contain elements and designs that both reflect our own time and preserve and uphold the traditions of the last millennia. Corporate bodies, too, can draw on heraldic tradition to proclaim the corporate identity of their institutions.

HERALDIC DESIGN

Because heraldry has its roots in military usage, the few rules that govern it were designed to promote visual clarity on the battlefield. The principal rule concerns color. The surface of the shield is known as "the field," and anything that is placed on it "a charge." It is vital that the color of any charge is distinct from that of the field to enable it to be seen clearly. To this end, the colors used in heraldry are split into three groups: "metals," "colors," and "furs" (See Figure 1). Metal must never be placed on on metal or color on color. (Furs are not bound by these restrictions.) In practice, gold and silver are not used because of their tendency to tarnish,

and so white and yellow are used instead.

With only this small number of colors available to the designer, it would be impossible to keep arms unique, and so it has become the practice to divide the field into different colors. Each of these division of colors has a name that can be described in two words (see Figures 2 and 3).

CHARGES

Any object that is placed on a field, be it of a whole or divided color, is known as a "charge." A charge is usually chosen because it has some significance for the person who is to bear it. It is impossible to list all of them here, but a few groups need a special mention: the ordinaries, the subordinaries, geometric shapes, crosses, animals, and birds.

THE ORDINARIES

This group of charges is so commonly used that it is known as "the ordinaries." It is thought that the designs were derived from the shield's original strengthening bars. (See Figure 4).

THE SUBORDINARIES

The subordinaries are a group of lesser ordinaries (see Figure 5).

GEOMETRIC SHAPES

A number of geometric shapes are used in heraldry (see Figure 6).

CROSSES

The cross is a very commonly used charge and may appear in over 150 different designs.

ANIMALS AND BIRDS

Animals are very commonly used and appear in a variety of postures (the more common are shown in Figure 7). Similarly, birds often appear in heraldic art and also have a variety of set postures which enable them to be described verbally (see Figure 8). Special terms are reserved for fish and deer, as well as for parts of the human body. The limbs of creatures and humans are

shown either "couped," as if cut off cleanly, or "erased," as if torn off. (see the illustration on page 31). The lion and eagle are traditionally considered the most noble of the animals and birds, and the mythical griffin (part lion and part eagle) is said to combine the best characteristics of both and to be the fiercest creature.

SUPPORTERS

Although the shield is the main vehicle for the display of heraldic devices, it is not the only item in a complete heraldic achievement. A pair of supporters – two figures, animal or human – standing on either side of the shield and holding it up are common. (These are derived from the days of knightly tournaments, when the contestants' shields were borne round the arena by two pages).

FIGURE 1

1, 2 THE METALS: GOLD (YELLOW) AND WHITE (SILVER).

3, 4 THE FURS: ERMINE (IN VARIETY), VAIR (IN VARIETY).

5, 6, 7, 8, 9 THE COLORS: RED, BLUE, PURPLE, GREEN, AND BLACK.

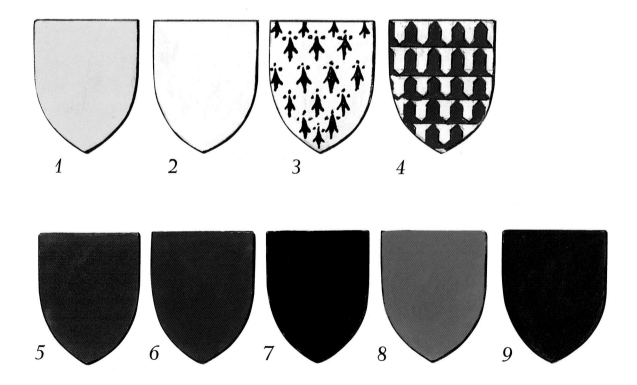

1   2   3   4

5   6   7   8   9

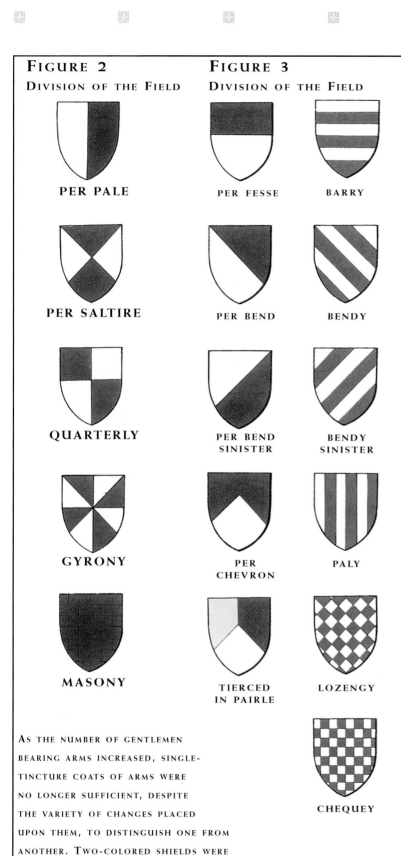

FIGURE 2
DIVISION OF THE FIELD

PER PALE

PER SALTIRE

QUARTERLY

GYRONY

MASONY

FIGURE 3
DIVISION OF THE FIELD

PER FESSE

BARRY

PER BEND

BENDY

PER BEND SINISTER

BENDY SINISTER

PER CHEVRON

PALY

TIERCED IN PAIRLE

LOZENGY

CHEQUEY

AS THE NUMBER OF GENTLEMEN BEARING ARMS INCREASED, SINGLE-TINCTURE COATS OF ARMS WERE NO LONGER SUFFICIENT, DESPITE THE VARIETY OF CHANGES PLACED UPON THEM, TO DISTINGUISH ONE FROM ANOTHER. TWO-COLORED SHIELDS WERE THEREFORE INTRODUCED.

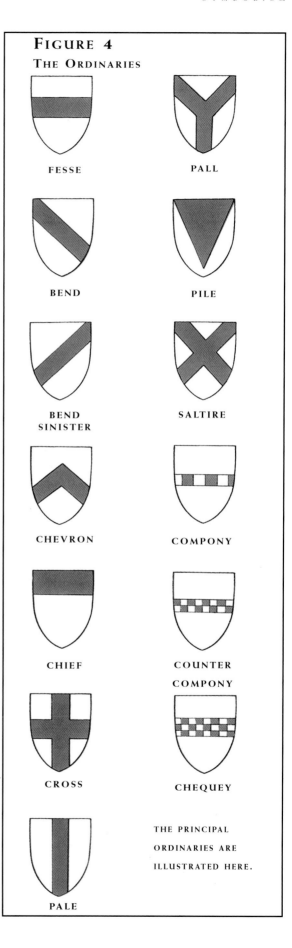

FIGURE 4
THE ORDINARIES

FESSE

PALL

BEND

PILE

BEND SINISTER

SALTIRE

CHEVRON

COMPONY

CHIEF

COUNTER COMPONY

CROSS

CHEQUEY

PALE

THE PRINCIPAL ORDINARIES ARE ILLUSTRATED HERE.

FIGURE 5
THE SUBORDINARIES

BORDURE

CROSS FIMBRATED

ORLE

CANTON

FRET

CROSS QUARTER-PIERCED

THREE CHEVRONELS

FRETTY

TRESSURE

FIGURE 6
GEOMETRIC SHAPES

MOLLET

BILLET

HELMETS AND CRESTS

Helmets appear in different forms, according to the rank of the person. The crest is displayed on top of the helmet. (In medieval times it secured the mantling that hung down behind the helmet to protect the back of the wearer's neck.) The mantling is secured by either a torse or wreath – usually material of two colors twisted into a band that fits round the helmet, coronet or cap of maintenance to keep everything in place. If the bearer is a member of the nobility, their coronet of rank may be displayed below the helmet.

The whole group may be shown standing on a "compartment," which may display a motto on a riband draped across it.

FIGURE 7
ANIMALS

A LION GARDANT HAS ITS FACE TOWARD THE VIEWER

A LION DOUBLE-QUEUED HAS TWO TAILS

A FORKED TAIL IS CALLED A QUEUE FOURCHY.

A LION LOOKING BACKWARD IS CALLED REGARDANT.

THE ANIMALS

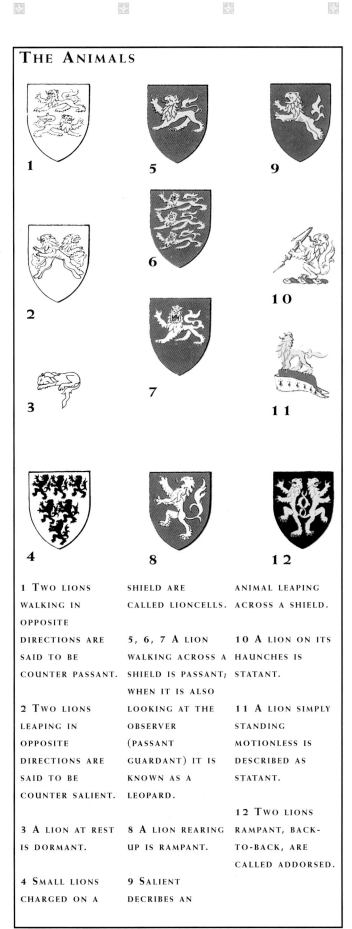

1 TWO LIONS WALKING IN OPPOSITE DIRECTIONS ARE SAID TO BE COUNTER PASSANT.

2 TWO LIONS LEAPING IN OPPOSITE DIRECTIONS ARE SAID TO BE COUNTER SALIENT.

3 A LION AT REST IS DORMANT.

4 SMALL LIONS CHARGED ON A SHIELD ARE CALLED LIONCELLS.

5, 6, 7 A LION WALKING ACROSS A SHIELD IS PASSANT; WHEN IT IS ALSO LOOKING AT THE OBSERVER (PASSANT GUARDANT) IT IS KNOWN AS A LEOPARD.

8 A LION REARING UP IS RAMPANT.

9 SALIENT DECRIBES AN ANIMAL LEAPING ACROSS A SHIELD.

10 A LION ON ITS HAUNCHES IS STATANT.

11 A LION SIMPLY STANDING MOTIONLESS IS DESCRIBED AS STATANT.

12 TWO LIONS RAMPANT, BACK-TO-BACK, ARE CALLED ADDORSED.

FIGURE 8
BIRDS

ADDORSED

DISPLAYED

DOUBLE-HEADED

INVERTED

THE LIMB ON THE LEFT IS COUPED; THE ONE ON THE RIGHT IS ERASED.

THE ACHIEVEMENT OF ARMS OF THE BOROUGH OF BECCLES, SHOWING IN THE FULL ACHIEVEMENT TWO SUPPORTERS STANDING ON A "COMPARTMENT" OF GRASS.

INSIGNIA OF OFFICE

PRINCE

MARQUIS

DUKE

VISCOUNT

EARL

BARON

EACH RANK OF THE ENGLISH NOBILITY HAS ITS OWN CORONET, AS ILLUSTRATED HERE.

GRIFFIN SUPPORTERS

FEMALE

MALE

THE GRIFFIN IS THE KING OF ALL THE CREATURES. WHILE THE LION IS THE KING OF THE BEASTS AND THE EAGLE IS THE KING OF THE BIRDS, THE GRIFFIN BEARS A COMBINATION OF THE BEST ATTRIBUTES OF BOTH THESE MAGNIFICENT CREATURES. THOUGH BOTH FORMS ARE SHOWN, THE MALE FORM IS RARE.

Basic Techniques

◆ ◆ ◆

MATERIALS AND EQUIPMENT

You may be surprised at how much equipment you will need to paint your own illuminated letters, but do not rush off to the art store and buy a basketful of different things, because in most cases you can initially use items that you already have to hand. As time goes by, you will develop your own way of working, using your own preferred selection of tools.

YOUR WORK STATION

It is very important that you make your work station as comfortable as possible. You will inevitably become enthralled with what you are doing and, before you know it, you will have spent several hours on your task. You do not then want to get up from your work with a cricked neck and stiff all over. It is also important that you have all that you need close at hand so that you do not have to keep getting up to select your tools. While this may have the advantage of preventing you from

becoming stiff, it will play havoc with your concentration and patience.

Where you work depends on both your preferences and your particular situation. I have a small studio with a computer stationed at one end and a glass-engraving desk at the other end of the same bench. My small adjustable drawing board fits exactly under the mantelpiece, so I keep all my equipment there, putting the things that I need for a particular project on a small table nearby. There is a large, full-length window, but I have become used to keeping the drapes shut as I found the extraneous light distracting when I was working at glass-engraving, and so I decided that it was better to work in the dark, with just a small light positioned in front of my face but below eye level. I sit on an old kitchen chair, which is just the right height for me; although it is not very beautiful, it is comfortable, solid, and does not wobble about.

LIGHT

Make sure that you have a good light with which to illuminate your work: a long-necked lamp is ideal. Position it so that it neither shines into your eyes nor throws shadows from your hands onto your work, thereby obscuring your view.

THIS SKETCH SHOWS
THE DRAWING BOARD
POSITIONED IN THE
LAP AND RESTING ON
THE TABLE.

TIPS

MAKING YOUR OWN DRAWING BOARD

THIS SKETCH SHOWS THE DRAWING BOARD POSITIONED AT THE EDGE OF THE TABLE TO PREVENT YOU FROM LEANING YOUR ELBOWS ON IT, SO LEAVING YOUR HAND FREE TO MOVE. IT ALSO DEMONSTRATES THE POSITIONING AND USE OF THE T-SQUARE AND RIGHT-ANGLED SET SQUARE.

TAPE

ALTERNATIVELY, YOU CAN BUY A READY-MADE DRAWING BOARD, WITH A VARYING ANGLE. THESE ARE ATTAINABLE FROM MOST GOOD ART-SUPPLY STORES.

BASIC EQUIPMENT

If you haven't got an adjustable drawing board, you can easily adapt something suitable to make one. If you have an ordinary drawing board, or a piece of plywood that is thick enough not to bend when you lean on it, you can set it up on a table, propped up on some books or a large can, or on anything else that you have at hand which suits the purpose. Make sure that the front edge of your board is aligned with the edge of the table to prevent you from resting on your elbows.

You could sit with the front edge of the board resting on your lap, but if you do this make sure that you have everything that you will need ready on a side table so that you do not have to keep putting the board down whenever you want anything. You could easily make a small board to stand on your table, using three pieces of plywood, some small battens, and a roll of masking tape (see above). Failing all these things, you could use the back of a big tray.

If you are not used to working on a sloping board, you may find it uncomfortable for a while. At first, everything seems to fall on the floor, but it is nevertheless worth persevering because it is not only much easier to view your work on a sloping board, but you can also ensure that you are keeping everything straight and that your vertical lines and strokes are truly vertical. If you are sitting comfortably and firmly on your chair, with your weight solidly distributed across the seat, you will more easily be able to resist the temptation to lean on your elbows. For if you lean on your elbows you restrict the freedom of movement of your arm, hand, and wrist, which obviously hampers your drawing ability.

Make sure that you have a side table on which to put everything that you will need so that your pens and pencils are resting on a level surface. Cut two or three pieces of paper to the size of your drawing board and tape these on with masking tape to act as a pad. You will find that all kinds of nibs will work better on this more yielding surface.

T-SQUARES

If you have not got a proper drawing board with a parallel rule attached, and you are using a board of your own devising, you can nevertheless set up your work with the aid of a T-square. If you have not got one of these, it is really worth buying because it will enable you to keep your work true, both vertically and horizontally. They are not that expensive and will always come in useful for future projects.

A T-square is literally T shaped. The head is short and thick and, when in use, overhangs the edge of the drawing board to which it is pressed so that it can slide up and down. The leg is both longer and thinner, and is, in fact, a ruler which is attached very carefully at right angles to the head.

Place the T-square on the board, making sure that it is pressed firmly against the edge. Slide the top of your piece of paper under the T-square so that both are lined up exactly. Next slide your T-square down the page without moving the paper, and stick down the paper lightly with some low-tack masking tape. By sliding the T-square up and down you will find that you can now make the parallel and horizontal lines and marks that you need.

RIGHT-ANGLED SET SQUARES

By taking a right-angled set square and sliding it along your T-square, you can make vertical lines and marks wherever you want. This will greatly facilitate any ruling and marking out that you may need to do. No doubt you will initially feel that you need as many hands as an octopus in order to do this, but after a bit of practice you will soon see that it is not as difficult as you first thought.

RULERS

You will need to use a ruler to measure your layout plan. Make sure that you can read the markings on your ruler easily – there is nothing more annoying than having to count along the ruler if the markings have become worn or obscured. You will also find a ruler useful for drawing the occasional straight line.

VELLUM, PAPER, AND CARDBOARD

When about to embark on a project, the first thing that you will need to consider is what material to use for your work. The answer usually lies in the question "What is the finished project to be used for?"

Whatever material you use, it needs to have some essential qualities. The surface must be smooth enough to allow the pen nib to glide easily across it without snagging and impeding the smooth execution of the stroke, or, even worse, catching in the surface and causing a splatter of ink to explode in all directions. The surface must also be of sufficient weight to support the work without wrinkling or sagging. If the completed work is to be framed, the material must furthermore be sufficiently strong to remain flat in the frame. If you are making a scroll, on the other hand, it must be limp enough to allow you to roll it up without creasing or cracking it. You want your completed work to look right, and so, while bearing the above considerations in mind, you should chose the material that you both like and feel is appropriate for the task.

VELLUM

Vellum has been used since Roman times and is still available today. Made from specially prepared sheep- or calfskin, it is a very durable material that is typically used for projects that are intended to last. It is also the preferred material for the very finest and most prestigious work.

If you intend to use vellum, choose your skins carefully and, if you need more than one for a project, try to match their colors. Vellum is quite difficult to store. Keep it flat in a dry drawer until you need to use it, but note that if it dries out it will become hard and cracked, and if it is too damp it will become moldy.

Vellum has a smooth side – the outer – and a rough side – the inner. It is not of a uniform thickness, so when you cut out the section that you want to use try to cut a piece that is of the same thickness. When cutting it, use a sharp craft knife and a steel rule to cut against. If you have a rubber cutting-down mat so much the better,

BECAUSE VELLUM IS A NATURAL PRODUCT, IT VARIES IN COLOR AND TEXTURE.

but you could use a piece of wood or hardboard or, for a small piece of work, a spare vinyl floor tile instead. If the finished work is to be framed, remember to leave enough round the edges to fill the frame when you cut your piece out.

POUNCE

First your piece of skin needs to be degreased. Even though it will have been extensively treated, it still has a greasy surface that will repel ink and water-based paint. In order to degrease it, you will need to rub the surface with a prepared powder called pounce. This acts as an abrasive and, as well as removing the grease, raises a fine nap on the skin which makes a key for your inks and paints.

Pounce can be prepared by mixing one part cuttlefish bone, two parts pumice powder, and a half-part of gum sandarac. These ingredients can be obtained from a specialist art supplier and should be mixed and ground together in a mortar and pestle. Sprinkle some of the pounce on your vellum and, using a scrap piece of skin, rub it all over the surface until it feels smooth. When you are satisfied, brush off all the powder into a jar to keep for future use (do not forget to put a label on it). Once the skin has been pounced, avoid touching it with your hands: even the cleanest person leaves greasy fingerprints which effectively reapply grease to the surface.

PAPER AND CARDBOARD

There is now a large variety of paper available from art stores. There are even papers that have been produced to look like vellum (but unhappily some of their colors are very bright and rather unsuitable for many projects). The paper needs to be smooth and of sufficient weight to bear the drawing; good-quality drawing paper is about as thin as you should go. You need to remember that decorative treatments are quite heavy and will cause the paper to sag. Water-based inks and paints will also cause light-weight paper to cockle – to form waves and dents.

Your choice of paper or board will depend on the size of your proposed project, and after careful consideration you may well have to settle for using a different material to your first choice, or otherwise modify your ideas.

For a big estate map that I once drew (see below), I needed paper that was 4 feet wide on the roll. I had to buy a whole roll of an Italian paper, Fabriano FA4. It is a heavy, smooth paper, which is nice to work on. It is a little stiff and very absorbent, so a drop of water spilt on it would raise a bump almost instantly. I soaked the paper, using a bowl of water and a shaving brush, and it subsequently accepted washes and other treatments. Luckily, I have since used up most of it, so it was a useful investment. If your work is to be framed, chose some bristol board, which is both smooth and stiff and will not sag in a frame.

KEEPING YOUR WORK CLEAN

However hard you try, you cannot avoid transferring grease from your hands to the working surface. This will repel ink and watercolor and will give a ragged and unclean look to your work.

It is a good idea always to place a piece of scrap paper underneath your pen hand, which will keep your fingers from making contact with the surface. Another tip is to tape or pin a piece of paper onto your drawing board, underneath the spot where your hand most comfortably rests. You can then place your work under this, leaving just that part protruding on which you are working. This will have the double advantage of protecting the piece from your hands and holding the work in place on the sloping drawing board. You could even go to the extreme of wearing gloves. I once drew a large estate map, 4 feet by 5 feet in size, containing pictures of all the houses on the estate, the village churches, views of the farms, the relevant heraldry, and so on. As this was fixed to a very large board that had to be stood against the wall while I worked on the top, and laid on the table while I worked on the bottom, it was not

A SELECTION OF PAPERS AND VELLUM. NOTE THE TRANSLUCENT QUALITY OF THE VELLUM.

practical to position pieces of paper under my hand and so I invested in a pair of white cotton gloves to wear while I was working. It was a revelation to see how soiled they became.

STORING PAPER

Try to store your papers laid flat if you can. It makes life much easier when working on a project, for there is nothing worse than trying to work on a fairly stiff piece that has been rolled up for some time – it is continually curling up and will make you very frustrated.

TRACING PAPER

You will need some tracing paper to trace your chosen designs or other elements that you may wish to incorporate into your own design. You can either buy tracing paper from an art store or you can use domestic baking parchment, which is not quite as transparent but is very much cheaper and, in most cases, serves very well. You can also use tracing-down paper.

Tracing paper is very useful, too, when you are working out a design. Draw your design and then, on a piece of tracing paper, trace over it, making any modifications and alterations that you feel are necessary as you do so. (You may have to do this several times before you are satisfied and it is ready to transfer to your project paper.)

You can also use tracing paper to produce symmetrical designs. Draw or trace one half of the design onto tracing paper. Fold the tracing paper exactly at the point where you want the center to be and then trace the design from your first drawing. Unfold your paper and you will see two identical halves which are now ready to transfer to your project paper.

TRACING-DOWN PAPER

Tracing-down paper is specially prepared paper, coated with a red powder, that you can buy from art stores. Place the sheet, powder side down, on your project paper, then place your drawing on top of it and draw over it with a fine, sharp pencil. The red powder will

make a clear mark on your project paper, which can be rubbed off with an ordinary eraser after you have inked it in.

Should you find yourself working on red project paper, you can make your own tracing-down paper in any color you want, to provide a contrast. Take a sheet of baking parchment and select a soft pastel in a contrasting color to the paper. Rub the pastel over the baking parchment and then, when you have covered it as well as you can, take a piece of scrap paper and rub it all over the baking parchment to smooth out the pastel. You can now use it as you would tracing-down paper.

FROM TRACING TO PROJECT PAPER

Take a 6B pencil and generously go over the back of your drawing on the tracing paper. When you have done this, place the tracing paper the right way up on your project paper and draw over it again, taking care to be accurate. The coating of 6B lead on the back will leave a clear impression on your project paper.

LEFT SHOWS THE USE OF TRACING-DOWN PAPER, WHILE BELOW YOU CAN SEE THE IMAGE OBTAINED.

PENS

If you intend to do your drawing in ink, you will need a pen with a fine, pointed steel nib. A steel crow quill is ideal. This has a very fine, soft, and flexible nib – the harder you press, the wider the line becomes. It is also possible to draw long, swelling lines with it that will give your work character and style.

As well as steel crow quills, other pens with thin, pointed nibs that are stiffer and make wider lines can be obtained from art stores.

TECHNICAL-DRAWING PENS

You can buy technical-drawing pens from stores that deal in art and drawing office supplies. As well as offering nibs in a variety of different thicknesses, they have a cartridge for ink which is fed to the paper through a thin tube that serves as the nib. When the cartridge is empty, it can be refilled from a special bottle (supplied with the pen).

When they work well, technical-drawing pens are wonderful instruments that will write for hours. They also have disadvantages, however. This first is that they make a continuous fine line that never varies in weight; this is ideal for technical drawing but lacks the style and elegant touch needed for fine artwork. The other drawback is that if you leave them unused for any length of time the ink in the little tubular nib becomes dry. They are very difficult to unblock and much valuable time can be lost in trying to wash them and get them working again.

CALLIGRAPHY PENS

You will not use calligraphy pens for drawing initials, but as you will need them to transcribe the accompanying text – which is as much a part of your project as the initial – it is important to know something about them.

Their nibs are chisel-shaped, which means that they make a thin line when moved sideways and a thick line when drawn downward. On no account try to push them upward, for the corners will stick into the paper and cause a disastrous splatter or even tear the paper. It is very important to hold calligraphy pens lightly when using them, so that the whole width of the nib rests on the paper and gives you a clean line of even thickness. You should also remember to maintain the correct pen angle when working across the page so that your thick and thin lines maintain the right proportions.

You can buy nibs for calligraphy pens in a variety of sizes. The size of nib that you will need depends on the size of the lettering that you require. Usually the ideal procedure is to rule two lines within which to contain your lettering that are four or five nib widths apart.

FOUNTAIN PENS

There is a variety of fountain pens made for calligraphy. Some of them write very well, others are awful. They have one drawback: most require ordinary, nonwaterproof ink to prevent them clogging up. If text is what your project is all about, this may be perfectly acceptable to you, but if you make any mistakes it is difficult to correct them.

PENS WITH SYNTHETIC NIBS

There are many such pens available for use for both drawing and calligraphy and they can be very good value. They tend to dry up if they are left unused, however, and many do not contain waterproof ink. It is also fatal to use them with watercolor when drawing, as they tend to run. But you could use them for outlining your artwork when it is dry, though they have a tendency to bleed into thick gouache paint.

QUILL PENS

Quills are as yet unsurpassed in terms of the quality of the work that they produce when properly cut and used. If you are right-handed, you should ideally chose the feathers from the left-hand wing of the bird because they curve away from a right-handed person. In practice, however, the quill is typically shortened and the barbs stripped off, so the curvature is of little significance to the user.

TIPS

MAKE YOUR OWN QUILL

THIS ILLUSTRATION SHOWS HOW TO CUT AND TRIM A QUILL ACCORDING TO THE INSTRUCTIONS GIVEN IN THE TEXT.

CUT

STAB

CUT

TRIM

CUT

THIS SHOWS HOW TO FIT AN INK RESERVOIR TO A QUILL PEN FOLLOWING THE INSTRUCTIONS ON THE OPPOSITE PAGE.

First take a sharp knife and scrape all around the end of the quill to remove the protective wax coating, then trim off the barbs and shorten the quill. Turn the quill upside down and cut off the tip with a long, diagonal cut, moving downward and away from yourself. Clean out the pith inside the quill. Now lay the quill down on a hard surface and stab the point that you have made with your cut from the back so that you make a neat split up the center. If the quill does not split far enough you may have to make the split longer by pushing the end of a paintbrush into the quill and stretching it so that the split increases. Make a second cut so that you shape two shoulders on your nib. Next trim the nib to the right thickness, taking care to keep the slit in the middle.

Now all that remains is to cut the point square – this is the most important cut of all and should be done very carefully. Turn the pen up the other way so that the front is facing upward, and place only the tip of the nib on a hard surface. With a sharp knife, cut downward at a long angle so that you leave a square-cut edge, but also one that is very thin where it touches the paper. Quills need periodic recutting to maintain their fine edges.

You can make pens from any hollow-stemmed plants – reeds, bamboo, and so on – in much the same way as shaping a quill. You can also cut notches into them so that they make double lines or produce other effects.

INK

A large variety of ink is available from all art stores. Ideally, you should use waterproof ink. India ink is both waterproof and dense: it does not become thin when you are drawing a long stroke and, best of all, it will not run. You can thus use it with watercolors and you can also make corrections.

There are all kinds of colored inks available, too, which are fun to use. One of their disadvantages, however, is that they tend not to be very dense, so at the point where one stroke crosses another you often get a darker patch of color which gives the work an uneven look. For colored work, it is therefore better to use gouache paint. Mix it carefully so that it is thick enough to remain opaque, yet thin enough to run from your pen. As well as being of a much brighter hue than colored ink, it is denser and remains constant in tone.

RESERVOIRS

One problem inherent in all pens which need to be dipped is that they very soon run out of ink – in some cases they will only write one letter. This obviously slows you up and breaks your rhythm. If you are using a steel nib, you can buy a little reservoir that clips onto the back of the nib and holds a good supply of ink, thus allowing you to write for some time. Some nib-holders also come with a little tongue that sits behind the nib and serves the same purpose.

If you are using a pen that you have cut yourself, you will need to be a little more enterprising, however. Cut a thin strip of soft tin (of the sort that is used for cigar tins) of the right thickness to go inside the stem of the pen that you have cut. Fold one end to make a hook and push it into the pen. This makes a little tongue that sits behind the nib and forms a very satisfactory reservoir.

PENMANSHIP

Excellence in penmanship is only attained by perseverance and practice. It is a skill that can be mastered, but if you are going to excel in it then you must be determined to do so and practice hard.

That point having been made, however, there are other things that you can do which will greatly assist you. You must be able to concentrate on your work, for example,

so leave yourself sufficient time either to complete the piece in one go or at least to write a significant part of it – a paragraph or sentence, perhaps – without interruption. If you stop work in the middle of a passage and then start again later you will clearly be able to see the point at which you stopped: no matter how hard you try, there will be discernible differences in your hand.

POSTURE

The importance of good posture cannot be emphasized enough. Chose a solid chair which is both comfortable and doesn't wobble. Sit upright, so that your hand can rest comfortably on the paper, and do not lean on your elbows. If your chair is not high enough, either get another or use a pillow.

SLOPING BOARDS

If you are not using one already, you will find that your work will improve immeasurably if you use a sloping board. When sitting upright in front of such a board, you will be able to see your work more truly and will thus be able to judge more easily whether it is straight. If your chair is of the right height (you may have to experiment with this), only your hand should rest on the board's sloping surface; your elbow should be free to move. You should never sit with your elbow or forearm resting on the board, as this results in a cramped style and restricts your freedom of movement.

At first, you will no doubt find that your paper keeps sliding to the floor whenever you lift your hand. To remedy this problem, sit comfortably in your chair with your feet flat on the floor and your weight firmly distributed over the seat; now take up your pen and place your hand on the board in a writing position. Next put a spare sheet of paper under your hand so that if you were writing you would write just above it. Now take some masking tape and stick the paper to the board at the sides. Slip your project paper under this, with just enough on which to write protruding. This serves three very important functions which will greatly help you when you are writing. Firstly, it stops your paper from falling to the floor. Secondly, and most importantly, it prevents your pristine piece of paper from picking up any grease and dirt from your hands. Thirdly, it ensures that you are always writing in the most comfortable position.

NIBS

Calligraphy pens' nibs are shaped like little spades or chisels. It is this shape that gives the form to the letter.

If you have a fountain pen, by all means use it, but note that these pens have an important drawback: they cannot use waterproof ink as it is too thick and blocks their little tubes. Waterproof ink enables you to make corrections, so it is preferable to use a dip pen.

Look at your nib. Chisel-ended calligraphy nibs have two sharp corners. They present a problem, however, in that if you push the nib up the page one or other of the corners will stick into the paper and make a splatter or

blot. When using this type of nib, it is therefore essential to form your letters using only those strokes that are pulled downward or sideways. Given this requirement, you will immediately appreciate that you will have to learn a completely new method of writing. Do not think of it as writing at this stage: regard it instead as drawing letters.

If you have a dip pen, you may need to "flame" it before you can use it. It may be that your nib is covered in a protective coating of lacquer to prevent it from rusting which, unless removed, will repel ink and thus prevent the nib from working as it should. To remove the lacquer, pass the nib briefly though a match or lighter flame and the lacquer will burn off with a little puff of smoke. As soon as you see this happening, plunge the nib into some ink to quench it. It should now write perfectly.

To start off with, I recommend that you use a medium- or 2'-sized nib. This will produce much larger letters than you are probably used to, but at this stage you are still learning how to form the letters, so you need to be able to see what you are doing clearly.

LOADING THE PEN WITH INK

These instructions apply only to dip pens; fountain and synthetic-nib pens have their own ink supplies already fitted.

It is very important not to try to write if there is any ink on the front side of the nib (the convex face) as this will cause overinking and blobs. You should load your pen

SHARP CORNERS

FRONT → ← **BACK**

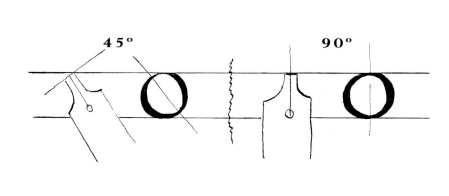

45°   **90°**

with ink using a brush kept in the bottle. Simply take a brushful and scrape the edge of the brush against the back of the nib; the ink is squeezed into the hollow of the nib, with none collecting on the front. This is also a very useful method when you have mixed up a small amount of gouache paint with which to write, say, just one capital letter and there is insufficient into which to dip the nib. However, I find this method far too slow for writing ordinary text.

When I am writing with my right hand, I hold a piece of tissue paper in my left hand. I dip the nib into the ink and scrape off as much of the ink adhering to the front side as I can on the side of the bottle and then I wipe the front side on my piece of tissue. This procedure removes

any ink from the front effectively, leaving me ready to proceed.

One last thing: if you are using waterproof ink, wash out your pen with clean water when you have finished, otherwise it will become clogged up and caked with encrusted ink.

WRITING

Lower your hand onto the paper and let the nib sit on the page at the angle that is most comfortable for you. (Ideally, the nib should touch the paper at an angle of approximately 45°.) Allow the nib to rest lightly on the page, for if you grip too tightly the whole width of the nib could be prevented from resting on the paper, resulting in a ragged, inconsequential line. So, relax and allow the pen to glide smoothly across the page. When you start to use a quill pen, which is much softer than a metal nib, you will have to be even gentler.

Draw the pen down the page so that it makes its thickest line. Now draw it across the page so that it makes its thinnest line. In this way, produce a series of dog-tooth patterns: thick, thin, thick, thin, and so on. This shows

you what the pen is capable of doing. As you inscribe the forms for the letters, it is vital that you do not alter the angle of the nib in relation to the writing line. It is this constant angle, and your careful manipulation of it, that produces graceful shapes.

LETTERS

I have drawn the alphabet to show you how to form the letters (see page 41). Look at the drawings and then carefully follow them. Practice the letters in groups of similar shapes. Start with the "O" shapes, then the "L" shapes, then the "N," and finally the oddments. Leave the "A" and "S" shapes until last, as these are quite tricky.

The letter "O" is the "mother" of the alphabet. You will notice that this "O" is thinnest at the top and bottom and widest at the two sides. You can replicate this effect exactly if you place your pen on the paper parallel to the writing line and draw first one curve downward and then the other. (Note that you should always make an "O" with two strokes, each starting from the thinnest part at the top and then pulling downward in a swelled curve so that they meet at the bottom.)

RULING THE PAGE

When ruling your page, remember that you need to allow space for the ascenders and descenders (stalks and tails). There is nothing more unsightly than a mess of ascenders and descenders inextricably entangled with each other. If the body of the text is to be of five nib widths, it is usual to allow four nib widths for ascenders and three for descenders, and so for each line of writing you need to allow four for the ascenders, five for the body text, and three for the descenders, making a total of twelve.

Make a mark at every twelfth nib width on a piece of scrap paper or on your backing sheet to use for future reference. Take the measurement with your dividers and mark it down the side of the project page. Now take a line marker made from two compasses and set the two pencils on the two lines that you drew to contain the body of the text. Rule a pair of lines – the bottom one must be ruled on the first of the twelve nib widths that you have marked – until all the lines have been ruled. It is a good idea to pencil a small cross within the lines intended for the body of the text at this stage.

SPACES AND COUNTERS

Spaces are the gaps between the letters and words and counters are the spaces within the letters. These are just as important as the strokes of the letters, for your aim is to produce a page of text that looks even. The text will look too dense if the spaces and counters are too close together and too loose if they are too far apart. The space between the letters should be equal to the size of a lower case "n."

MAKING CORRECTIONS

Provided that you have used waterproof ink, if you have written a wrong letter you can write the correct letter over the wrong one and then paint out any remaining parts of the wrong one that still show with permanent-white gouache.

If you are using colored paper, you will have to adjust the color of the permanent white to match the paper by mixing it with gouache. If you have made a mistake on a drawing, paint out the bits that are wrong; if you intend to color it afterward, however, you may have to cover the whole area that is to be that color with paint so that the white does not show up as a patch in your final color. If you are working on vellum, you can scrape off the ink with a scalpel or craft knife (but do so with care).

If you are using nonwaterproof ink, however, you have a bit of a problem, because the ink will bleed into any pigment that is painted over it. You could try painting over the offending ink with some diluted white glue to seal it, and then paint over that with white.

PENCILS AND ERASERS

You can get by with only one pencil, but a selection will serve you better. Use an HB for normal work and a 2H for drawing and tracing. A 2B is probably the most useful for general-purpose drawing, while a 6B can be used for blackening the back of tracing paper. You must also have a good pencil-sharpener.

It is vital that you have an eraser which you can rely on to do a good, clean job without leaving a greasy smear on the paper. I like a soft, white one and cannot get on with a putty eraser, but if it suits you then by all means use one. The main thing is to keep it clean and to throw it away when it starts to get hard. If it gets very dirty, rub it on a clean piece of paper, which should clean it up. Be very careful if you are using your eraser near gouache paint as it will smudge the paint.

PAINTING TOOLS

Your work will usually be done in watercolor and gouache, so choose your brushes from among the watercolor selection. Watercolor brushes come in a rather daunting variety of sizes and qualities. The sizes that I have found most useful are Nos. 6, 2, 1, 00, 000, and 00000. As regards quality, buy the best that you can afford. Sable brushes are the best, being the most springy and retaining a good load of paint. I find camel-hair brushes altogether too soft and "lazy." There are some good synthetic brushes available at a very reasonable cost, and I also use these; they work very well and last for some time, as long as I treat them carefully. It is worth getting a larger brush for applying washes if you wish to tint large areas, and also for wetting large pieces of paper so that you can stretch them.

When you have finished using your brush, wash it out carefully with some warm, soapy water and draw it to a point through your fingers. Then stand it upright in a jar or some other receptacle to dry.

Ultimately, you will use whatever receptacle takes your fancy as a water pot. You can buy special pots with wide bases that are not so likely to be knocked over as others or, like me, you can use an old preserve jar. Fill it about half full so that you can swish your brush around without the danger of splashing everything in the vicinity.

Remember that a good artist never works with dirty water. If you try to use blue paint with water that is tinted yellow, for example, you will produce a shade of green. If your water is anything other than clean it is not water but weak paint, which will spoil your clean tints.

There are numerous types of palettes that you can buy, but if I want to make up a quantity of gouache to use instead of ink I do so in a white plastic bottle top which gives sufficient depth in which to dip with nib without having to mix up a huge quantity. When I have finished, I leave the mixture to dry; when I need it again I add water and more pigment if necessary.

If I want to mix colors, I use a clear-plastic tray, of the type that supermarkets often pack four items of fruit in and which thus has four convenient divisions. Because the tray is very light, I can attach it to my drawing board with a piece of masking tape and thereby keep it close at hand. Being clear, the white paper shows through it and I can easily see the tone of color that I am mixing.

WATERCOLORS

Watercolors come either in cake form or in tubes. The colors are clear and allow the paper to glow through, which gives them a translucent effect. If you are going to paint miniatures within your letters, you will need some watercolors.

If you buy a set of paints, you will be given a range of colors to work with. If you intend to buy individual colors, however, chose crimson alizarin, light red, yellow ocher, cadmium yellow, ultramarine, and cobalt blue, as well as ivory black. You will notice that this selection gives you two different reds, yellows, and blues – you should be able to mix all the colors that you will need from these. The black will help you to tone your colors. If you cannot be bothered to mix up your own colors, you should also buy burnt sienna and Vandyke brown. These two browns will both save you some time and help you tone other colors in a less muting way than black.

Do not forget that watercolors are transparent. You do not need white, as your paper will generally be white and will shine through your washes, lightening the colors.

GOUACHE

Gouache is essentially a watercolor that is sold in a tube, but it is more thick and opaque than watercolor proper. When it is correctly diluted with water, it should give a dense, even color, allowing no trace of the paper to show through. (If you have difficulties getting the correct consistency, mix a little permanent white with your chosen color – not enough to change the tone radically, but sufficient to make the density thicker.)

Because gouache colors are opaque, they do not mix as well as ordinary watercolors, which means that you will need to buy some extra colors, especially those in the purple/violet range which are difficult to create by mixing.

Gouache colors are used in the majority of our projects as they have a clear and bright brilliance that cannot be matched by watercolors. If I want a pure color, I take the paint straight from the top of the tube, mixing in a drop of water to make it creamy enough to use. If I need to mix colors, I squeeze small amounts of the required tones onto a palette and then mix them together on this. (Note: gouache is a little like mustard, however, you nearly always take more than you need and so end up wasting more than you use.)

TEMPERA

Tempera consists of finely dried pigment mixed with egg yolk and a little water to make it usable. It is quite difficult to handle and apply satisfactorily. It is, however, a very durable medium, and was used on ancient manuscripts with the result that they are as luminous and brilliant today as when they were first created.

GOLD

Specks and larger areas of burnished gold on the page give little flashes of light that illuminate the work and give it a touch of exotic luxury.

POWDERED GOLD

When powdered gold is applied to the work, it adds a rich glow to the design that highlights the colors – particularly the lighter ones – with a mellow luster. When dry, powdered gold has a gritty appearance, but because the particles are very small the little glints of light that they give off are subtle. If this gives the desired effect all well and good, but by carefully burnishing the gold it will appear smoother and not so dull nor as sparkly.

Powdered gold can be purchased in both liquid and paste gouache forms and is very easy to apply with a small brush. You can also buy it made up as either poster paint or ink. Traditionally, you could buy loose powdered gold, which was mixed with a little distilled water and gum arabic. These ingredients can still be purchased from art stores today if you want to work in the traditional way. It is also possible to buy powdered gold (shell gold) that has been prepared in little cakes which can be used like cakes of watercolor.

However it has been prepared, it is very important to keep stirring the medium in order to keep the gold in suspension. Do not dip your brush too deeply into the mixture, or it will simply clog up. Paint with short, almost dabbing, strokes and take care to cover the work evenly, unless it is your intention to allow the background color to show through. (This can be a very effective treatment which adds considerable richness to the work, so it is worth experimenting with it.)

Powdered gold is useful for small details, as it is easier to apply than gold leaf. It is also very useful for painting a diaper (a decorative, brocadelike pattern painted over a base color which breaks up the latter and adds greater richness).

When washing your brushes, do so in a small pot with only a little water, to prevent wasting the gold and literally pouring it down the drain. As the gold sinks to the bottom, the water can be poured off every so often.

You will eventually accumulate a usable amount of gold that would otherwise have been lost.

GOLD LEAF

Gold leaf gives a flashing, brilliant effect. Considerable skill and a lot of practice is required to lay it effectively – indeed, it is much easier to describe than to do. Perseverance and patience are the watchwords.

Gold leaf is sold in little books or in loose-leaved packets. It comes in two forms: transfer gold and gold leaf proper. Transfer gold looks like a coating of finely powdered gold mounted on a tissue backing sheet. Gold leaf is a leaf of gold that has been rolled so thinly that it cannot sustain its own weight and therefore has to be mounted on a sheet of tissue paper. It is extremely fragile and will collapse very readily. It also tends to stick to itself, so you must take great care not to let the sheets of gold leaf fold in on themselves.

When applying it to the work, the gold leaf can either be laid flat on the paper or else the form to be gilded can be raised. (It is these raised forms that reflect the light to provide the flashing appearance of fire when they have been properly burnished.) Gold leaf will only stick to your work with the help of adhesive.

LAYING FLAT GOLD LEAF

First paint the area to be gilded with a suitable sizing substance. (Traditionally, this was made with gum-ammoniac crystals dissolved in a little hot water; white glue, diluted with some water, will do just as well.) Paint two coats of sizing, allowing the first coat to dry well, since it soaks into the paper. After about half an hour, take the sheet with the gold leaf on it and lay it on the paper, gold side down. Carefully and thoroughly rub and press over the area. The gold will stick to the sizing and come off the backing paper. Ideally you should use a burnisher to do the rubbing. Its versatile shape allows you either to rub gently, using the broad side, or delicately, using the tip.

If you are not satisfied with the result, lay another coat of gold directly onto the first – the gold will stick to the gold on the page. Now put away your sheet of gold carefully and take up either a piece of baking parchment or some tracing paper and lay it over the gilded image. With the burnisher, gently burnish the gold through the covering paper, taking particular care with the edges. Continue until you are satisfied with the level of brilliance.

LAYING GOLD ON A RAISED FIGURE

When it has been carefully gilded and thoroughly burnished, a raised capital letter attracts and reflects the light in such a way that it makes the page appear to be alight.

The item must first be carefully drawn in pencil. The body of the form must now be built up with the application of a material to give it weight and shape. This is usually done by painting on two or three coats of gesso.

Gesso is a thick, creamlike substance which, when dry, leaves a raised surface on the page; a second or third coat will raise the surface even higher. Gesso is quite tricky to use. It needs to be of a sufficiently thick consistency to form a raised body of material when dry, but it also has to be runny enough to flow off the brush or nib when it is being applied. Unfortunately, these requirements are not compatible, so it is better to opt for a thin consistency in order to apply it, and then add a second coat.

When you are laying it on, ensure that there are no bubbles, for when it is dry these will look like little craters. (If you make any such bubbles while applying the gesso, prick them with a pin.) When it is dry, scrape it carefully to remove any unevenness. When you are satisfied that your raised form is as good as you can make it and it has dried out properly, you can

then apply the gold leaf. (If you use a commercial gesso you will also need to buy some prepared sizing, which you should first apply to your dry form and then leave for a couple of hours.) In order to make the gold leaf adhere to your form, you need to moisten it. Make a small tube from a rolled-up piece of paper and blow three or four soft breaths through it onto your figure.

If your gold leaf is in book form, carefully cut off a piece of gold and backing paper of the right size; use a pair of tweezers or a small paintbrush to manipulate the cut fragment into place. If it is in loose-leaf form, take the loose page and lay it over your form with the utmost care, allowing as little waste as possible.

With the burnisher, gently rub over the backing paper. Continue until all the gold has become separated from the backing paper and has adhered to the form. Remove the backing paper and examine the result – it may be that another coat of gold is needed. If only a small area of the form is still wanting, use some of the pieces of gold that may still be adhering to the backing paper. When you are satisfied that you have covered all the form, trim it with a craft knife if necessary.

PROJECTS

The projects presented in this book have been chosen to give an overview of the development of the art of illustrated initials, from the time when simple pen-drawn decorations were used up to the time when they were superseded by the advent of printing and the concurrent use of reusable wooden printing blocks for forming letters. I recomend that you work through them, gradually building up your skills.

The skills required for these projects will both tax your patience and satisfy your creative urges, demanding as they do a wide range of required talents. You will need to develop your abilities of both penmanship and draftsmanship. You will have to extend your ability to be meticulous and consider fine detail. You will need to develop your skills as a colorist and miniature painter. You will be able to put all these skills together to extend your abilities as a designer when you start to use what you have learned to adapt some of these marvelous pieces of work for your own use.

Projects

◆ ◆ ◆

PATER NOSTER
qui es in cælis
sanctificetur nomen
tuum. Adveniat regnum tuum.
Fiat voluntas tua, sicut cælo
et in terra
panem nostrum
quotidianum danobis
hodie. Et dimitte nobis
debita nostra, sicut et nos
dimittimus debitoribus
nostris.
Et ne nos inducas in
tentationem.
Sed libera nos a malo.
AMEN.

Roman Capitals

❖ ❖ ❖

The Roman letters A.M.D.G. stand for the Latin words *ad majorem dei gloriam:* "to the greater glory of God." I have put them at the beginning of the projects to remind us that our study of illuminated letters is more than simply the pursuit of an artistic whim, and that if we can see it in a more spiritual light we will find the patience to persevere when things get difficult. They also remind us that the basis of the script that we use today is founded upon the Roman capital letters that were carved in stone two millennia ago.

The transcription of these Roman letters makes a very useful first exercise. It will allow you to practice using some of your equipment on an easy project that has a good chance of success. Completing the project will boost your confidence.

YOU WILL NEED

❖ Paper

❖ Masking tape

❖ T-square

❖ Right-angled set square

❖ Sharp 2H pencil

❖ 6B pencil

❖ Eraser

❖ Masking fluid

❖ Nos. 1, 6 and 0000 brushes

❖ Palette

❖ Gouache paint: yellow ocher, permanent white, red ocher

❖ 4 thumb tacks (optional)

1 Place your paper squarely on the drawing board using a T-square or parallel motion. Lightly tape it down.

2 Draw in the horizontal lines at the top and bottom of the rectangle that will contain the letters and mark the positions of the top and bottom of the letters. (If using a T-square, make sure that the head remains in contact with the edge of the board or your lines will be neither parallel nor straight.)

3 Keep a diagram of Roman capital letters to hand. Note the different proportions of the various letters, but use them as a guide rather than an exact measurement.

4 Slide the T-square down the paper so that your drawing area is a little above it. Take up the right-angled set square and rest it on the T-square. By sliding it back and forth you can draw all the vertical lines that you need to complete the rectangle and the position of the letters. (Note that it is easier to mark the middle of the letters.)

5 Untape the paper. You should work on a flat surface from now on.

6 Lightly draw the rest of the letters, taking care to define the thick and thin strokes. If you get it wrong, make your alterations with an eraser, but note that if you have drawn thick, bold lines by pressing down hard you will not be able to do so. Draw the curves of the "D" and the "G" freehand, remembering that they should fit into an "O" shape.

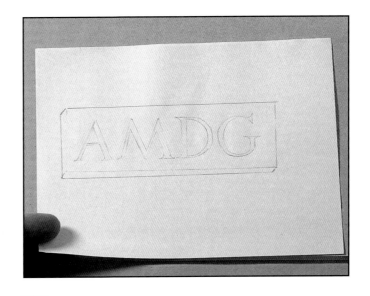

9 Place tracing paper on your final working paper (shaded side down). Tape down, and copy over your drawing – making sure the tracing paper does not move.

7 Carefully trace the design from the original using a 2H pencil.

8 Turn over the tracing paper and go over the back of the design with a 6B pencil. Now turn it up the right way.

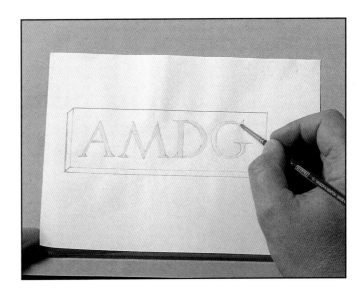

10 With the No. 1 brush, carefully paint masking fluid onto the letters. It is important that you cover the letters but get no masking fluid on any other part of the paper.

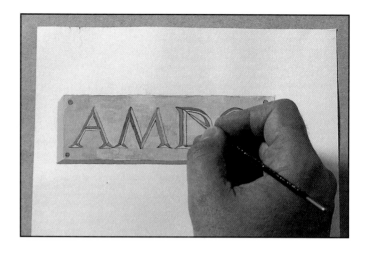

11 Mix a little yellow ocher with enough water to make a milky consistency and paint all over the rectangle with the No. 6 brush to make a good, even wash.

12 When the wash is dry, carefully rub off the masking fluid with an eraser.

13 The letters should appear to be cut into stone; these "cuts" have a dark and a light side. With a pencil, lightly draw the central line of the "cuts" in the middle of each of the limbs of the letters. Mix a little permanent-white gouache with some of the previously prepared ocher wash and paint the light side of the letters and the end of the slab, using the No. 1 brush.

14 Mix a little red-ocher gouache with the wash and paint the dark side of the letters and the bottom of the slab.

15 Take up a little clean water with a No. 0000 brush and drop it into the mouth of a tube of permanent white to make the paint creamy enough to paint a highlight onto the exposed edges of your letters and the part of the slab facing the light. You only need to make the lightest indication of a line.

16 When it is dry and you are satisfied with it, pin your work to the wall as a reminder in the future that your hard work can have successful results!

Seventh-century Fish

❖ ❖ ❖

The two fish depicted in this project are from a seventh-century Italian gospel. Fishes are very adaptable creatures to use in letter forms, as they can be straight or curved.

YOU WILL NEED

❖ Tracing paper

❖ Project paper

❖ 2H and 6B pencils

❖ Masking tape

❖ Gouache paint: ultramarine, crimson lake, brilliant yellow, flame red, lamp black, purple lake, madder carmine

❖ Crayons in the same colors as the gouache paints (above)

❖ Nos. 2 and 0000 brushes

1 Trace the design from the original using a 2H pencil. Turn over the tracing paper and go over the back of the design with a 6B pencil. Now turn it up the right way.

2 Remove the tracing paper and quickly trace the design again onto a piece of spare paper. Color the design on the spare piece of paper with crayons to test that you are satisfied with the color scheme that you intend to use. (You may feel that this step is unnecessary and be quite happy with the colors as they are. However, it is worth doing, because as well as testing the colors for this particular project, you can keep the crayoned roughs for reference and as source material for future projects. Note: I may not specify this step in future projects.)

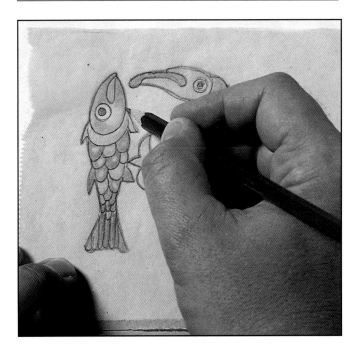

TIP

OUTLINING

Outlining requires practice. However, it is worth mastering the technique because it draws everything together, tidies up the loose edges, and adds a crispness to the work. Paint straight from the tube, adding water to the mouth until the paint is the consistency of thin cream. Use the smallest brush that you have. Hold quite close to the tip so that it is almost vertical when you use it. Steadily stroke your way round the outlines, overlapping each stroke as you go. You need to paint the thinnest line that you can manage and keep constant. Do not worry if you end up with a slight irregularity in width, but try to avoid painting an overly heavy line as this spoils the whole effect. You can correct or tidy up the odd wobble or stray whisker on the outside with permanent white.

5 Paint the red, yellow, and green areas using a No. 2 brush and flame red, brilliant yellow, and a mixture of ultramarine and yellow. Take the color directly from the tube, introducing just enough water to make the paint a thin, creamlike consistency. Take care not to paint outside the segments of color so that the hues are kept clean and the striking effect of the pattern is not diluted.

6 Outline the design with madder carmine and a No. 0000 brush (see tip).

3 Tape down the tracing paper. Draw over the design again with a sharp 2H pencil. An impression of the design will be left on your paper from the 6B lead on the back.

4 Mix a little ultramarine and crimson lake, well diluted with water, to make a violet color, and paint these areas. Leave the white of the eye unpainted. Fill in the black of the eye with lamp black or a pen.

Ninth-century "M"

❖ ❖ ❖

This handsome "M" has been copied from a ninth-century gospel. It is a good project to help get you started because it requires you to be neat and exact, so that all the lines which make up its shape are properly parallel to each other and all the blocks are straight. You should do your best to paint and finish it without the aid of a ruler. In this way you will preserve the essential correctness of the design but retain the individuality of hand-done work, which gives freshness and interest.

1 Trace the outline with a 2H pencil and go over the back with a 6B pencil.

2 Trace the design onto a piece of rough paper and color it with crayon to test the color scheme.

3 Trace the drawing onto your project page, checking the image against the original and making corrections as necessary.

4 Paint the red, blue, and green areas straight from the tube, using flame red, ultramarine, and permanent green (light) and a No. 2 brush. Now mix a lavender color from a watery solution of ultramarine and crimson lake and paint the appropriate areas.

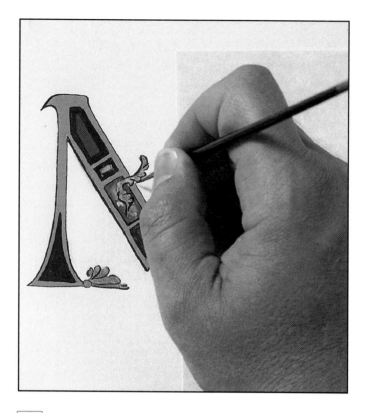

5 Mix a little yellow ocher with some water to make a creamy consistency and then paint the yellow areas, making sure that you preserve the integrity of the straight and parallel lines.

6 Mix some madder carmine with a little water to make a thin, creamy consistency and, with the greatest possible care and using a No. 0000 brush, outline the design with a slim, slender line.

7 You may now need to correct the outline from within, using the color that it covers; use permanent white on the outside.

Eleventh-century Spanish "A"

❖ ❖ ❖

hese two fish form an elegantly simple letter "A," and were taken from a copy of an eleventh-century Spanish Bible. They offer a good opportunity for you to practice your outlining. As the project is quite short and the design uncluttered you will be able to work on your outlining without having extra visual distraction. With the longer projects that come later on in the book, where maintaining a crisp outline is so important, it is better to leave this task until you are fresh. However this design will not take long to complete, so you can finish it in one go. Furthermore, the color scheme is bright and clear, so you will easily be able to see and correct your outline.

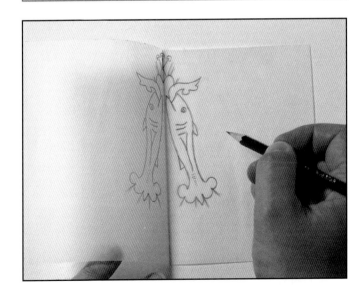

YOU WILL NEED

❖ Tracing paper
❖ Project paper
❖ 2H and 6B pencils
❖ Nos. 2 and 0000 brushes
❖ Gouache paints: yellow ocher, madder carmine
❖ India ink
❖ Steel crow quill

1 Trace the fishes with a 2H pencil. If you want them both to be identical and symmetrical, trace only one on one side of your tracing paper. Fold the tracing paper in half, at the point where the middle would have been had you traced the pair. With the first fish on the underside, trace over the outline of the second fish on the top side. You should now find two identical fishes nose to nose when you open up the paper. (This is a very useful method if you have to draw anything that has two symmetrical elements, such as swags, cartouches, shields, hearts, and so on.)

2 Pencil over the back of your first tracing with a 6B pencil. Place the tracing on your project paper and trace down the design.

3 Take some yellow ocher mixed with enough water to make a weak wash and quickly but carefully paint over each fish with a No. 2 brush, leaving out the eyes.

4 While the wash is still wet, paint the fishes all over, using a No. 2 brush and taking paint directly from the tube of yellow gouache. The damp surface will create an opaque, all-covering coat that is both dense and even.

5 Mix some madder carmine with water until its consistency is like soft cream. (It needs to be runny enough to flow onto the work easily without picking up the yellow ocher underneath. It also needs to be thick and opaque enough to cover both the yellow pigment and the white of the paper.) Outline the images using a No. 0000 brush. If necessary, tidy up the outline on the inside with yellow ocher and on the outside with permanent white. Paint the pupil of the eye with madder carmine.

6 With a steel crow quill and India ink, draw in the fish scales. (Take care not to have too much ink on the pen or it will bleed into the paint. Also try to make sure that you do not press too hard when you are drawing on the paint, otherwise you will cut into the surface with the sharp nib.) Finally, draw the fountain.

Twelfth-century German "S"

❖ ❖ ❖

This elegant "S" comes from a twelfth-century German Bible, and is a test of your drawing skills as much as your coloring ability. The creatures in this letter put one in mind of two puppies disputing over a leash. Whether they had any symbolic significance, we no longer know.

1 Trace the design using a 2H pencil. Go over the back with a 6B pencil and then trace it down onto your project paper.

2 Paint the two creatures' heads as follows. (Note that they are painted with yellow ocher on one side and red ocher on the other.) First paint both heads with water, using a No. 1 brush, to dampen them. Paint a little yellow ocher, diluted with water, on the top side and a little diluted red ocher on the bottom side. With a wet No. 1 brush, blend the two together, so that the dark hue – the red – is on the bottom and the light – the yellow – is on the top and they gradually blend into each other.

3 Join the two heads together with red ocher, carefully painting round the area to be occupied by the blue scales.

4 Mix some ultramarine and permanent white to make a bright pale blue and paint the scales.

5 Change your water and mix it with some permanent white to the consistency of thin cream. Use this to outline the blue scales and to paint the white dot in each.

6 Use alizarin crimson and yellow ocher to paint the leash.

7 Paint the two leaves, one with yellow ocher and the other with permanent green. If you wish to draw out some highlights where the veins go, do so with a squeezed-out brush, but make sure that you do it quickly.

8 Outline the image in red ocher.

TIPS

LIFTING OFF COLOR

If the creatures appear to be too dark after step 2, and also so that you can work some highlights into the folds of the necks, wet the painting with clean water. Squeeze out your brush between your fingers and then, with the squeezed-out brush, paint over the area where you wish the lightening of tone or highlight to be. Only use one stroke: if you use another you will simply replace the paint that you have just removed. If you still wish to remove more paint, clean the brush, squeeze it out again and only then make a second pass. If you want to remove still more, wet the brush again and repeat the process. You need to be quick when doing this as the color soon soaks into the paper and then cannot be removed. This lifting-off technique is very useful and has many applications, especially when painting around objects or where you wish to indicate light shining on an object. It can also come to your rescue when you find yourself with a wash that is about to swamp everything, or when two wet areas of different colors are bleeding into each other. In the latter instance you need to be very quick indeed in order to reverse a potential disaster.

CLEAN WATER

Whenever you want to use a lighter color, always change your water, especially when you intend to use white. Even the slightest coloring in your water will dull your white, while a touch of blue will turn your yellows green.

Eleventh-century Dutch "R"

◆ ◆ ◆

This eleventh-century capital "R," from the Chronicles of William of Jumieges, appears alive with writhing animation. It represents a slightly more ambitious project, building on the drawing skills that you practiced in the last project. Study the image carefully before trying to draw it so that you have worked out exactly what is happening.

TRACING FROM A BOOK

If possible, do not trace directly from a book or other type of document. Photocopy the image and trace over the photocopy instead. If you are not permitted to photocopy the book or document, either because you would thereby be infringing copyright regulations or because to do so would stress the book's binding or damage the document, draw the image freehand and then make a tracing from that.

DRAWING YOUR OWN COPY

When you first try to draw a copy of something, you may find it quite difficult. The following tip may help. Draw the image at one end of a piece of tracing paper. Fold the paper over and compare it with the original. Trace off the parts which are good, but alter the elements which are not so good. Fold the tracing paper over your second attempt, as before, and repeat the process. (You may have to do this four or five times.) You may end up with one or two sheets of tracing paper that are folded up like a concertina, but on the top copy you will have a drawing that is as close to the original as you can make it.

1 Trace the image. (I found it quicker to scribble all over the back rather than draw over it with a 6B pencil.) Transfer to your final paper.

2 Mix some ultramarine and permanent white and paint the pale-blue areas.

YOU WILL NEED

❖ Tracing paper

❖ Project paper

❖ 2H and 6B pencils

❖ Gouache paints: ultramarine, permanent white, brilliant yellow, flame red, red ocher, Prussian blue, black, permanent green, gold, burnt sienna

❖ Nos. 1 and 0000 brushes

❖ Burnisher

3 Mix some brilliant yellow into your ultramarine and
permanent-white mixture to paint the green colors on
the frog and the dragon.

5 Paint the shadows on the tongues and tail with
red ocher.

6 Paint the shadows on the blue areas with Prussian blue
(or ultramarine and black).

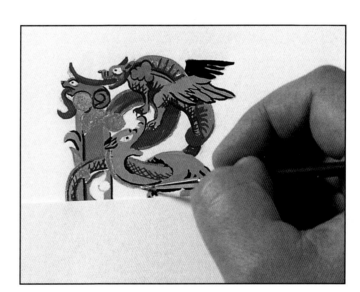

4 Change your water and mix some flame red and
permanent white to make the pink for the top dragon
and the main stem.

7 Paint the shadows on the green areas with
permanent green.

8 Paint the gold detailing with gold gouache. (If you
want to give it a slightly smoother and more shiny
appearance, you can burnish it with a burnisher. If you do not
like the effect, apply another coat of gold paint, which you
could reburnish if you wanted to. Experiment and see how
you get on.)

9 Mix some burnt sienna and black to make a very dark brown and add a little water to give it a consistency like thin cream. With a No. 0000 brush, outline the image.

10 Draw in the highlights with permanent white.

Eleventh-century English "Q"

❖ ❖ ❖

This capital "Q" is taken from an eleventh-century manuscript of the Winchester school. The skillful juxtaposition of primary colors, together with the small touches of gold, give this capital letter a stunning, jewellike brilliance.

YOU WILL NEED

- ❖ Tracing paper
- ❖ Project paper
- ❖ 2H and 6B pencils
- ❖ Gouache paints: ultramarine, flame red, brilliant yellow, permanent white, burnt sienna, black, cadmium primrose yellow
- ❖ Nos. 0, 1, and 0000 brushes
- ❖ P.V.A. gilding medium
- ❖ Transfer gold
- ❖ Paper tube
- ❖ Burnisher

TIP

TRACING

Take care that you do not move your tracing paper while you are working. It is worth sticking the tracing paper down with low-tack masking tape so that it cannot move.

1 Trace the design. (Take care, because the original is not symmetrical.) Trace the image down onto your project page.

2 Apply the P.V.A. gilding medium to the parts that will receive the gold. Use a No. 0 brush to apply the sizing. Resist the temptation to apply a thick drop because when it dries it will shrink and wrinkle. First apply one thin coat and then allow it to dry and sink into the paper. When it is dry, build up the letter form with as many additional thin coats as you need to create the right thickness, allowing each to dry before applying the next.

4 Burnish the gold through the backing paper or a piece of tracing paper and then burnish directly onto the gold.

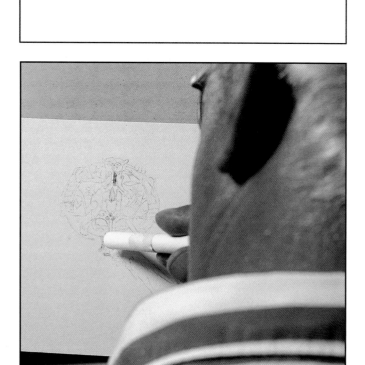

3 Apply the transfer gold. Before it will stick to the P.V.A. gilding medium the glue in the medium needs to be resoftened. To do this, roll up a little tube of paper to about the size of a cigarette and breathe onto the medium gently. Lay your transfer gold onto the medium, backing paper upward, and rub it gently with the pointed end of the burnisher. The gold will stick to the letter form and come off the backing paper. Apply another coat directly on top of the first, and then a third. (Note that gold will stick to gouache paint if it has been moistened by a warm breath, so do the writing first, then the gilding, and finally the painting.)

5 Mix a weak mixture of cadmium primrose yellow and ultramarine and paint the background using a No. 1 brush. (Alternatively, you could use gold gouache paint for this, which would contrast quite well with the burnished gold.) Note that it is important to do the background first, so that you do not leave any little corners of unpainted white paper showing through.

T I P

PREPARING P.V.A. GILDING MEDIUM

P.V.A. gilding medium is a pink color. It consists of a glutinous liquid that contains a thickening agent held in suspension. This tends to settle in the bottle and needs to be stirred up. Do not shake the bottle and thereby make it full of bubbles, however. (If you get bubbles on your paper you should pop them with a pin or brush.) Instead, turn your bottle upside down, end to end, until the medium has been well mixed, or else stir the medium with a brush – but make sure that you do not create any bubbles.

6 Paint the red areas with flame red and the pink with permanent white added to the red.

7 Change your water and paint the blue areas with ultramarine. Add a little cadmium primrose yellow to the ultramarine and paint the green areas.

8 Outline with a mixture of burnt sienna and black and paint the seeds in the pods using a No. 0000 brush. Then add the highlights by making a threadlike line on the light side.

9 Apply the white dots to the blue areas using a No. 0000 brush. (Your paint needs to be fairly thick and stiff for this; if it is too wet it will run into the blue.)

Eleventh-century English "N"

❖ ❖ ❖

This eleventh-century initial is from a Bible illustrated in the Durham style. The poor man is entangled in the snares of life and seems beset by all the cares and worries of existence, which are epitomized by the strange creatures that surround him. Enjoy the challenge of working this delightful initial.

YOU WILL NEED

❖ Tracing paper

❖ Tracing-down paper

❖ Project paper

❖ Sharp 2H pencil

❖ Nos. 1, 0, and 0000 brushes

❖ P.V.A. gilding medium

❖ Transfer gold

❖ Burnisher

❖ Gouache paints: cadmium primrose yellow, yellow ocher, ultramarine, dark green, burnt umber, red ocher, flame red, permanent white, black

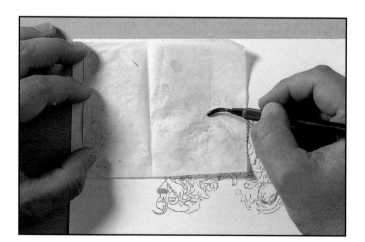

1 Trace the initial with a sharp 2H pencil. Use a piece of tracing-down paper to transfer the image to your project paper. If you pencil over the back with a 6B pencil or scribble extensively over it you will find that it is difficult to see what you are doing when you trace it down.

2 Apply the P.V.A. gilding medium to those areas that will be gilded. Allow the first coat to sink in and dry and then apply two or three coats, depending on how raised you want the gold to appear. Allow each to dry before applying the next. Then rub down three coats of transfer gold over the medium, working around the edges with the point of your burnisher. Burnish the gold thoroughly.

3 Paint the creatures in olive green, mixed from cadmium primrose yellow, yellow ocher and ultramarine.

4 Outline the creatures in dark-green with a No. 0000 brush.

5 Paint the man in the following colors. *Coat:* a mixture of burnt umber, red ocher and yellow ocher; dark tones in burnt umber. *Hair:* a mixture of burnt umber and yellow ocher. *Skin:* a mixture of yellow ocher, flame red, and permanent white.

6 Paint the blue areas with ultramarine.

7 Mix a little yellow ocher into your blue color and paint the green areas.

8 Outline the image in a burnt-umber and black mixture, using a No. 0000 brush.

9 Highlight the green areas with yellow ocher and the blue with permanent white. Tidy up the edges with permanent white.

TIPS

TRACING-DOWN PAPER

Tracing-down paper is essentially a sheet of tissue which is coated on one side with a powder (usually red) that comes off when under pressure. You place a sheet of tracing-down paper under your tracing and then go over it again with a sharp pencil. The pressure of the pencil causes the powder to stick to the paper, leaving a copy of the image on it. Take a piece of baking parchment and a set of soft chalk pastels. Select a pastel of a contrasting color to that of your project paper. Rub it all over the baking parchment and then rub over it thoroughly with your finger (wrapped in a piece of paper).

Twelfth-century English "I"

◆ ◆ ◆

This bold capital "I" has been copied from a twelfth-century English manuscript. I have used it as the basis of my designs for four Christian sacred monograms. Copying them will give you a chance to practice what you have learned so far and to brush up on your technique.

IHS: the Latin form of the Greek letters IHC, the first three letters of the Greek word *IHCOYC*, meaning "Jesus."
PX: the first two letters of the Greek word *XPICTOC*, meaning "Christ" (this may be written in different ways, often with the X on the stem of the P).
AO: Alpha and Omega – the first and last letters of the Greek alphabet. Jesus said "I am the Alpha and the Omega . . ."

MARIA: the monogram of the Virgin Mary, mother of Jesus Christ.

The treatment of these initials is quite straightforward, but this often has a greater impact than a more complicated decorative scheme. These simply designed capitals can be very useful for secondary initials within a project, such as those used at the beginning of paragraphs and sentences.

By way of an embellishment I have tried to make the middle node of the "I" look as if it is made of shimmering material.

LIFTING PAINT

The light parts of the nodes were made by lifting the paint off the surface with a squeezed-out brush. Paint the color, then quickly wash out the brush and squeeze it dry. Next paint over the area that you want to appear lighter, and the brush will suck up the color, leaving the area looking paler. It is important to be positive when you do this: the more you dither the more ragged and messy the result. You must also be quick, or the pigment will soak into the paper.

PAINT THE AREA WITH MEDIUM-STRENGTH COLOR.

QUICKLY WASH OUT THE BRUSH AND SQUEEZE IT BETWEEN YOUR FINGERS. WITH THE DRY BRUSH, QUICKLY GO OVER THE CENTER OF THE AREA AGAIN, LIFTING OFF THE COLOR AS YOU GO, LEAVING A LIGHTER TONE WITH SOFT, GRADUATED EDGES.

PAINT THE OUTSIDE OF THE AREA WITH DARKER, FULL-TONE COLOR WHILE IT IS STILL WET, SO THAT THE TONE BLENDS IN. WHEN ALL IS DRY, CAREFULLY PAINT THE TWO PIECES OF WHITE HIGHLIGHT.

Twelfth-century Flemish "E"

• • •

This project is from a twelfth-century Flemish Bible. The illustration shows Jonah being spewed out of the whale's body. Jonah and the whale are incorporated into the capital letter "E," from the Latin word *et*, meaning "and." The cunning combination makes a very telling design. If you can make it half as interesting as this example, you should be pleased with your ingenuity and skill!

YOU WILL NEED

❖ Tracing paper or baking parchment
❖ Sharp 2H pencil
❖ Eraser
❖ Gouache paints: ultramarine, brilliant yellow, red, pink-flame red, dark brown, black, gold
❖ Transfer gold
❖ P.V.A. gilding medium
❖ Nos. 1, 2, and 0000 brushes
❖ Burnisher
❖ Paper tube

1 Trace over the design with tracing paper and a 2H pencil, and then trace it onto your project page.

2 Paint the bands on the capital "E" with P.V.A. gilding medium. You will probably have to apply two coats; allow each coat to dry before proceeding further. Take care to make sure that you paint well into the corners so that you do not leave them ungilded.

3 While the two coats of P.V.A. gilding medium are drying, carefully paint the gold in the central areas of the big capital "E," and also in the turned ends of the foliage. (I have additionally embellished the whale with a few gold scales, a gold eyebrow, and some gold fins.) You may have to leave all the gold to dry before you can proceed further.

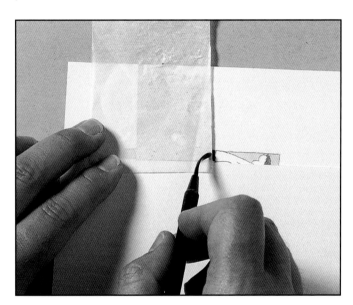

4 When all is dry, have your paper tube, sheet of transfer gold, and burnisher to hand. Gently puff through the tube onto the P.V.A. medium on the first strap of the capital "E," so that the gum in the medium is moistened. Lay your sheet of transfer gold onto the strap, placing the edge of the gold as close to the edge of the design as possible. Holding the paper still with your spare hand, burnish the backing paper over the strap with even, circular strokes. Repeat the process with each of the other straps, working from the top downward. When all the straps are done, burnish directly onto the gilded areas until a deep shine is produced.

5 Mix a pale solution of ultramarine and brilliant yellow and dilute it with enough water to obtain the correct color. Paint the pale-green area outside the initial.

6 Paint the red and blue areas carefully. Mix a little pink-flame red with lots of water to dilute it into an appropriate color.

7 Paint the whale in your own mixture of brown gouache.

8 Mix some dark-brown and black gouache to make a thin, creamy consistency and outline the image. Leave Jonah unpainted.

9 The brown color which I painted on the whale looked boring, so I mixed up some gold gouache with water and gave the whale a weak wash. I felt that this added considerable richness to the whole composition. (Remember, when you do this, to leave the eye white, which gives it a piercing brightness.)

Fourteenth-century French "T"

❖ ❖ ❖

The little miniature used in this capital letter comes from a fourteenth-century French manuscript. This method of design is such a common feature of the decoration of letters from the fourteenth-century onward that it is worth trying to emulate it.

You will have to make up your own mind about the little monk. Is he the cellar master making sure that his brew is fit to be placed before the abbot, or is he taking the opportunity to have a swift draft himself?

This letter is straightforward in its treatment and, provided that you take each step at a time and that you are thoughtful and patient, you will be surprised at how well you progress.

YOU WILL NEED

- ❖ Tracing paper
- ❖ Sharp pencil
- ❖ Gouache paints: black, burnt umber, red, yellow, ocher, gold, green, ultramarine, and permanent white
- ❖ Brushes

1 Make a tracing of the image and transfer it to your project page. When you draw the barrel, make sure that you preserve the rounded shape of the staves and hoops.

2 First paint the miniature. Mix a little black and burnt umber with enough water to make a weak mixture and paint the background of the dark cellar.

3 With a wash of burnt umber, paint the barrel, the stand, and the archway. With a squeezed-out brush, quickly lift the color off the top of the barrel and then paint a second coat onto the underside of the barrel. With a squeezed-out and rewetted brush, blend the dark and light shades together so that the barrel appears round. Paint the stonework on the arch with a second coat of burnt umber; also paint the jug with the same color.

4 Take a little black and mix it with water to produce the pale tone of the monk's habit. Paint the habit all over and, while it is still wet, paint the dark tones, blending and softening them a little with a clean, wet brush to show the folds. Paint the hoops of the barrel with the same shade of black, lifting the color off the top with a squeezed-out brush to make these areas look lighter and preserve the rounded effect.

5 Mix a touch of red and yellow to make the skin color and paint the hands and face. A second coat under the chin and where the arm protrudes from the sleeve will provide shadow.

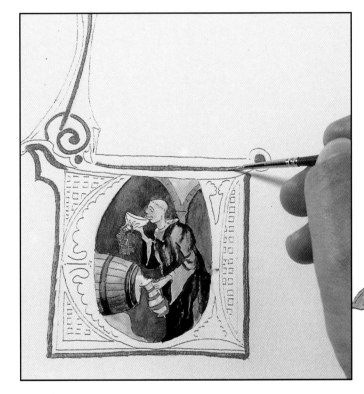

6 Paint the gold areas, including the keys and the hoops on the jug, with gold gouache.

7 Paint the red and green areas, taking care with the little green squares around the initial letter.

8 Mix some ultramarine and permanent white to make a pale blue and paint the whole initial, leaving a thin white line between the blue and the red.

9 With neat ultramarine, paint the dark-blue parts of the image.

10 Mix some permanent white with water until it is the consistency of thin cream. Paint all the white lines on the blue areas and also between the other colors, painting over the gaps that you left. Note that the little green squares are highlighted with white at the bottom and on the right-hand side. (Correct any wiggles using the color that the highlights are painted on.) Be patient with the white dots on the red: if they are placed correctly, they will lighten the tone.

11 Mix some black and burnt umber to make a dark brown and outline everything. Paint the shadowed top and left-hand side of the little green squares.

T I P

DEALING WITH SPLODGES

If you get paint in the wrong place when using gouache, it is possible to remove it. Wet the offending spot and gently stir it with a brush until you see the paint lift up from the surface. Squeeze out your brush and pick up as much as you can. Repeat the process as often as possible, but be careful not to damage the surface. When you feel that you can do no more, leave it to dry, but first try blotting out the last attempt with a tissue or some blotting paper.

When it is completely dry, paint over it with a strong coat of permanent white, which you should lay on gently to ensure that you do not mix in any of the offending pigment that lies below. Allow to dry. When it is totally dry, repaint the lost image, taking care to lay the colors on gently so that you do not disturb the permanent-white pigment lying below.

Fourteenth-century English "I"

❖ ❖ ❖

This amazing capital "I" comes from the English Luttrell Psalter, which was written in the fourteenth-century for Sir Geoffrey Luttrell, a Lincolnshire knight. I have copied this letter because of its bizarre extravagance. You can certainly enjoy stretching your painting and drawing skills with this!

The lesser initials have also been included to make the point that it is not only the great capital letters that interest us. The other capitals that appear on the page can be given a decorative treatment as well, in varying degrees according to their importance. These capitals,

drawn in a fat, Lombardic style, are plainly drawn and simply colored, but are made more significant by the pen-drawn decoration that surrounds them, forming white dots and a trifoliate decorative design. At first sight this looks rather complicated, but provided that you keep calm it is actually quite straightforward. If you draw round the letters, leaving a white line and drawing round the trifoliate leaf shapes at the appropriate places as you progress, you will find that it is not as difficult as it first seemed. Next draw the irregularly scalloped outer edge, and you subsequently only have to fill in the rest carefully, leaving out the little white dots as you do so.

1 Trace the large capitals and, if you want, also the lesser capitals.

2 Transfer the image to your project paper with a sharp pencil.

3 Ink in the lesser initials, leaving the coloring until last.

YOU WILL NEED
- ❖ Tracing paper or baking parchment
- ❖ Sharp pencil
- ❖ Ink or gouache paints: brilliant yellow, yellow ocher, burnt umber, light red, ultramarine, black
- ❖ Brushes

4 This project has been drawn in ink, but there is no need to ink the main design. Make a thin wash of brilliant yellow and water and wash over the top half of the character. Leave the eye white. Squeeze out your brush and lift the highlights off the beak, forehead, cheek, and folds of material. Paint the tail.

5 While the yellow is still wet, mix yellow ocher and a little burnt umber and paint the dark parts on the back of the head and the folds.

6 With a weak solution of light red and water, blend the dark tones with the lighter yellow, lifting off paint to provide the modeling on the face and the folds of the cloth.

7 Paint over the tail with the same brown-reddish color.

8 Paint a light wash of ultramarine and water over the lower half of the creature and quickly lift off the highlights on the face and the leading thigh. Leave the eye white.

9 Paint the dark parts with neat ultramarine and blend it with the light parts with a wet brush, lifting off paint if needed.

10 Paint the white lines, dots, and circles on both halves of the creature and on the flowers.

11 Make a soft and creamy mix of black and burnt umber and carefully paint the outlines. Place a dot of the mixture in each circle.

Sixteenth-century English "S"

• ◆ •

This capital "S" is striking in the imagination of its design and in the vigor of its style. The interwoven strapwork is typical of the penmanship of the sixteenth century. It appeared on an uncolored document, the capital being simply drawn with a pen.

USING COLORED PAPER

You can produce some very striking effects with colored paper. There are some problems that you should be aware of, however. If you are tracing down a design you may find that the red tracing-down paper does not show up. In this case, make yourself a sheet of contrasting color with some baking parchment and a chalk pastel of an appropriate color. To do this, lay the pastel on its side on the baking parchment. Rub it all over the sheet to get as even a color as you can. Then wrap a piece of paper around your finger and rub it all over the baking parchment, spreading and working in the pastel until the surface of the baking parchment is completely covered.

1 Trace the design with a sharp 2H pencil and then go over the back with a fairly sharp 6B pencil.

2 Mix some pale green with ultramarine, cadmium pale yellow, and water. Paint the head and lower body of the two dolphins.

YOU WILL NEED

❖ Sharp 2H pencil and 6B pencil

❖ Tracing paper or tracing-down paper

❖ Brushes

❖ Gouache paint: pale green, ultramarine, cadmium pale yellow, permanent white, flame red, gold, black, burnt umber

❖ Pen and ink

3 Mix some light blue, permanent white, and ultramarine and paint the top of the back, the bottom jaw, and fin and tails.

4 Paint the tongues and small mid-sections with a light red.

5 Paint the dark colors on the green, blue, and red areas, and the fins and tails with dark blue.

6 Paint the gold areas with gold gouache, carefully placing the dots on the interwoven section.

7 Make a soft and creamy mix of black and burnt umber and carefully outline the whole image, taking particular care over the interwoven areas.

8 I have drawn the interwoven areas separately in pen and ink. It makes it easier to see the pattern and is also handy to keep for future reference.

TIP

STRAPWORK

Strapwork is a very common and attractive element of designing letters and borders and has been used in different styles over the centuries. At first sight it looks very complicated, but patiently follow each part through. It helps to remember that the design is often formed by two interlacing parts combining from different directions. Sometimes a third, unconnected, unending strap is interlaced with the two ends. If you like these designs, it is worth collecting tracings and keeping them in a scrapbook for future reference and adaptation.

Fourteenth-century "D"

• • •

This capital "D," copied from a fourteenth-century manuscript, shows the amazing beauty and simplicity of form of the Lombardic capitals, and also emphasizes their suitability for decorative treatment. The treatment and design is quite simple and straightforward, but the effect is brilliant.

It is a good idea for you to get into the habit of drawing initials freehand and, if you are not doing this already, this is a simple project which gives you a chance to try out your ability. Once you can do this, your work will become much more spontaneous, and will also have your own stamp on it rather than mine. Another advantage is that you can easily make the capitals whatever size you want, without having to go to the trouble of enlarging or shrinking the design.

YOU WILL NEED

❖ Pencil

❖ Tracing paper

❖ Gouache colors: light blue, ultramarine, permanent white, red, green, gold, creamy white, black, burnt umber

❖ Brushes, including No. 0000 brush

1 Trace, transfer, and color in as before.

2 Paint the blue areas.

3 Paint the red and green areas.

4 Paint the dark-blue areas with neat ultramarine and then, with a clean, wet brush, blend the ligh dark areas to try to give the effect of a rounded su

5 Paint the gold border and roundels in the fi gold gouache.

6 Mix some soft, creamy white with permanen white and water and, using a No. 0000 brusl carefully paint all the highlights on the blue and green leaves.

7 I felt that the four green triangles looked to plain, so I painted a diagonal crosshatching over them in a darker green. This made them look more interesting, but still very dull. To alleviate tl I painted a very tiny gold dot into each diamond i was very pleased with the result. You could do the same.

8 I thought that the center of the letter looke too dull, so I painted the white dots in grou of three, adding only one where there was not enough room for three. This made the middle lool more interesting and also much brighter. You migl wish to do the same.

9 Mix some black and burnt umber into a runny, creamy consistency and carefully outline the image, tidying up with permanent white as you go.

Fifteenth-century Border

◆ ◆ ◆

This project is something of a summing-up exercise, and presents an opportunity to test what you have learned so far with a complete project. I have chosen this particular prayer because it is probably the only piece of prose that is known to almost everyone. I have chosen to write it in Latin, because although this is now regarded as a dead language, it is nevertheless still used universally. If you do not like the idea of writing in Latin, try it in your own preferred language. You could also use another short item of text that you know well; the important point is that you choose something that you are very familiar with, so that you do not have to think about the words. The border that I have used is taken from a fifteenth-century French model, and the capitals have been adapted from an example of work from the same period.

LAYOUT

You will first have to decide upon the size and shape of paper you are going to use. You will next have to think about the amount of decoration you wish to apply, and how much of your efforts will be devoted to the text, capitals, and decoration.

Make the size of your capital letter relate to the writing lines: the size is up to you, but if it does not match the lines it will look odd. You need to establish how much room you will have for writing your text. If the text is very wordy, you may have to spend some time working out how you are going to fit it onto the page, and then see how much space is left for decoration and capital letters. As these projects are about capital letters, however, it would be better to chose a text that displays them to good advantage. You will have to decide how many lines will be needed to accommodate the words, and you may have to make several drafts on rough paper before you have a satisfactory layout.

Having worked out the number of lines you will need, you then have to rule up the available space to accommodate your words within the required number of lines within the decorated area, leaving enough space between each pair of lines of text for the ascenders and descenders. Now chose a nib that will give you lettering of the right size to fit the lines, working on the basis of four or five nib widths for the body of the text.

You will next need to consider how you are going to arrange the words within the lines on the page. They can be aligned to the left- (A) or right-hand margin (B); both approaches look effective, especially when combined with a scheme of decoration that emanates strongly from one side or the other. You could also center them (C). This looks good, too, and will allow you to employ a symmetrical scheme of decoration which is the same on both sides of the text. It is quite difficult to get this right, however. Count the letters and spaces in each line (allow one character space equivalent to the letter "n" between each word), then find the middle of the line and mark this on the center of the line on your page, spacing out the rest of the characters of the line on either side of this. Do the same with each line. (If you have a computer, you can, of course, command it to do this for you. Provided that you can print it out in the same size that you are going to use to write the text, you can simply trace off the layout, which will be perfectly correct.)

A

B

C

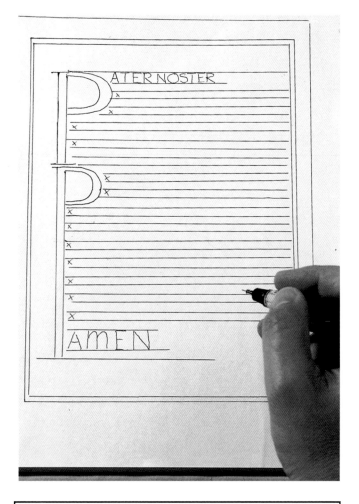

1 Once you have worked out all your rulings on a sheet of rough paper, place this on your project page and trace them down lightly.

2 Before you start transcribing your text, carefully spell out the alphabet on a piece of rough paper and put it on a board in front of you. This will help you to focus your brain and hand on the job and will give you time to make sure that your pen is working properly.

3 When you are satisfied that all is well, try to write all the piece in one go; it will improve the continuity of your letter forms.

4 Provided that you have used waterproof ink, you will be able to make some corrections to ill-formed letters with permanent-white gouache.

5 Once you are satisfied with your text, put it away to make sure that it is thoroughly dry before applying the decoration.

6 Draw in the capitals and decoration in the spaces round your text.

YOU WILL NEED

❖ Rough paper
❖ Project paper
❖ Waterproof ink
❖ Pen
❖ Pencil
❖ P.V.A. gilding medium
❖ Paper tube
❖ Burnisher
❖ Gold leaf
❖ Gouache paints: green, red, blue, dark red, dark green, dark blue, white, black, burnt umber
❖ Brushes, including No. 0000 brush

7 Paint on P.V.A. gilding medium in two coats, allowing each to dry completely before proceeding with the frame, the center of the main capital, and the berries.

8 Working from the top downward, take your paper tube and breathe onto the medium to moisten it. Rub down two coats of gold leaf onto each gilded part, burnishing them carefully through the backing paper before you proceed further.

9 Gently but thoroughly burnish each gilded piece until it takes on a dark shine.

10 Paint the two pieces of green decoration. As you paint them, also lift off a sweep of pigment from the center of each part of the leaf so that it is highlighted.

11 Paint the leaves in the center of the top initial and also paint the center of the lower initial, but in this case leaving out the leaves.

12 Paint the red letters of the "Pater Noster," the two capitals, and the "Amen," as well as the leaves in the lower capital.

13 Paint the blue decoration, lifting out the color in the center of the leaves as you proceed. You will need to do this quickly, or the paper will become stained.

14 I decided that I did not like the green center of the second capital, and that I would rather gild the "Pater Noster" than have it in red, so I did another version, making the center red, the leaves green, and gilding the letters.

15 Paint the red decoration, lifting off the pigment in the central areas as you go.

16 With some dark red, dark blue, and dark green, work around the decoration as appropriate, painting in those parts that should really be in shadow.

17 Take some permanent-white gouache and a No. 0000 brush and work over the whole project, painting in the highlights.

18 With a black and burnt-umber mix, outline the work, painting in the whiskers on the berries to make them stand out more.

PATER NOSTER
qui es in cælis
sanctificetur nomen
tuum. Adveniat regnum tuum.
Fiat voluntas tua, sicut cælo
et in terra
panem nostrum
quotidianum danobis
hodie. Et dimitte nobis
debita nostra, sicut et nos
dimittimus debitoribus
nostris.
Et ne nos inducas in
tentationem.
Sed libera nos a malo.
AMEN.

Fifteenth-century White Vine

• • •

This style of design, known as the "white vine," first appeared in the tenth century. It became very popular on its reappearance in Italy in the fifteenth century. The pen-drawn vine-and-leaf design is picked out in different colors and is enhanced by the colors that surround it. The vines were usually left white, but some were colored cream and some green; some were even multicolored, especially when the vine design was drawn as a geometric spiral. The design was often drawn both within the letter and spreading round it and down the page.

1 Take a piece of tracing paper or baking parchment and draw two horizontal lines (between which the inscription will be written) and two vertical lines (which will contain the vine design). Draw in the lettering, the outlines of the capital letter, and the design. Retrace and alter as often as you feel necessary to achieve the size and shape that best occupies

YOU WILL NEED

- ❖ 2H pencil
- ❖ Tracing paper or baking parchment
- ❖ Project paper
- ❖ Tracing-down paper
- ❖ Eraser
- ❖ Ruler
- ❖ Masking tape
- ❖ Nos. 1 and 0000 brushes
- ❖ P.V.A. gilding medium
- ❖ Paper tube
- ❖ Gold leaf
- ❖ Burnisher
- ❖ Gouache paints: ultramarine, blue, red, brilliant yellow, yellow ocher, gold, black, burnt umber
- ❖ Waterproof ink
- ❖ Lettering pen

2 Draw the vine design in detail, making sure the tracing paper does not move.

3 Rule two guidelines (for the lettering and design) on your project paper. Using waterproof ink and a lettering pen, write the word, leaving out the capital. Trace down the capital letter and design.

4 Paint two coats of P.V.A. gilding medium onto the capital letter, flower centers, and little buds. Allow each to dry.

5 Breathe on the area to be gilded through the paper tube to make the medium sticky and lay the gold leaf onto the form, rubbing it down with a burnisher.

6 Paint the blue and the red areas.

7 Paint the green areas with a mixture of brilliant yellow, yellow ocher, and ultramarine.

8 Paint the gold areas on the outside of the initial and the vine area, making sure that the gold gouache is thick enough.

9 Outline everything with a mixture of black and burnt umber. Apply spots of gold leaf to any bare patches in the gilding and reburnish if necessary.

Using the same design, I have written a different word, taking some liberties with the text to make it fit in the space. I have also experimented with the color pattern to give a stained-glass effect. Instead of gold leaf I have used gold paint on the initial and have also experimented with outlining in gold paint.

10 "Greetings," written in French. I have used the same tracing, adapting it to a capital "S." I have painted the whole design in the one color. The effect is so strong that I did not outline it – even adding gold to the buds and flower centers would diminish the impact.

11 "Greetings," written in German. I again used a single color for this (the green was mixed from ultramarine and yellow ocher).

Fifteenth-century French "A"

❖ ❖ ❖

This initial was adapted from a fifteenth-century French manuscript and relies mostly on penwork for its effect. The drawing and painting of the initial are simple tasks, but the penwork around the initial and in the stem needs a little thought. I drew it with a technical drawing pen, but a steel crow quill would do just as well. It is important both to make all the hoops the same size and to produce fine lines.

When I first looked at this initial, I was attracted by its design possibilities. According to the demands of the text, the stem could be made any length and the branches could be placed in any suitable position. The design could be adapted to fit a left- or right-hand margin or could go in the middle of the page, while a small miniature or heraldic device could be used in the place of the initial.

YOU WILL NEED

❖ Tracing paper

❖ Project paper

❖ Pencil

❖ Ruler

❖ Right-angled set square

❖ Compasses

❖ Eraser

❖ Steel crow quill

❖ Waterproof ink or gouache paint

1 Draw a vertical line on a piece of tracing paper to act as the backbone of the design. Draw in a series of crossbars, making sure that they are at true right angles to the stem. Using your compasses, draw a series of circles centered on the stem. Rub out the part of the stem where the capital letter will go.

2 Trace down the design onto your project paper.

3 To do the penwork, you will need waterproof ink of your chosen color or gouache paint. (If you are using gouache, mix it with water and and transfer it to your pen with a brush.) Draw the initial and the surrounding penwork.

4 Draw in the design, trying to keep the work as fluid and neat as you can. Then, to finish, color the initial.

Fifteenth-century "Q"

◆ ◆ ◆

This project is copied from a fifteenth-century musical score. I was attracted by the miniature – what is it all about? In any event, the capital "Q," which is simply drawn in gold strapwork and decorated with acanthus leaves and pen-drawn "stamens," makes a very attractive project. It does, however, need to act as the frame for a miniature illustration of some kind, but whether you copy this one or devise and execute one of your own is entirely up to you.

YOU WILL NEED

❖ Tracing paper

❖ Tracing-down paper

❖ 2H pencil

❖ Project paper

❖ Gouache paints: gold, red, ultramarine, permanent white, black, burnt umber

❖ Watercolor paints: burnt umber, Prussian blue, crimson lake

❖ Nos. 1 and 0000 brushes

❖ P.V.A. gilding medium

❖ Paper tube

❖ Gold leaf

❖ Burnisher

1 Make a tracing of the image and trace it down onto your project paper, ensuring that it is upright.

2 Paint the P.V.A. gilding medium onto the capital letter with the No. 1 brush and allow thirty-five minutes for it to dry.

3 Puff a breath through the paper tube onto the top of the letter. Lay the gold leaf on the area that you have just moistened. With the burnisher, rub over the area so that the gold adheres to the letter and is detached from the backing paper. Work all round the letter and down the tail, making sure that you do not rub away the area that you have just completed.

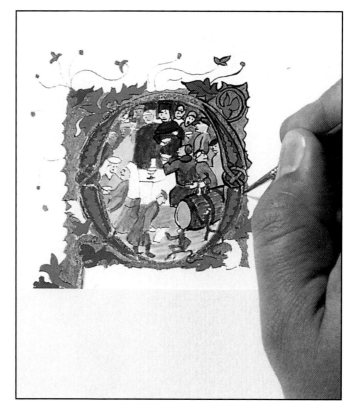

4 Paint the gold gouache (diluted to the right consistency) on the outer parts of the design.

5 Paint the red and blue areas, as well as the fat cardinal at the top of the group.

6 Paint the miniature with watercolors. Start by painting the dark area at the top, behind the heads, with a mixture of burnt umber and Prussian blue. Then paint the floor with light brown, along with the barrel, darkening the paint with a little burnt umber. Darken the fat cardinal's color with some crimson lake, and then paint the rest of the figures, working from the largest parts to the smallest. Finally, paint the animals.

7 Outline the image with a mixture of black and burnt-umber gouache, as well as some of the figures in the miniature.

8 Highlight the blue areas with some permanent white. Use a No. 0000 brush and make sure that the paint is the consistency of thin cream.

THIS CAPITAL COULD BE ADAPTED IN MANY
WAYS. THE STEM COULD BE LONGER OR SHORTER,
ACCORDING TO NEED. IT COULD EVEN BE DRAWN
THE OTHER WAY UP, IF YOU WERE USING A
DIFFERENT LETTER. THE LACEWORK AT THE
BOTTOM COULD BE PLACED IN THE MIDDLE, IF
THIS SUITED THE TEXT BETTER. YOU COULD
HAVE MORE OR FEWER WHISKERS AND DRAW ON
THE ENDS. AS FOR THE MINIATURE, YOU COULD
PAINT ANY SUBJECT YOU LIKED.

Fifteenth-century "K"

❖ ❖ ❖

This exotic pink "K" is taken from another fifteenth-century musical score, this time from a French book of hours. Although it looks quite large here, it would originally have been drawn much smaller than this. Books of music were placed on a stand for a choir of monks to gather around; books of hours, however, were very small and could be slipped into a pocket. This capital letter starts a prayer of supplication – "Lord have mercy" – that would have been sung in Greek at the beginning of every Mass.

I have included this project to introduce the effect of raised gold and also to point out some interesting developments that occurred while I was experimenting with different materials.

YOU WILL NEED

❖ Tracing paper or baking parchment

❖ Tracing-down paper

❖ Project paper

❖ 2H pencil

❖ Eraser

❖ Gouache paints: permanent white, ultramarine, alizarin crimson

❖ Gesso

❖ P.V.A. gilding medium or spirit-based gilding medium

❖ Nos. 1 and 0000 brushes

❖ Gold leaf

❖ Paper tube

❖ Burnisher

1 Make a tracing of the image and trace it down onto your project paper. If your image is sharp enough, you will not need to draw over it.

2 With a No. 1 brush, take up some prepared gesso and paint round the form, taking care to paint into the points and corners. Now take a good brushful and start to fill in the form. Pushing, rather than painting it, gradually work over the form, filling in the area with gesso, so that any surface irregularities are removed. Work from the top downward. When you have finished, put your work away in a warm spot to dry for at least a couple of hours.

3 When the gesso is smooth and hard, paint a coat of gilding medium over it. Leave it to dry. (If you use P.V.A. gilding medium, you will find it difficult to paint a thin coat without leaving brush marks, which will show through the gold leaf and spoil the mirrorlike surface for which you are aiming. You may prefer to buy a prepared, spirit-based gilding medium which dries quite smoothly, leaving no brush marks, but takes several hours to do so. If it is painted directly onto the paper, it makes it look transparent, so take care round the edges of the form.)

5 Paint the letter as follows. (Keep a piece of paper under your hand to prevent damage to your gilding.)

The light-blue parts: with a permanent-white and ultramarine mixture.

The pale-pink part: with an alizarin crimson and permanent white mixture.

The dark-blue parts: with neat ultramarine.

The dark-pink parts: with neat alizarin crimson.

Highlighting: highlight the pale-blue and pink parts with permanent white.

This letter is not outlined. If you want to do so, I suggest that you outline the pink areas with madder carmine, the blue areas with Prussian blue, and the gold areas with a black and burnt-umber mix.

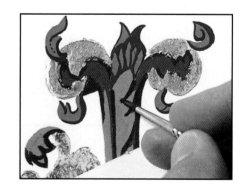

4 Breathe through the paper tube onto the medium at the top of the page to moisten it. Lay the gold leaf on the area and burnish the backing paper. Rub down another layer of gold to make good any splits. When you have finished, burnish the gilded work through a piece of tracing paper, working over and round each piece. Then burnish the gold directly.

TIP

GESSO

Gesso (which is made of plaster of Paris or a similar material mixed with a binder) is painted over the area to be gilded, leaving a raised area. When it is dry, gold leaf is applied to it. The gilded raised form glitters and catches the light, illuminating the page. You can make gesso yourself, but if you will only be needing a small quantity use ready-made acrylic-based gesso that you can buy in small jars.

If you are going to apply gesso, the secret is to lay a smooth, even base coat. When you open the jar, you will see that it contains a thick, white, creamlike substance which will need to be diluted with water if it is to be used for lettering. If it is too thin and runny, it will not stand proud of the paper. If it is too thick, you cannot lay it smoothly. By constantly adding a little more water you can get the right consistency. Dip a brush into the gesso and lift it out, letting the water drip back onto the mix. If the water sits on the surface, the mixture is too thick, so add a couple more brushfuls of water. Keep on testing and adding water until the drip settles into the mix. When the mix has reached this stage, it is ready to use.

Fifteenth-century Borders

◆ ◆ ◆

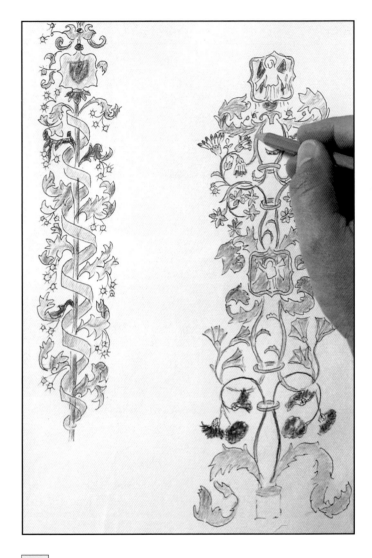

These two borders are taken from a fifteenth-century manuscript, and show how two dissimilar designs can be combined on the same page. They are relatively simple in composition and can be adapted, lengthened, or shortened according to the needs of the project in hand.

The left-hand border, the inner one, is composed of acanthuslike elements that have been expanded to resemble heraldic mantling, with gold fruits and a ribbon winding round them. It has an uncomplicated dignity and could be used on either side of the page, or even between two columns of text. The ribbon could display a motto, piece of text, or message. The little escutcheon at the top could carry a heraldic device, monogram, or miniature.

YOU WILL NEED

- ❖ Tracing paper
- ❖ Project paper
- ❖ 2H pencil
- ❖ Ruler
- ❖ Gesso or P.V.A. gilding medium
- ❖ Brushes
- ❖ Gold leaf
- ❖ Paper tube
- ❖ Burnisher
- ❖ Gouache paints: yellow ocher, permanent white, black, burnt umber, colors of your choice
- ❖ Pen
- ❖ Waterproof ink

1 Either trace the design onto your project page or draw it yourself. If you do the latter, rule a center line and mark it at regular intervals to show where the top of the ribbon crosses it. Rule guidelines to the left and right to make sure that the acanthus leaves and gold fruits are the same width either side and all the way down.

2 Apply gesso or P.V.A. gilding medium to the fruits. (If you use P.V.A., resist the temptation to apply a fat drop of it, which will shrink and wrinkle as it dries. Instead apply two or three coats.) Burnish on the gold leaf, starting at the top and working down.

3 Paint the ribbon to make it look as if it is made of a lustrous material, at least on the front side. Make a wash of yellow ocher and paint each section, lifting off the color in the center by squeezing out your brush and soaking up the color before it has soaked into the paper. You could also apply some clean water to the center and lift it off. Treat each section in turn in this way. Mix a little of your wash with more yellow ocher to make it darker and paint two or three small vertical stripes at either end of each section. Finally, paint a thin strip of neat ocher at the downhill end of each section, to give the illusion of shadow. You could treat the reverse of the ribbon in the same way; this one has been painted blue, but you could chose a different color.

4 When all is dry, write your text. Remember to write the letters at right angles to the direction of the ribbon, not vertical to the page.

5 Paint the acanthus leaves in the color of your choice. A useful tip is to mix your main colors with a little white, making them paler in tone. You can then use the neat color to apply the darker shadow tones.

6 Highlight the outward-rising curves of the acanthus leaves with permanent white.

7 Outline the image with a mixture of black and burnt umber. Remember to paint in the "eyelashes" round the fruits.

Fifteenth-century "P"

❖ ❖ ❖

This initial has been adapted from a fifteenth-century missal and displays a flamboyant Lombardic capital "P," as well as some delicate filigree pen decoration. I have also drawn the coat of arms of the city of Paris within the "P." This is a very good way in which to display heraldic devices. The rest of the word is written in the Ronde style, a round letter form used in the French tradition, but you could use any other style that suited your particular project.

YOU WILL NEED

- ❖ Tracing paper
- ❖ Project paper
- ❖ 2H pencil
- ❖ Ruler
- ❖ Steel crow quill or technical pen
- ❖ Black waterproof ink
- ❖ Gesso
- ❖ Brushes
- ❖ Gouache paint: yellow, ultramarine, permanent white, red, black, burnt umber
- ❖ Gold leaf
- ❖ Paper tube
- ❖ Burnisher

1 Rule lines on your project paper to contain the word and capital. If you intend to include any other text, rule the lines for that, too, and write the text.

2 Make a photocopy of your design, and use it to work out your color scheme

3 Make a careful tracing of the capital and transfer it to your project page. Draw the black penwork in waterproof ink around and outside the letter.

4 Paint the area to be gilded with gesso, pushing it into place with your brush and filling all the little points and corners. (The little fleurs-de-lys on the coat of arms are particularly fiddly, so you may prefer to paint these in yellow paint.)

5 Apply the gold leaf with the burnisher.

6 Mix some ultramarine and permanent-white gouache and paint the blue areas.

7 Using neat ultramarine, paint round the inside of the center of the "P," shading outward and then, with a wet brush, blending it into the pale-blue area.

8 Paint the red areas.

9 Outline the image with a mixture of black and burnt umber. Highlight the blue areas with permanent white.

Fifteenth-century English Border

❖ ❖ ❖

This project involves a capital letter taken from a fifteenth-century poem about St. Edmund, which is thought to have been written in the *scriptorium* of the abbey at Bury St. Edmunds, England. The decorative elements are fairly simple, but their effectiveness depends on a crispness of execution. The work needs to be done with flair and panache.

YOU WILL NEED

- ❖ Tracing paper
- ❖ Project paper
- ❖ 2H pencil
- ❖ Gesso
- ❖ P.V.A. gilding medium
- ❖ No. 1 brush
- ❖ Gold leaf
- ❖ Paper tube
- ❖ Burnisher
- ❖ Gouache paints: gold, red, ultramarine, green, brown, black, burnt umber, permanent white

1 Trace the image and transfer it to your project paper. (Remember that this should serve only as a guide.) The position of the box for the second capital depends on the text.

2 Mix a little P.V.A. gilding medium with gesso and apply a drop of the mixture to each berry using an old No. 1 brush.

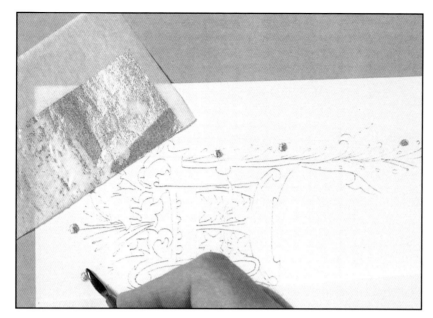

3 Breathe through the paper tube onto each berry in turn, starting at the top of the page. Take a sheet of gold leaf and, using the burnisher, rub it down over each berry.

4 Apply gold paint round the capital and down the stem.

5 Paint the blue, red, and green areas, having first mixed a little white with each color.

6 Paint the blue of the capital. Mix a lighter shade of the blue and paint the lighter part of the capital and the other light-blue areas. Paint the blue tips of the stamens.

7 Outline all the areas of color with the appropriate, undiluted color.

8 Paint the brown shadows on the red-acanthus stems and trumpet shapes.

9 Outline the gold areas with a mixture of black and burnt umber.

10 Highlight the blue areas with permanent white.

Thirteenth-century Border

❖ ❖ ❖

No study of illuminated and illustrated capital letters is complete without considering borders. Their variety is as diverse as the different styles of lettering and ranges from a simple colored line drawn down the margin, or between the columns of text, to almost a whole page of the most brilliant and complicated miniature and decorative work, with space allowed for only a word or two. How far you go on this path is up to your artistic inclination and ability, the time that you have to devote to the project, and probably the depth of the your purse. The borders that I have used in this work are relatively simple, but also complicated enough to add great decorative effect to your work, and to give you great personal satisfaction when you have successfully completed them.

This example is from a thirteenth-century book of hours and includes a frame for a miniature picture. The original had the capital letter "D," which I have included so that you can have some idea of the scale of such a letter, used in this way. You will see that there is very little room left for text and that this would have been confined to a few opening words or title and that the bulk would have appeared on the following pages.

The design is of the well-known ivy-leaf pattern and the leaves can be colored green or any other color of your choosing, or they can be gilded. You can mix them up, or you can use a different color for the leaves on each of the branches.

In my project I have just used red, blue, and green and have produced a solid and robust effect. You will see that I have applied white lines to the leaves and to the frame on the right-hand side of the design. By comparing the two sides, you can see what a difference this makes and how that side looks much lighter and more sophisticated than the left-hand side. Both treatments have their place. The one that you use depends on the effect that you wish to obtain.

Whether you paint a miniature in the frame, or use it to contain some significant text is up to you and the use to which the project will eventually be put.

It is worth remembering, that the original page was probably only 6 inches high and would have required the utmost patience and diligence to complete.

YOU WILL NEED

❖ Sharp 2H pencil

❖ Ruler

❖ T-square/parallel motion

❖ Right-angled set square

❖ Project paper

❖ Tracing paper or baking parchment

❖ Gesso or P.V.A. gilding medium

❖ Paper tube

❖ Gold leaf

❖ Gouache: gold and selected colors

❖ Brushes

❖ Burnisher

1 Draw the framework with a ruler and set square onto a piece of tracing paper or baking parchment. It is worth drawing it up in ink when you are satisfied, as it can be used at a later date, either as it is, or modified, for some other project. Draw it in a size that suits you and then use a photocopier either to enlarge or reduce it to the size needed for your project. (Remember that it is always worth drawing things bigger, if possible, and then reducing them down on a photocopier. This makes them look much neater and tighter.) When you are satisfied, trace your guidelines down onto your paper, marking the center and the diagonals with dotted lines. Clip the tracing to your project paper with paper clips, so that it does not slide about, and use a ruler to guide you as you trace down. Once you have finished tracing down, do not use the ruler again. Do the rest of the work freehand. The little irregularities that will inevitably occur, despite your best efforts, help to give the project a natural spontaneity that is the mark of hand-done work.

2 Within the guidelines that you have traced onto your project paper, carefully draw up your scheme of decoration. You may want to do this on a second piece of tracing paper so that you can make any necessary corrections without making messy erasures on your paper. If you do this, trace your finished design down onto your page. You should not need to draw over it: the traced outline should be sufficient.

3 Carefully stir up your P.V.A. gilding medium. (If you roll it on the desk, you will mix it well without causing any air bubbles.) Paint all the areas you wish to have gold. One coat will be enough, but it does soak into the paper, and so if you wish the gold to appear slightly raised you will need two coats. Each of these will take about thirty-five minutes to dry.

4 Take your paper tube and puff a warm breath onto a section to be gilded. It is important to do this before you apply any gouache paint or you will find that your hot breath will also soften the gum in the gouache and the gold will stick to that as well. While the P.V.A. is moist and sticky, take a sheet of gold leaf and carefully lay it over the spot. Take your burnisher and rub the leaf, especially round the edges, so that it sticks to the form and peels off the backing paper. You can see through this, and so can tell when the gold has stuck down. You may need to apply another coat if your cover is less than satisfactory. The gold will stick to itself, as well as any uncovered patches of the gilding medium. With a little practice you will be able to place your gold leaf down on the page so that you waste hardly any of it.

Start at the top of the page and work your way down, so that you do not lean on any of the parts just gilded. When all is completed, take a piece of baking parchment, lay it on the work and burnish all the gold to raise a deep, lustrous shine. Finish off with a light burnishing directly onto the gold. Take particular care to work with the point of your burnisher round the edges of each form. From now on, make sure that you have a piece of scrap paper between your hand and the work, so that you do not cause any damage to your completed work.

5 Take gold gouache and paint the four corners of the frame. When this is dry, you can burnish it to improve the shine, but the contrast between the paint and the gold is quite effective. You may find that you need two coats to obtain a satisfactory cover.

6 Carefully paint the border and the capital "D" with your choice of colors. I used two tones of blue. I mixed some ultramarine with some permanent white to make the pale blue and straight ultramarine to provide the darker tone.

7 With great care, do the outlining. The paint must be of the right thickness: too thin, and it spreads and does not cover; too thick, and it blobs and will not spread and cover evenly. Usually, outlining is done with a mixture of black and burnt sienna, which makes a very dark brown: too black, and it looks severe; too brown, and it looks pale and anemic. You could try a dark tone of each of the colors used: green leaves outlined with dark green and so on, reserving your black-brown outline for the gold areas. This is not as daunting as it may seem, as you can do all the green bits, then all the red bits, and so on.

8 You will need to decide how much you intend to highlight with white. This will depend on the effect that you seek and so I deliberately left some areas unhighlighted so that you can make up your own mind. You will also see that I have highlighted the leaves in different ways, some more, some less. This, too, will help you to decide what effects please you best.

111

Sixteenth-century Italian "R"

❖ ❖ ❖

This massive capital "R" comes from a sixteenth-century book of Italian music. It contains two miniatures: one at the top and the second under the arch of the leg. At first sight this is a daunting project, but take it calmly, step by step, and it will gradually organize itself.

YOU WILL NEED

- ❖ Tracing paper
- ❖ Project paper
- ❖ 2H pencil
- ❖ Gouache paints: ultramarine, red, brilliant yellow, green, permanent white, Prussian blue, gold, burnt umber, black
- ❖ Brushes

---

1 Make a tracing of the main elements of the design and transfer it to your project page using a very sharp pencil.

2 Block in the colors one by one: first the blue, then the red, and then the green, mixing each color with a little white.

3 Paint the darker tones, taking each color in turn. (Prussian blue made the very dark tone.)

4 Blend a little more white with each color and paint the lighter tones. Where necessary, use a wet brush to blend the tones together.

5 Highlight the green areas with brilliant yellow.

6 Highlight the blue and red areas with white.

7 Paint the small gold areas.

8 Highlight the top of the ribbon with white and use a little burnt umber to shade the underside.

9 Outline the design with a mixture of black and burnt umber.

Fifteenth-century "P"

❖ ❖ ❖

This project introduces the idea of writing the entire first word of the text within the capital, a concept that could have all kinds of applications. This example is based on a fifteenth-century model.

YOU WILL NEED

❖ Project paper

❖ 2H pencil

❖ Gesso

❖ P.V.A. gilding medium

❖ Brushes

❖ Gouache paint: yellow ocher, ultramarine, red, brilliant yellow, permanent white, gold, black, burnt umber

❖ Gold leaf

❖ Paper tube

❖ Burnisher

1 Make a tracing of the design and transfer it to your project paper. (If you want to modify the design, alter the tracing first.)

2 Mix the gesso with a little yellow ocher so that you can see it and apply it to the strapwork of the capital "P," the doves on the finials, and the letters that make up the word. You may want to lay on a second coat to raise it a little more.

3 When the gesso is dry, paint a thin coat of P.V.A. gilding medium over it and leave it to dry.

4 Blow on the gilding medium through the paper tube and then apply the gold leaf using your burnisher. Start in the corner farthest from you and do a small bit at a time, making sure that you cover the medium well as you proceed.

5 Paint the blue areas using neat ultramarine.

6 Paint the red areas using neat red.

7 Paint the green areas with a mixture of brilliant yellow, ultramarine, and white.

8 Paint the gold area in the center of the letter.

9 Outline the design in a mixture of black and burnt umber.

10 Outline the red and blue areas in white.

11 Apply a powdering of white dots to the red areas.

12 Highlight the green leaves in white and paint white dots along the green stems.

13 Paint gold dots onto the blue areas.

Fifteenth-century "W"

◆ ◆ ◆

This "W" was copied from a fifteenth-century manuscript and was originally an "M." I traced the letter and then turned the tracing paper upside down and traced the decoration, adapting it as necessary. This kind of adaptation will help you if you cannot find the exact letter or style of decoration needed.

I painted the letter using light and dark tones on all the colors, which adds greatly to the richness. It is highlighted in white and outlined in a mixture of black and dark umber.

Notice that I have drawn the bottom right-hand point of the gold square outward a little to give it more style and take the plainness out of the straight line.

Fifteenth-century "W"

♦ ♦ ♦

This impressive capital "W" was developed from a fifteenth-century capital "M." It was drawn freehand from the example, the different elements being reversed as necessary. The muted colors give it a subdued dignity, which is extremely attractive.

1 Take a careful tracing. Note that the black center is not symmetrical. You can leave it as it is or you can correct it in the tracing. The tail has a tendency to drift to the right and would look stronger if it were straighter. Correct this as you trace it.

Rule a grid on your tracing paper to contain the stem and the shape of the capital. Also rule a cross through the middle of the letter on your tracing paper. You will quickly see which parts you need to alter. As you trace it off, move the tracing paper about, so that the part you are tracing is correctly located in the grid that you have drawn. Thus, when you have finished, the whole will be correctly located on your tracing paper and you will be able to trace it down onto your project paper with every part located in the right place.

2 I chose to paint the green areas first as this seemed to be the predominant color. Mix up some yellow ocher and ultramarine. Carefully paint the green areas. Mix in a little white and paint the light tones.

3 Mix a little ultramarine with a little white and dull it down with some of the green mixture. Paint the blue elements. Add a little more white and paint the lighter parts.

4 Similarly, paint the red with madder carmine and then mix in a little white to paint the lighter parts

5 Paint the black with a 0000 brush. Take care to work neatly, using it to tidy up and delineate the green leaves and the gold elements in the center.

6 Take some of your green mix, add a little black and use this to paint the inside of the letter.

7 Highlight with white lines and dots.

8 Enliven the dark-green background color in the middle of the letter with gold dots. Notice that they are placed in threes.

9 Paint the rest of the gold areas.

10 Outline with a mix of black and burnt umber.

Simple Floral Treatments

♦ ♦ ♦

These little examples have been drawn to show how effective simple flower decorations can be. They have been drawn in ink and painted with watercolor. Because this is transparent, the pen line shows through and there is no need to outline. Were they painted with gouache, which masks the pen line, they would have to have outlines to neaten and tighten them up. They would, however, look brighter and more jewellike. The letters would have looked better had they been outlined with paint, but they point out the folly of trying to outline in pen more eloquently than a written warning.

Sixteenth-century Border

• • •

This border is an adaptation of the ivy-leaf pattern. The miniature was copied from one by the Italian master Guilio Clovio, who worked in the first half of the sixteenth century. He is regarded as the Michaelangelo of miniature painting, one of the finest illustrators of manuscripts who has ever lived. His borders typically contain classical figures, armor, architectural features, urns, and diverse decoration, all delicately and excellently drawn and colored. I have added the birds and creatures both to signify creation and to add some color and interest.

TIP

DRAFTING YOUR DESIGN

When you embark on a project, it is important to consider the text and the decoration together, so that you do not spend hours on one part only to find that you have created an irreconcilable conflict with the other. The size of the miniature, the disposition of the frame, and the location of the little box for the capital letter will be determined by the length of the text. Experiment with drawing draft shapes and layouts on a piece of rough paper. Keep all your drafts: if they have not worked for this project, they may well help you with another. Do not be afraid to try something new. Learn from the past, but develop that knowledge.

Templates

• • •

K

Templates

• • •

Q

Templates

• • •

G

Templates

◆ ◆ ◆

E

Glossary

◆ ◆ ◆

Ascender
In calligraphy, the stroke which ascends above the height of the lower-case letters.

Base
The medium used to adhere loose gold onto vellum or paper – gesso, size. or P.V.A.

Bestiary
A natural-history book, popular in the twelfth and thirteenth centuries, containing tales about animals, both real and imaginary.

Burnish
To polish or shine. In illumination, a burnisher (*see below*) is used on the gold to achieve maximum reflectivity and smoothness.

Burnisher
A smooth-ended tool, formerly a dogtooth or agate, now made of hard, smooth plastic or mineral.

Carpet page
Ornamental page of decoration, often cross-shaped, found in Celtic gospels.

Cursive
Informal style of script, with the letters linked. Used for letters and documents rather than manuscripts.

Descender
In calligraphy, a stroke which carries on below the height of the lower-case letters.

Diaper
To decorate with a small, uniform pattern – often used for the background to a scene or in the depiction of drapery.

Gesso
A mix of fine plaster and adhesive, which is used as a base to bind loose gold to the support in raised gilding.

Gloss
A commentary written alongside a text.

Gouache
Water-based, opaque paint often used in contemporary illumination instead of traditional tempera.

Gum arabic
A type of gum, added to powdered gold as a binder.

Gum ammoniac
A resin, purchased in crystal form, which is melted down with hot water to make size, the traditional base for flat gilding.

Gum sandarac
A resin used as a fine powder in the preparation of vellum for calligraphy and illumination.

Half uncial
A script using ascenders and descenders with the pen held at a slanted angle.

Historiated initial
An illuminated initial where the void of the letter is painted with a scene relevant to the passage it heads.

Insular
Refers to work produced in the British Isles c.550–900.

Interlace
A type of pattern where several lines or bands are plaited over and under each other.

Loose gold
Gold beaten into delicate, fine sheets, applied to a base in gilding.

Majuscule
Upper-case script.

Minuscule
Lower-case script incorporating ascenders and descenders.

Papyrus
Earliest form of support (*see right*), made from the stem of the papyrus plant.

Parchment
Sheep- or goatskin prepared to make a delicate support for calligraphy and illumination.

Pounce
A fine, abrasive powder which is used to prepare vellum for calligraphy.

Powder gold
Pure gold, sold by the gram, which has been ground to a powder. It is mixed with gum arabic and used for illumination.

P.V.A.
Polyvinyl acetate glue, which can be used as a base for raised gilding.

Rubrication
To emphasize part of the text in red. It is used in this book to describe the application of rows of red dots around the outline of illuminated letters in the insular style.

Serif
The strokes which end the main strokes of a letter, sometimes wedged or hooked.

Shell gold
Powder gold combined with gum arabic and allowed to harden in a pan (originally sold in a half mussel shell).

Size
Traditional base for flat gilding.

Support
The material used as a surface for calligraphy and illumination – paper, vellum, and parchment.

Tempera
A medium consisting of ground pigment and egg yolk, diluted with water.

Transfer gold
Sheets of gold manufactured as a transfer (i.e., with a backing sheet).

Trompe l'oeil
An illusionistic representation of a subject on the two-dimensional page which deceives the eye into thinking that it is three dimensional.

Uncial
A script used in manuscript writing by the Romans and Celtic peoples, such as Celtic uncial.

Vellum
Calfskin that has been prepared for calligraphy and illumination.

Versal
A capital letter from an alphabet of Romanesque origin, so called because it was used to plot the opening of a new verse.

Index

◆ ◆ ◆

CREDITS
Winchester Cathedral, Hampshire/Bridgeman Art Library, London/New
York
  p.14 Initial letter 'P' Prevaricatus Moab – The Moab Rebelled, II Kings:
illustration shows Elijah intercepting the messengers sent by King
Ahaziah, from the Winchester Bible (c.1150–80)
  p16 Initial letter 'V' Visio Abdie – The Vision of Obadiah: illustration
shows Obadiah of I Kings 18, v4 from the Winchester Bible, (c.1150–80)

Project artwork and calligraphy by Stefan Oliver
Photography by Nigel Bradley
Additional illustrations by Rob Shone

The Brontës

The Brontës

Brian Wilks

A STUDIO BOOK

The Viking Press · New York

For Marie
and
In memory of John

Acknowledgments

I am grateful to the Council of the Brontë Society for their kindness in allowing me to consult and reproduce material from the collection of manuscripts, paintings, drawings and books in their care at the Brontë Parsonage Museum at Haworth. In particular I would like to thank Miss Amy Foster, the Brontë Society Archivist, for her most patient and sympathetic help in searching out all manner of curious details. I am also indebted to Mr Norman Raistrick, Custodian of the Brontë Parsonage Museum, for his many kindnesses over frequent visits.

Any biographer of this extraordinary family owes much to Elizabeth Gaskell's biography of her friend Charlotte; I have an equal debt to the detailed studies of individual members of the family produced by Winifred Gérin in recent years. Fanny Ratchford's *The Brontës' Web of Childhood* remains an authoritative handbook of the children's writing. J. Lock and W. T. Dixon's *A Man of Sorrow* and Annette B. Hopkin's *Father of the Brontës* provided me with a most stimulating exploration of the Rev. Patrick Brontë's life.

At Leeds University I would like to thank the Keeper of the Brotherton Collection for allowing me to consult the Brontë material in his care, and my colleagues Paul Sharp and Robert Unwin who encouraged my tentative excursions into their more proper fields of study, and generously offered help with sources for my study of the nineteenth century and the history of Yorkshire.

I would thank the many people at Haworth who found time to humour yet another visitor, and especially Tyson Mather for his particular help.

My most lasting debt is to the late John F. Danby, the best of teachers and the kindest of friends, who taught me to appreciate the personal nature of literature and to consider the people behind the words.

Marie will know the measure of my gratitude, which extends to Jonathan and Jessica, whom I thank for the cheerful manner in which they accepted life with a father who was at times lost in the 1800s, bothering about some other children in a room full of papers and books.

Finally I thank Michael Stapleton, who has been the most understanding, encouraging and patient of editors.

Brian Wilks
Leeds 1974

Contents

Chapter 1

Introduction:
Romance and Reality

On Saturday, 9 November 1861, Charles Hale from Boston, Massachusetts set off to walk the four miles from Haworth to catch a train at Keighley. He was carrying, as souvenirs of his visit to Yorkshire, 'the whole lower sash of the window of Charlotte Brontë's bedroom', several 'panes of glass', some 'moulding or woodwork' and the 'entire wire and crank of Mr Brontë's bell pull'. Such was the spell that the family of writers had cast over the literary world. A few months before Mr Hale's acquisitive visit at a time of convenient renovation, the Rev. Patrick Brontë had died, and the contents of the parsonage, including his top hat and walking stick, had been put up for auction as mementoes and souvenirs.

Two reasons can be found for Mr Hale's pilgrimage: the popularity of the novels *Jane Eyre* and *Wuthering Heights*, and the world's fascination with Mrs Gaskell's biography of Charlotte Brontë. Since 1861 many have made similar expeditions to the modest moorland parsonage.

The homes of great writers are often the setting for legends and fanciful anecdotes about the people who lived in them, and Haworth is no exception. The nostalgia that prompts people to honour an old lady because once 'as a little girl she was privileged to knit the Rev. Nicholls a sock, under his wife Charlotte Brontë's instruction' tends to obscure the authentic story of the writer's life. This is a pity, for unadorned, the story of Patrick, Charlotte, Branwell, Emily and Anne Brontë is deeply interesting.

No family of writers can have attracted more attention than the Brontës. The tragic death of Mrs Brontë, leaving six children under the age of eight, and the subsequent untimely deaths of the children—not unusual at the time—have cast a tinge of pathos over most that is written about them. Knowing the whole story of their sufferings it is easy to forget that the parsonage was a home where four children grew to maturity, a place that at times would be filled with laughter as well as tears.

The years that the Brontës lived in Haworth were years of momentous social change. Almost every aspect of life was to alter during the first fifty years of the nineteenth century. The Rev. Patrick Brontë's life, from 1777 to 1861, began before the French Revolution and ended after the Crimean War. His lifetime covered the period of change from the ordered hierarchical society governed by an élite, to the thrusting industrial society ruled by competition and the dictates of trade. Through enclosure, the drift to the towns, and a series of desperate depressions, he was to see the poorest classes become 'the undeserving poor' condemned as 'moral failures responsible for their own condition' in a world where progress disregarded people. During his lifetime the population of the country was to treble, with more than three quarters of the population living in towns and working in industry. Epidemic diseases, starvation and unemployment were never far away while society was brutal and violent with no forces for law and order, other than military, until 1856.

Patrick's eighty-five years were years of contrasts and conflict. On the one hand there was astonishing progress and a growing sense of responsibility among those who governed; on the other, there was widespread prejudice against any attempts to change the *status quo*. It was still customary for gentlemen to fight duels to protect the honour of a lady. Indeed in 1821 John Scott, the editor of the *London Magazine*, which the Brontës read, was shot and fatally wounded by a friend of the editor of *Blackwoods*, which they also read. While little boys still climbed chimneys and worked till they were maimed or worn out in mills and mines they were still thought to be 'God's lambs'. A widespread problem with drunkenness faced a stiff temperance campaign: brutal violence and high moral principle were close fellow-travellers of industrialisation.

As an ordained clergyman in the Established Church of England Patrick Brontë had a social responsibility for everyone in his parish. As chairman of the Parish Vestry, the committee that ran the affairs of the parish, he was to concern himself as much with a campaign for piped water and higher standards of hygiene to combat cholera, as he was with spiritual matters. A glance at the minutes of this Vestry Meeting at any time during his forty-one years shows him organising vigilantes to protect people and property as well as appointing churchwardens. A builder of churches and Sunday schools where literacy was taught, he must have taken his enthusiasm and involvement home to his children. Charlotte was to teach in the church school; Branwell to serve on parish committees (one of them, ironically, the Haworth Temperance Committee) and in every way the children would be aware of the affairs that concerned the parish in which they lived. When trouble came to the village the parson would be in the thick of things. Of peasant stock himself, Patrick Brontë had a sympathy with the farmers and weavers of Haworth, knowing the problems of Chartism and the Luddite riotings as events happening in his own parish.

Perhaps of all the revolutions that he was to witness it was the revolution in transport that was the most profound. First the canal system and then the great railways ensured that a network of communications gradually covered the country. When in 1835 he sent his son to London it was by stagecoach and a journey that took two days; some ten years later his daughters were able to travel first class by overnight train from Leeds.

Yorkshire, during this period of industrial growth, was a grim county. With *habeas corpus* suspended Palmerston several times garrisoned troops in Leeds against possible riot and in fear of Civil War. Leeds itself became the unhealthiest city in England, with a foully polluted river, 15,000 people on poor relief attending soup kitchens and devastating outbreaks of cholera and typhoid.

It was in this world that the Brontë children grew up. A world where the average age for a Leeds working man at death was nineteen years. It was a world where the little boy who carried Mr Hale's baggage from Keighley Station had difficulty with parcels because he had severed his left thumb in the mill where he worked. As children of the parsonage the Brontë children were in no way sheltered from the realities of the world. Accompanying their father about the village they would have some idea of the problems facing people less fortunate than themselves. An educated man, their father took both the Tory and the Whig newspaper, and it was his custom to discuss the news with his children in order that they would grow up with an interest in events beyond Haworth and Yorkshire.

The nineteenth century was not wholly a time of misery, cruelty and repression. Steadily, social progress was being made. Men like Sir James Kay-Shuttleworth who lived but a few miles from Haworth carried on a great battle for reform and for the provision of education for all. Charlotte was to stay at Sir James' home and could scarcely have avoided concerning herself with his philanthropic interests. During her lifetime she was to see the first Public Health Act passed, the first Factory Acts and the Great Reform Bills in Parliament.

The Brontë Parsonage Museum, as it is today. The extension built after the Brontës' time can easily be identified. The older part of the house, though much restored, is still substantially the house they knew.

A stagecoach at the turnpike. At some time or another every member of the Brontë family was to travel by this means, an experience that Charlotte found most disagreeable, finding herself jolted and jostled among strangers. It being cheaper to travel 'outside', coaches were often top-heavy and on poor roads liable to overturn.

The Menai Suspension Bridge and the Britannia Tubular Bridge across the Menai Straits. These two great engineering achievements serve to indicate the transformation that almost every aspect of life in Britain underwent during the Brontës' lifetime. Sail made way for steam, the stagecoach for the railway train, craftsmanship and timber to mechanics' skill and steel.

A dinner plate, typical of the souvenirs that flow from Haworth. From the immediate success of Jane Eyre to the present day, tourism has lent its ingenuity to find ways of commemorating this remarkable family.

SELECT PIECE.

DUET.

How beautiful are thy dwellings, O Lord of Hosts ! My soul hath a desire and longing to enter into the courts of the Lord.

CHORUS.

Blessed are they that dwell in thine house : they will always be praising thee.

Before the Sermon.

Sing, ye parents, poor and lowly,
　Let your praises daily rise ;
Jesus knows your cases wholly,
　Jesus sends you kind supplies
　　For your offspring,
　To enrich and make them wise.

Sing, ye children, Jesus hears you,
　Jesus loves your artless lays :
Sure the glorious prospect cheers you,
　To be train'd in wisdom's ways ;
　　Let your voices
　Echo round the Saviour's praise.

Christian teachers, join your praises,
　Sing in elevated strains ;
Barren heaths, and dreary mazes,
　Soon shall all be fruitful plains :
　　Your Redeemer,
　Lo ! he lives—he lives and reigns !

AFTERNOON SERVICE.

HYMNS
TO BE SUNG IN THE
CHURCH OF HAWORTH,
On Sunday, the 19th Day of July, 1840,
WHEN
TWO SERMONS
Will be preached ; one in the Afternoon, by the
REV. JAMES CHEADLE, M. A.,
VICAR OF BINGLEY ;
And one in the Evening, by the
REV. G. R. ANSTEY, M. A.,
PERPETUAL CURATE OF WILSDEN.
Collections will be made in aid of the Church Sunday School,
Service to commence at Two o'clock in the former instance, and at Six in the latter.
In order to prevent crowding in the Gallery, Silver will be thankfully received at the entrance.

KEIGHLEY :
PRINTED BY R. AKED, BOOKSELLER, LOW-STREET.
1840.

Hymn sheet for a service in the old church during Patrick Brontë's ministry. The words of the hymn exemplify the burden of Patrick Brontë's own preaching: they are addressed to the common people of the parish, are homely, and offer comfort.

Other factors also affected the life of the Brontë family. They were a tightly knit group of people all sharing exceptional gifts, interests and ambitions. As Charlotte tells us:

My home is humble and unattractive to strangers, but to me it contains what I shall find nowhere else in the world–the profound, and intense affection which brothers and sisters feel for each other when their minds are cast in the same mould, their ideas drawn from the same source–when they have clung to each other from childhood, and when disputes have never sprung up to divide them.

Consequently their story is the account of a family growing up together towards a dependent maturity.

Another force which must have enfolded them was the sheer vitality of the evangelical brand of religion fashionable in the early nineteenth century. The singing of the great Wesleyan hymns and the hectoring tones of the preachers would be heard through the walls of church and parsonage alike. No wonder that their religion should be part of the fibre of their being, and that Anne should write hymns that typify the grim life that confronted the would-be Christian.

The Narrow Way

Believe not those who say
　The upward path is smooth.
Lest thou shouldst stumble in the way,
　And faint before the truth.

It is the only road
　Unto the realms of joy ;
But he who seeks that blest abode
　Must all his powers employ.

9

Bright hopes and pure delights
    Upon his course may beam,
And there; amidst the sternest heights,
    The sweetest flowerets gleam.

On all her breezes borne,
    Earth yields no scents like those;
But he that dares not grasp the thorn
    Should never crave the rose.

Arm—arm thee for the fight!
    Cast useless loads away;
Watch through the darkest hours of night.
    Toil through the hottest day.

Crush pride into the dust,
    Or thou must needs be slack;
And trample down rebellious lust,
    Or it will hold thee back.

Seek not thy honour here;
    Waive pleasures and renown;
The world's dread scoff undaunted bear,
    And face its deadliest frown.

To labour and to love,
    To pardon and endure,
To lift thy heart to God above,
    And keep they conscience pure;

Be this thy constant aim,
    Thy hope, thy chief delight;
What matter who should whisper blame,
    Or who should scorn or slight?

If but thy God approve,
    And if, within thy breast,
Thou feel the comfort of His Love,
    The earnest of His Rest.

Anne Brontë. 27 April 1848

We may flinch at the austere message of Anne's hymn, but we shall not begin to understand the Brontës if we fail to see the importance for them of the ideas it contains. The proximity of the parsonage and the church, within the single embrace of the same graveyard, was of deep significance in their lives.

Whatever the sources of the Brontës appeal may be, they have never ceased to be the centre of curiosity and interest. Within Charlotte's lifetime they had become part of English folklore and she was to see the first visitors seek out the parsonage:

> Various folks are beginning to come boring to Haworth, on the wise errand of seeing the scenery described in *Jane Eyre* and *Shirley* . . . but our rude hills and rugged neighbourhood will I doubt not form a sufficient barrier to the frequent repetition of such visits . . .
> (Charlotte, 1850).

Nowadays more than 50,000 people every year take the place of the 'various folks' who made their way to Haworth Parsonage and caused Charlotte to comment. Fortunately, few are as insistent as Mr Hale of Boston in carrying off such substantial mementoes of their visit.

The church of St Michael and All Angels as it was at the time of Patrick Brontë's ministry as perpetual curate, 1820–1861. This building and the pattern of life it established through the liturgy of the church was to dominate the family's upbringing, education and intellectual life.

Chapter 2

Patrick Brontë

THE POOR SCHOLAR

Patrick Brontë's influence upon his children was profound. Directly and indirectly his style of life and deeply held views were to shape their development as people and as writers. To know them we must first try to know him.

Variously described as selfish, cruel, eccentric; as a recluse and a bigoted tyrant, he has come to represent the popular idea of a typical Victorian father. The shortage of reliable information has allowed too much scope for good stories. The truth is more complicated than the convenient caricature of a bullying, narrow-minded parson. The Rev. Patrick Brontë has been a much misunderstood and maligned man.

Patrick was born in Ireland on St Patrick's day in 1777, the eldest of ten children. His father, Hugh Brunty, and mother Elinor (sometimes called Alice) were peasant farmers eking out a living at a time of poverty and hardship. Very little is known about his life in Ireland and it is uncertain whether the family name was Brunty or O'Pronty. At fourteen Patrick was to sign his name as Prunty on the flyleaf of an arithmetic book.

It is believed that a small two-roomed whitewashed cottage at Emdale near Loughbrickland in County Down was his birthplace, and the ruins of a cottage within sight of the Mourne Mountains have been honoured with a plaque to record this claim. Some say that his father Hugh was a 'storyteller' as well as a farmer. We do know that he was a Protestant who married a Catholic and that his children were brought up as Protestants. It is widely believed that the young Patrick was at one time apprenticed as a hand-loom weaver and later as a blacksmith; but in his own account of his early life, given in a letter to Mrs Gaskell a few years before his death, he makes no reference to these occupations. Whether from pride or forgetfulness the only career he mentions is teaching.

At sixteen he appears to have been an assistant school teacher. How he came to read and write, coming from a peasant cottage, we shall never know but somehow he did and turned it to good effect: 'I shew'd an early fondness for books, and continued at school for several years. At the age of sixteen–knowing that my father could afford me no pecuniary aid–I therefore opened a public school–in this line I continued for six years.'

It is thought that the school referred to is in Drumballerony.

To become a school teacher was in itself a remarkable achievement: it was, however, to be but the first of a whole series of surprising advances. From teaching at the Drumballerony school which was attached to the Glasscor Presbyterian Church, he was invited to become tutor to the sons of the Rev. Thomas Tighe, vicar of Drumballerony.

There can be no doubt that the three years this peasant's son spent living in Thomas Tighe's vicarage were to provide the main impetus for Patrick's life's work, for he now lived in the home of an educated man with books and the social contacts appropriate to a priest of the Established Church; moreover, Tighe's vicarage was the house

The cottage near Drumballyroney in northern Ireland where it is believed Patrick was born of peasant stock in 1777:
Well thatched, had a good earthen floor
One chimney in the midst of the roof
One window and one latched door.
(Patrick Brontë, 'The Cabin of Mourne')

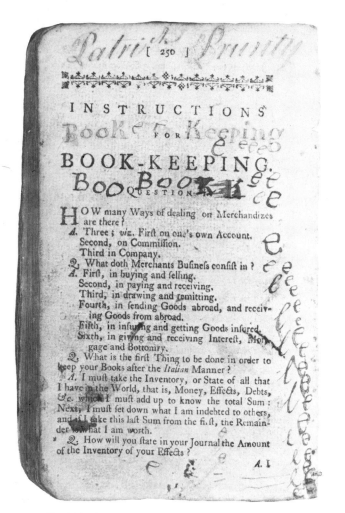

Patrick's signature as Prunty *or* Brunty *before he adopted the spelling of Brontê—which eventually became the Brontë used today.*

where John Wesley stayed during his regular preaching tours of Ireland. Whatever we may surmise of the influence such contacts in the religious and cultured household might have had on the young man, the facts are that Thomas Tighe was a graduate of St John's College, Cambridge, and that in 1802 it was to this college that Patrick, the son of an illiterate and poor Irish peasant, was admitted.

The missionary Henry Martyn describes Patrick's arrival at St John's: 'He has twice given me an account of his outset to college which for its singularity has hardly been equalled, I suppose, since the days of Bishop Latimer. He left his native Ireland . . . with seven pounds having been able to lay by no more after superintending a school for some years. He reached Cambridge before that was expended, and then received an unexpected supply of £5 from a distant friend. On this he subsisted for some weeks before entering St John's and has since had no other assistance than what the college afforded.'

It would be interesting to know how Patrick made his way to Cambridge, it was an extraordinary journey to make at all. To rise from the lowest class in Ireland was almost unheard of in the nineteenth century: it is a measure of Patrick's determination and courage that he not only became a school teacher but also an undergraduate at Cambridge. When he took his place at the

college it was as a 'sizar', that is, as a student who contributed to the cost of his place by acting as a personal servant to the noblemen undergraduates. One such nobleman in residence at the same time as Brontë was John Temple, who succeeded to his father's title in the same year and became Lord Palmerston.

All the signs are that the red-headed Irishman, at twenty-five some six or eight years older than his fellow students, was an able undergraduate. Today, in the Parsonage Museum at Haworth we can see two college prizes that he was awarded. Each is stamped with the college crest, and inscribed: 'My prize book. For always having kept in the *first class* at St John's College, Cambridge. To be retained semper.' To achieve the first class speaks well of his ability for his prizes would be won in competition with scholars from the English Public Schools, where boys would have had a rigorous classical education. His industry and ability combined to serve him well and he won further exhibitions and grants which, together with payments from tutoring other students, financed him for the rest of his time at college.

St John's, which Wordsworth had only recently left, was traditionally associated with the north of England. It is tempting to wonder whether its connection with Yorkshire was to influence Patrick's later decision to settle in the north after his ordination. Sir Roger Ascham, tutor to Queen Elizabeth I, one of St John's most illustrious men, was himself from Yorkshire and at times as many as half the St John's students were northerners. Be that as it may the mature Irish student made good use of his time there.

We cannot know for certain what subjects he studied, the traditional course would be theology, philosophy and classics. He later maintained that he had studied some medicine and he certainly continued an interest in that field. In 1806 the poor scholar achieved his ambition, he graduated with the degree A.B. (the modern Bachelor of Arts).

During the Cambridge years, England was under threat of invasion from France. Together with Lord Palmerston, Patrick joined a small volunteer force at the college, and long after it was his proud boast that he had once drilled and taken part in 'mimic military duties' with a Secretary for War. His interest in military affairs was to stay with him all his life, and there is at least one recorded instance of him corresponding with Palmerston about local civic matters.

It was while at Cambridge that Patrick changed the spelling of his name from Prunty to Brontë. The entry of his name in the college books is confused: whether Patrick's accent proved too much for English ears, or whether, as some would have it, he sought to sever his connection with his Celtic forebears or not, he took to spelling his name as Bronte with some kind of accent over the last letter in order to signify that it was not silent. Throughout his life he used a variety of marks over the 'e', never consistently using the form Brontë which his printed works carry, and which his children were to use exclusively.

There is some support for the belief that he adopted the form Brontë after his hero Nelson who was created Duke

of Brontë by the King of Naples in 1799. There is no
evidence to support the view that he wishes thereby to
give the impression that his own and Nelson's families
were related. It may simply be that he was the first
member of his family ever to need to write his name
frequently, and consequently to formalise its spelling.
Today it is customary to use the form *Brontë*, the form
that Charlotte always used but which her father used
little. Perhaps Charlotte copied this spelling from the
printed version given on the title pages of her father's
books?

'THE ROLLICKING, HANDSOME, INFLAMMABLE YOUNG IRISH CURATE'

Patrick Brontë was ordained as deacon by the Bishop of
London in the Bishop's Chapel at Fulham Palace in 1806.
Later in 1807, as was the custom, he was ordained as
priest in the Royal Chapel in St James Palace by the
Bishop of Salisbury. So the great ambition was achieved;
with Cambridge behind him the young Irishman was
finally launched, and freed from the poverty of his upbringing.

Rapidly moving from one curacy to another he made
himself a popular and welcome figure. First at Wetherfield in Essex, later in Wellington in Shropshire and then
in Dewsbury, he quickly familiarised himself with clerical
duties and his new station in life.

At Wetherfield he fell in love with Mary Burder and
appears to have been engaged to her–until her guardians
warned her off the young curate with the thick Irish
accent and no reputable family connections. There are
traces of bitterness in Patrick's letters about these events
although he admitted that he was perhaps trying to step
over class barriers. Some years later his interest in Mary
was to revive but not enjoy any happier reception.

At Wellington he met William Morgan, a fellow curate,
who was to become his lifelong friend and who was to share
his passion for Wesley's brand of religion. It was Morgan
who was to introduce Patrick to the Methodist Fennell
family, an introduction that was soon to solve Patrick's

*An entry in a prize copy of Horace won by Patrick Brontë at
St John's College, Cambridge, where he studied Classics,
Philosophy, Theology and some Medicine. Patrick made a
a habit of writing in the margins and fly leaves of books so that
many of those he owned show amendments and notes. This was
a practice his children readily copied in their search for paper
on which to write or draw. Many of their books are covered with
scribbled sketches, poems, lists of names and doodling.*

*The young Lord Palmerston. A fellow student of Patrick's at
St John's. It was Patrick's boast that at the time of the
threatened invasion of England by France, he and Lord
Palmerston had taken part in 'mimic military manoeuvres' as
a form of Home Guard training. It was probably from such
activities that Patrick's love of firearms grew. Shooting was as
much a part of university life in the nineteenth century as
study.*

matrimonial problems. It was also through Morgan that Patrick first came to Yorkshire. In the early 1800s the county was a legend amongst preachers; it was the centre of the great evangelical revival noted for its fine preaching and its fearless parsons. The young Patrick jumped at the chance of going to the county of Grimshaw, where Atkinson and Robertson were still active.

In December of 1809 he arrived to be curate to the Rev. John Duckworth, vicar of All Saints, Dewsbury. Duckworth was two years younger than Patrick, with an even younger wife. Lodged in the ancient parish house by the church, Patrick quickly came to enjoy the young couple's company and to discover his full powers as a clergyman. Beyond his duties as a priest, he also found inspiration of another kind from his new vicar's example. Duckworth was a celebrated writer of hymns and his love of literature was to be a spur to his curate's ambition to be a writer.

From the earliest times Patrick had written verses. Now in John Duckworth he found practical help and a successful model. It was some time, however, before he was to follow his vicar into print.

The duties of a clergyman in 1810 were far wider and altogether more secular than we nowadays imagine. In

The Chapel Royal in St James's Palace, London. The chapel where Patrick was ordained priest by the Bishop of Salisbury in 1807, and where many years later Charlotte's publisher escorted her to a service so that she might catch sight of the Duke of Wellington, who was both Charlotte and her father's great hero (see Chapter 16).

gaining the priesthood Patrick had also become part of the hierarchical structure for the maintainance of law and order. In a country that was divided into parishes, each with a large measure of responsibility for its own affairs, the parish priest undertook a high degree of responsibility for all the public affairs of the folk in his care. At a time of poor communications, no constables or policing of any kind, it was to the parish committee and the parish priest that people deferred for help and advice with their day-to-day problems. Throughout the nineteenth century the parish continued to play a vital part in the affairs of small communities, and it was through these means that the Established Church maintained its influence. One event with which Patrick concerned himself while at Dewsbury illustrates his readiness, and indeed his ability, to accept this function of his office.

A young man called Nowell had been thrown into the town lock-up as a deserter from the army. Local people knew that he had never *joined* the army and that he had been wrongly apprehended. With determination, and some skill, Patrick organised Nowell's defence and ultimately, by writing to Palmerston, saw that justice was done.

Nowell was released and Brontë's reputation amongst the Dewsbury parishioners rose. Under the pseudonym of 'Sydney' and with a quotation from Shakespeare's *Measure for Measure* as his text, Patrick wrote to the *Leeds Mercury* and published Lord Palmerston's pledge that Nowell's case should be remedied. Patrick's defence

THE COTTAGE.

of Nowell was no flash in the pan; his zeal for justice and his outspoken views earned him a popular following in the parish.

When Charlotte was writing *Shirley*, her novel set near Dewsbury at the time of the Luddite riots, she was to draw heavily upon events that took place during her father's time there. One pleasant but probably embroidered story tells of Patrick's encounter with a drunken man on the occasion of a Sunday School children's procession (or 'Walking Day' as it is known in the north of England). As the procession of hymn-singing children set off, their way was barred by an obviously drunken man. With no more ado, Patrick pitched him into the hedgerow and the children were able to continue. The problem of the return journey remained. The affronted man, a well known troublemaker, gathered his friends and determined to block the way as the children and the 'rollicking fiery' curate returned. Patrick, however, with a fierce eye and no doubt a ready shillelagh, defied the rascal and once more the Whitsun procession passed unharmed. Such are the tales that good clergymen could inspire in an age that reached back to legends and super-

Punch *cartoon of 1871 commenting upon the plight of cottagers who lived in great poverty. It is to Patrick Brontë's credit that sixty years before this cartoon he showed a deep concern for the cottagers in the parishes where he served. Ahead of his time he was pioneering forms of adult education, writing for, preaching to, and teaching the poorest of families and championing their cause. This he continued to do all his life, much to the chagrin of the mill-owners and the more wealthy people of his parish. His first book was entitled* Cottage Poems *and dedicated to 'all those who sweat in honest toil'.*

stition. By whatever means, it appears that Patrick became a popular figure in the parish and a byword for his humour, temper and courage. His habit of always walking with a stick earned him the nickname of 'Old Staff'.

One of Patrick's early poems has survived, and it gives us an insight into the kind of man he was. It originates from a time when John Duckworth and his wife Esther had gone away from Dewsbury and left the vicarage and their dog 'Robin Tweed' in Patrick's care. Patrick's concern for the dog's health prompted a letter which was in a form that he was to use again some forty years later when writing to Charlotte.

The dog addresses his mistress to plead his own case in a poem entitled *Tweed's letter to his Mistress*. The ability to compose in this way may account for the reports of his great appeal to children. It is not hard to see that the author of Tweed's letter (and also later, of Flossie's to Charlotte) must have been able to charm children in an age when so much teaching was forbidding and purposefully harrowing.

Tweed's letter to his Mistress

Ah! Mistress dear,
Pray lend an ear,
To simple Robin Tweed;
I've been to you,
Both kind and true,
In every time of need.
I have no claim,
To rank or name,
Amongst the barking gentry;
No spaniel neat,
Nor greyhound fleet,
To grace the street, or entry.
But then you know,
I still can shew,
A bonny spotted skin,
Can watch the house,
Kill rat or mouse,
And give you, 'welcome in'.
How oft have I,
With watchful eye,
And fondly wagging tail,
And bark, and whine,
And frisk so fine,
Said, 'Mistress dear, all hail'.
Rap! at the door—
I soiled the floor,
With capering, and with jumping,
Whilst on my back,
With lusty thwack
Fierce Esther was a thumping!
My love for you,
Still bore me through,
Whatever my disaster;
If you said 'Tweed'!—
And stroked my head,
Each wound had then a plaster.
Each night I lie
With sleepless eye,
And longing wait the morrow;
And poke my nose
And smell your clothes,
And howl aloud for sorrow!
The other night
By clear fire-light
I saw your gown a drying,
So, on the stones,
I stretched my bones,
And spent the night in sighing!
But all in vain!
I thus complain,
Alas! there's none to heed me,

You have not sent
As you were wont,
To Esther for to feed me.
Hard is my lot!
Since I'm forgot,
By one I'll love for ever!—
But mankind change
As round they range—
A dog, he changes, never.
A long farewell!—
The gloomy knell,
Will soon inform the neighbours,
That Tweed is dead,
And has got rid
Of all his cares and labours.
Your kind, trusty and humble dog, Robin Tweed, at my kennel near the Vicarage, Dewsbury, the 11th June, 1811.

COTTAGE POEMS, AND UNLAWFUL EVENTS IN THE MANUFACTURING DISTRICTS

Nothing illustrates the troubled times of Patrick Brontë's early ministry more fully than the Luddite rioting that took place on the borders of his first parish.

Leaving Dewsbury in 1811, he was appointed Vicar of the ancient church of St Peter's at Hartshead-cum-Clifton, a parish near to Dewsbury and overlooking the Calder valley. It was a widely scattered community with many cottages set in woodland. When Patrick began his incumbency the fourteenth-century church was in a bad state of repair and a tree was growing from the squat tower. However, nothing could spoil the new minister's pleasure as he considered the prospect of his own parish.

He came to Hartshead with a reputation for common-sense, learning, and strongly held principles; but above all he was respected for his sympathy for the poorer classes of society. During the four years that he was vicar three events took place which were to affect him deeply. They were the publication of his first books, meeting and marrying his wife Maria, and the riots that brought a detachment of cavalry to Dewsbury. By the time he left Hartshead he was to have acquired a wife and two daughters, written two books of poetry, and become the owner of a pair of flintlock pistols.

The publication of his first book is of great importance as an indication of the character and thought of the man who was to father and educate three novelists. He was the first Brontë to publish a book.

It has been customary to dismiss his writing as very bad and boring. But this judgement arises from a failure to understand the author's special intention and self-imposed aims. His careful and specific writings were not intended as bids for the crown of poet laureate. If we ignore Patrick's stated aim we do him the injustice of criticising his poems for their failure to be that which he never sought to make them. In the nineteenth century verse forms were used far more frequently and with far less pomp and awe than they are today. Poems with short lines, simple words, rhyme, and a plain subject were very popular, being easily memorised in a world where many could neither read nor write. The immense popularity of Robert Burns' poetry bears witness to this.

Patrick's book, published in 1811, was a collection of verses entitled *Cottage Poems*. The title is important, for 'cottages' were the homes of the illiterate and the semi-literate 'labouring poor'. Patrick's slim volume was not offered for the salon or the literary critic's palate. The aim of the collection of poems was to provide a 'reader' for the humblest, slowest and poorest of students. To this end the anthology was printed with a clear well-spaced type, and with no more than sixteen lines to the page. On the title page it bore the following address:

All you who turn the study soil,
 Or ply the loom with daily toil,
And lowly on, through life turmoil
 For scanty fare:
Attend: and gather richest spoil,
 To sooth your care.

Clearly the book had a specific audience in mind, it was for a very special market – indeed for a readership that many of Patrick's fellow clergy would claim did not exist and, what is more, *should not* exist. As he explained in the Advertisement, Patrick was pioneering in the field of popular adult education. In this respect he was many years ahead of his time: 'Cottage Poems is a title which the Author has prefixed to the following work, because it is chiefly designed for the lower classes of society.' He claimed that none of the poems were 'above the compre-

hension of the meanest capacities. For the convenience of the unlearned and the poor, the Author has not written much, and has endeavoured not to burthen his subjects with matter, and as much as he well could, he aimed at simplicity, plainness, and perspicacity, both in manner and style.'

He was attempting to provide the kind of book that Charles Dickens' Joe Gargery of *Great Expectations* would find helpful once Pip had started him reading. Patrick knew that what he was attempting was unique: 'As the Author has not seen any work of exactly the same nature, he has been obliged to think and speak for himself.'

For the next twenty years the need for specially suitable books for the labouring poor was to go unheeded. Already alert to the need in 1811, Patrick Brontë was to continue to write in this manner for the rest of his life. His *Cottage Poems* is one of the earliest attempts, albeit a modest one, to offer the soothing benefits of literature to the poorest people. As late as 1850 this was seen to be a dangerous undertaking which would inevitably lead to dissatisfaction

17

and rebellion. In his conclusion Patrick spiked his critics' guns: '. . . Though the delicate palate of Criticism might be disgusted . . . the business . . . might be rendered useful to some poor soul, who cared little about critical niceties, who lived unknowing and unknown in some little cottage . . .'

It was not for nothing that Patrick had studied at the same Cambridge college as Wordsworth; a glance at 'The Leech gatherer' or 'Michael' will indicate his model. The level of life in 'cottages' was for many little higher than that of beasts. With a few others Patrick Brontë believed that their lives could be made something better.

The man was a natural teacher. This little book amply demonstrates his high regard for the value of literature, derived no doubt from his 'early fondness for books' and also shows his concern that *all* should share its benefits.

A cartoon caricaturing the Luddites, starving unionists driven to desperate remedies for their real and imagined grievances. Rioting in protest at the introduction of machinery led to violent attacks on mills and people in the manufacturing districts. Patrick's first parish, St Peter's Hartshead, was the scene of ugly riots.

Here was the man who years later could rely on his nine years old daughter, Charlotte, to proof-read a sermon he was to publish while he chatted to his printer. The love of teaching that moved him to print the *Cottage Poems* would be present again in the education he provided for his children in the parsonage at Haworth.

Closely following the date of publication of the little book of poems, Patrick Brontë found himself at the centre of events that were to earn his parish and its neighbours a place in English social history. In 1812 a Luddite raid took place within a few miles of his church.

Our knowledge of this raid has two sources, we meet it in history books but it is also related in great detail in Charlotte Brontë's *Shirley*, a novel which deals with the problems facing the mill owners and their workers in the early nineteenth century. While still quite young Charlotte was to attend school in a house very close to the mill that the rioters attacked. With the impetus of the story that her father told her as a child and with her own knowledge of the place of the events she found ample material for her imagination to work upon.

Throughout the industrial revolution the old structure

Maddened men, armed with sword and firebrand, . . . rushed forth on errands of terror and destruction.

RAWFOLDS MILL.

of cottage life was to be gradually eroded. In this respect Patrick Brontë's poems may have come too late. The cottage weavers to whom they were addressed were to find themselves in a state of distress that it would take more than verses to soothe or dispel. For there was revolution in the air. The war with Napoleon, a failed harvest, rocketing prices for corn, high unemployment and widespread poverty all coincided with the introduction of machinery into the mills which were the only hope of employment for the desperate weavers. Rightly or wrongly they became obsessed with the belief that it was 'the frames' or machines, that were taking away their livelihood. Throughout the manufacturing districts of the north of England bands of desperate men were preparing for violent attacks upon property and people. Equally, the government, by suspending *habeas corpus*, were preparing to deal very firmly with any signs of disorder or civil war.

At any time of civil disturbance it was the clear duty of the clergy to support the rule of law. No man of the established church could condone rebellion. Some of Patrick Brontë's fellow clergy soundly denounced the Luddites from their pulpits and generated an animosity between the 'rebels' and the clergy that may have been one of the reasons why Patrick bought himself a pair of pistols.

Gradually matters near Hartshead came to a head. At first a consignment of machines was ambushed and the machines wrecked. Next an attack on a local mill was mooted and weapons were stolen throughout the parish. The mill owners made their arrangements for the defence

The mill within Patrick's parish where a Luddite raid led to the murder of Horsfall and savage reprisals by the law. Accounts of this riot, combined with Patrick's reminiscences were the source of Charlotte's Shirley, *her only overtly 'social' novel where she attempted to deal with the problems confronting the hard pressed mill-owners and the wretchedly impoverished mill-hands. Her account is compassionate, accurate and informed; the battle of Rawfold's Mill being portrayed in considerable detail.*

of their property and a detachment of cavalry was sent into the district.

At last the attack came. On Saturday, 11 April 1812, some hundred men attacked Rawfolds Mill near Cleckheaton. William Cartwright, with five soldiers and six loyal workmen, withstood the siege until more soldiers arrived. Two of the rioters died from their wounds almost at once, others were hurriedly hidden in various cottages in the area. The attack was a failure, but the diligence with which the mill owners pursued the rioters generated so much ill feeling that the Luddites determined to assassinate them. An attempt on Cartwright's life failed but Horsfall, who owned a mill near Huddersfield, was ambushed and fatally wounded. This murder was the signal for a ruthless hunt to bring all the rioters to trial. Later that year, at York, some men were acquitted, some sent to prison hulks, some transported, fourteen men were hanged. The judge suggested that because of their great number 'they might hang more comfortably on two beams'. The vicious treatment of the weavers had its desired effect, the Luddite cause had lost its impetus.

As the parish priest close to the events Patrick Brontë must have known some of the men involved in the rioting

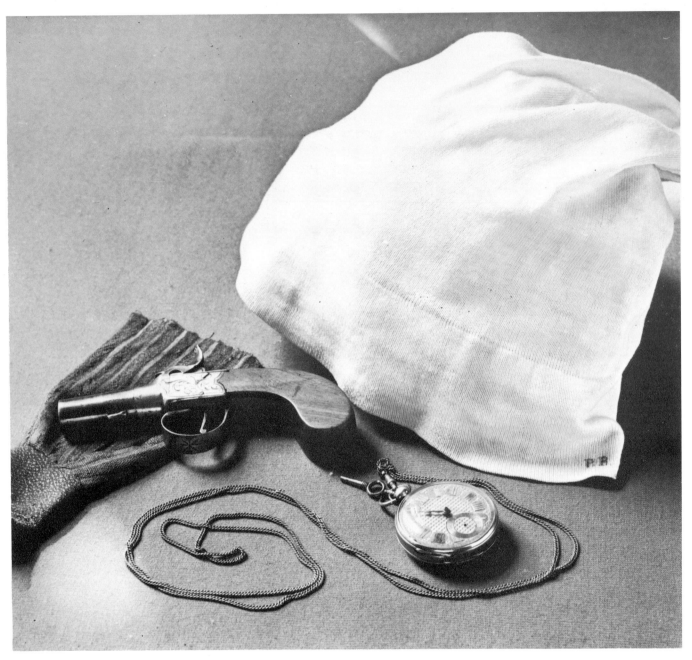

Patrick Brontë's pistol, nightcap and watch. It is thought that he first took to carrying a loaded pistol, in a pocket specially made in his greatcoat, at the time of the Luddite troubles in his parish. It was not unusual for a householder to keep firearms, there being no organised police or even night-watch at the time. Too much has been made of the fact that Patrick fired off the pistol each morning after leaving it loaded by his bedside through the night. This is the pistol he fired through the bedroom window, and, some say, made the 'bullet holes' which are to be seen on the church tower opposite the parsonage at Haworth.

and also their stunned and grieving families. The story is told that when one night he stumbled upon some men digging in a corner of his churchyard, he had the good sense to realise that it was an illegal burial of rioters who had died from their wounds while in hiding. He turned a blind eye.

The Leeds newspapers carried full accounts of the attack and the subsequent trial of the rioters, and we know that Charlotte sent to Leeds for all the relevant newspapers when she was researching material for *Shirley*.

Ironically Cartwright, who was awarded a medal for his gallant defence of Rawfold's Mill, lived to a ripe old age and was to become famous in Charlotte's portrayal of him in the character of Robert Moore, a man who 'did not sufficiently care when the new inventions, which he employed in his mill, threw the old people out of employ: he never asked himself where those to whom he no longer paid weekly wages found daily bread . . .' Here the daughter shows an imaginative sympathy for those very same cottage weavers for whom her father had intended his little book of 'plain sentiments in plain words'.

As a parson Patrick Brontë would have supported the rule of law over that of violent men. But he must also have puzzled over the desperation that drove his cottagers to hurl themselves so recklessly upon the muskets of the militia.

Chapter 3

Maria

Maria Branwell of Penzance in Cornwall when a young girl. Maria married Patrick Brontë on 29 December 1812 after a whirlwind courtship. Mother to his six children, she died of cancer within nine years of marriage.

Maria Branwell, the Brontës' mother, was born in Cornwall in 1783. She belonged to a genteel and much-respected family of Penzance merchants, was well educated and, having been brought up as a Methodist, a devout Christian. In almost every respect her childhood and upbringing was in marked contrast to Patrick's long struggle.

After the death of her parents, who left her with a small private income, she continued to live in Penzance with her maiden sisters Elizabeth and Charlotte, until the summer of 1812 when she left the temperate climate of Cornwall for a visit to an aunt and uncle in the harsher landscape of Yorkshire. It was during this visit that she met Patrick Brontë and they fell in love.

The uncle that Maria came to visit was John Fennell, first headmaster of the newly-established Wesleyan School at Woodhouse Grove near Bradford and it was to help her aunt run the domestic side of the boarding school that Maria came to stay. But she had also come to be a companion for their daughter Jane, and it was through cousin Jane that she was to meet Patrick, for Jane had recently announced her engagement in marriage to the Rev. William Morgan, Patrick's old friend and fellow curate. Naturally enough Morgan introduced Patrick to the Fennells and their work. So aptly had he fitted into their society with his own evangelical interests and experience in teaching that Fennell had appointed him as an examiner at the school. Thus the scene was set for Patrick Brontë, the curate in charge of St Peters, Hartshead, to walk ten miles to Woodhouse Grove to examine schoolboys' knowledge of the Bible, meet Maria Branwell and, in meeting her, find himself walking the twenty-miles round trip more willingly and more frequently than the inspecting of schoolboys' learning could ever require.

Their courtship was swift. Meeting in August, they were married in December, after an exchange of letters which chronicles their first friendship, their hopes, and their deepening mutual love. Nine of the letters written by Maria are all that we have of those months of earnest courtship: they tell its story from the first confirmation of friendship to the detailed description of the arrangements for the baking of wedding cakes. Maria was twenty-nine when they met; a small, delicate, rather shy lady with brown hair and hazel eyes. Shortly after their first meeting she wrote confirming their friendship:

Woodhouse Grove
August 26th, 1812

My Dear friend,
This address is sufficient to convince you that I not only permit, but approve of yours to me–I do indeed consider you as my *friend*; yet, when I consider how short a time I have had the pleasure of knowing you, I start at my own rashness, my heart fails and did I not think that you would be disappointed and grieved, I believe I should be ready to spare myself the task of writing . . . . If you knew what were my feelings whilst writing this, you would pity me . . . My uncle, aunt and cousin write in kind regards. I must now conclude with again declaring myself to be

Yours sincerely,
Maria Branwell.

She thus confirmed the 'friendship' that Patrick hoped had begun. From this reserved but committed tone Maria's letters grow rapidly more warm and candid as she confesses her deepening affection for her curate:

September 11th, 1812.
. . . Be assured, your letters are and I hope always will be received with extreme pleasure and read with delight. May our Gracious Father mercifully grant the fulfilment of your prayers! Whilst we depend entirely on Him for happiness, and receive each other and all our blessings as from His hands, what can harm us or make us miserable . . .

Again, on the 18th:

... How readily do I comply with my dear Mr B.'s request! You see you have only to express your wishes, and as far as my power extends I hesitate not to fulfil them. My heart tells me that it will always be my pride and pleasure to contribute to your happiness ...

Within a month, having accepted Patrick's proposal of marriage, she was able to write of their love in the most open terms:

October 21st

... I entreat you that you will do me the justice to believe that you have not only *a very large portion* of my *affection* and *esteem* but *all* that I am capable of feeling, and from henceforth measure my feelings by your own. Unless my love for you were very great, how could I so contentedly give up my home and all my friends – a home I loved so much that I have often thought nothing could bribe me to renounce it for any length of time together and friends with whom I have been so long accustomed to share all the vicissitudes of joy and sorrow? Yet these have lost their weight and though I cannot always think of them without a sigh, yet the anticipation of sharing with you all the pleasures and pains, the cares and anxieties of life, of contributing to your comfort and becoming the companion of your pilgrimage, is more delightful to me than any other prospect which this world can possibly present ...

Patrick clearly had won her heart. He became 'him whom I love beyond all others' who was to have no doubt that he possessed all her heart.

In November, Maria declared that she loved him 'above all the world besides', and in a most moving letter – when we consider the fate that lay before her – she forecast:

I think if our lives be spared 20 years hence I shall then pray for you with the same, if not greater, fervour and delight than I do now.

She was only to live nine of those twenty wished-for years.

The letters tell of picnics, walks by the river Aire and family excursions into the pleasant countryside around Woodhouse Grove. In the age of the motor car it seems hardly credible that Patrick would first walk some ten miles to meet Maria, only to spend the time with her 'walking'. But walk they did and it was on such an excursion, to the ruined Cistercian Abbey at Kirkstall, that Patrick proposed to Maria and was accepted, an event which he duly celebrated by composing a poem: *Kirkstall Abbey, a fragment of a romantic tale* which was published in his next book of verses. Of all Maria's letters the most endearing, and perhaps startling, is one which begins 'My dear Saucy Pat' and gives as good an insight as any into the character of the spirited lady who was to be the Brontës' mother:

Woodhouse Grove,
November 18th, 1812.

My Dear Saucy Pat,
Now don't you think you deserve this epithet far more than I do that which you have given me? I really know not what to make of the beginning of your last; the winds, waves, and rocks almost stunned me. I thought you were giving me the account of some terrible dream, or that you had had a presentiment of the fate of my poor box, having no idea that your lively imagination could make so much of the slight reproof conveyed in my last. What will you say then when you get a *real downright scolding*? Since you shew such a readiness to atone for your offences, after receiving a mild rebuke, I am inclined to hope you will seldom deserve a severe one. I

Woodhouse Grove School near Bradford. The school where Patrick, the visiting examiner, met Maria, the Headmaster's niece, and they both fell head over heels in love.

A page from a love letter from Maria to Patrick, which together with a few others and a brief essay on 'Poverty', represents almost all we can ever know about the mother of the Brontës. Clearly Maria was a woman of culture and some spirit. Note the postscript.

accept with pleasure your atonement, and send you a free and full forgiveness; but I cannot allow that your affection is more deeply rooted than mine. However, we will dispute no more about this, but rather embrace every opportunity to prove its sincerity and strength by acting, in every respect, as friends and fellow-pilgrims travelling the same road, actuated by the same motives and having in view the same end. I think, if our lives are spared twenty years hence, I shall then pray for you with the same, if not greater, fervour and delight that I do now.

I am pleased that you are so fully convinced of my candour, for to know that you suspected me of a deficiency in this virtue would grieve and mortify me beyond expression, I do not derive any merit from the possession of it, for in me it is constitutional. Yet I think where it is possessed it will rarely exist alone, and where it is wanted there is reason to doubt the existence of almost every other virtue. As to the other qualities which your partiality attributes to me, although

I rejoice to know that I stand so high in your good opinion, yet I blush to think in how small a degree I possess them. But it shall be the pleasing study of my future life to gain such an increase of grace and wisdom as shall enable me to act up to your highest expectations and prove to you a helpmeet. I firmly believe the Almighty has set us apart for each other; may we, by earnest, frequent prayer and every possible exertion, endeavour to fulfil His will in all things. I do not, cannot, doubt your love, and here I freely declare I love you above all the world besides! I feel very, very grateful to the great Author of all our mercies for His unspeakable love and condescension towards us, and desire 'to shew forth my gratitude not only with my lips, but by my life and conversation'. I indulge a hope that our mutual prayers will be answered, and that our intimacy will tend much to promote our temporal and external interest.

I suppose you never expected to be much the richer for me, but I am sorry to inform you that

Kirkstall Abbey near Leeds where, it is believed, Patrick proposed to Maria and was accepted. Patrick followed Wordsworth in his love of romantic ruined abbeys and celebrated Kirkstall Abbey in lines published in his third book of verse.

I am still poorer than I thought myself. I mentioned having sent for my books, clothes, etc. On Saturday evening, about the time you were writing the description of your imaginary shipwreck, I was reading and feeling the effects of a real one, having then received a letter from my sister giving me an account of the vessel in which she had sent my box being stranded on the coast of Devonshire, in consequence of which the box was dashed to pieces with the violence of the sea and all my little property, with the exception of a very few articles, swallowed up in the mighty deep. If this should prove the prelude to something worse I shall think little of it, as it is the first disastrous circumstance which has occurred since I left my home, and having been so highly favoured it

and if you complied with his request it is likely that we shall see you both here on Sunday evening. As we intend going to Leeds next week, we should be happy if you would accompany us on Monday or Tuesday. I mention this by desire of Miss F., who begs to be remembered affectionately to you. Notwithstanding Mr F.'s complaints and threats, I doubt not but he will give you a cordial reception whenever you think fit to make your appearance at the Grove. Which you may likewise be assured of receiving from your ever truly affectionate –
would be highly ungrateful in me were I to suffer this to dwell much on my mind.

Mr Morgan was here yesterday, indeed he only left this morning. He mentioned having written to invite you to Brierley on Sunday next,

Maria

Both the Dr and his lady very much wish to know what kind of address we make use of in our letters to each other. I think they would scarcely hit on *this*!

Many years later Charlotte wrote a moving account of how her father showed her these very letters:
'The papers were yellow with time, all having been written before I was born. It was strange now to peruse for the first time the records of a mind whence mine own sprang; and most strange and to me sad and sweet, to find that mind of a truly fine, pure and elevated order. They were written for Papa before they were married. There is a rectitude, a refinement, a constancy, a modesty, a sense, a gentleness about them indescribable. I wish she had lived and that I had known her.'

Maria and Patrick were married on 29 December 1812 at St Oswald's, Guiseley near to Woodhouse Grove School, in an unusual double wedding. The curates had hit upon the happy and convenient scheme of conducting each other's marriage by turns. Patrick married Jane Fennell to William Morgan while Maria acted as bridesmaid, and William married Patrick and Maria while Jane acted as bridesmaid. The wedding is commemorated by a plaque in the side chapel at Guiseley by the high, Jacobean altar rails at which the brides and their grooms knelt.

Only nine years after the marriage, Maria died of cancer, her death abruptly ending a very happy partnership as Patrick was to tell Mrs Gaskell:
'In a modest competency my wife and I lived in as much happiness as can be expected in this world – for nine years. At the end of that time, alas! She died, which occasioned great sorrow of heart to me and was an irreparable loss to both me and my children.'

Their short life together, however, was by no means a sad one. Patrick could be optimistic about his career, and their growing family would bring them great pleasure. From that December in 1812 Maria and Patrick set out on their path to Haworth blessed with a deep love for one another, good friends and the comfort of close and sympathetic relations.

Until the bleak September in 1821 when Maria died, after a prolonged and painful illness, all had gone well. Their first home, Clough House at Hightown near to Patrick's church in Hartshead, was comfortable and spacious and they were able to employ local girls as servants. It was while they lived here that their first children, Maria (1814) and Elizabeth (1815), were born.

At Hartshead Patrick was in his element. His zeal for popular education and his gift for getting on with people made him a popular parson. In his preaching, his teaching, his cottage meetings and his writings he found a ready and appreciative audience. For Maria the story was different. In coming to live at Clough House she had made a social journey which was in complete contrast to Patrick's progress from poverty to the priesthood. Having earlier forsaken the genteel security of her comfortable upbringing in Cornwall for the secluded country estate of her uncle's school at Woodhouse Grove, Maria now exchanged its riverside walks and romantic abbey ruins for a harsher landscape of poor farms and scattered cottages. She found herself close to the crippling poverty, social injustice and latent violence that prevailed in Yorkshire and many parts of the north of England.

Their stay at Clough House was, however, brief. After two years Patrick negotiated to exchange livings with the Rev. Thomas Atkinson, later to be Charlotte Brontë's godfather, who was then curate in charge of the Bell Chapel at Thornton near Bradford. The only reason ever given for this exchange tells us that Atkinson wished to move to Hartshead in order to pursue the courtship of a lady who lived there more conveniently.

For whatever reason, the livings were exchanged and in 1815 the Brontës moved to a house in Market Street, Thornton, and Patrick took charge of the old and rather unusual Bell Chapel, the ruins of which are still to be seen opposite the new church of St James. It was while they were living at the parsonage in Market Street, a rather drab little house which still stands, that their four remaining children, who would survive to adulthood and would so bemuse the world with their various talents, were born: Charlotte in 1816, Branwell, the only boy, in 1817, Emily Jane in 1818 and Anne in the January of 1820. The Brontës lived at Thornton for five years, long enough for Patrick to organise and complete the renovation of the dilapidated old chapel and to publish two more books: *The Cottage in the Woods* in 1815 and *The Maid of Killarney, or Albion and Flora* in 1818. The latter, whatever its value as a piece of literature, was published in London and is the first Brontë novel to appear in print. William Morgan

The birthplace of Charlotte, Patrick Branwell, Emily Jane, and Anne Brontë at Thornton. The butcher's shop was a later addition to what was once the vicarage.

25

reviewed his friend's book *The Cottage in the Woods* in his *Pastoral Visitor* of 1817 giving us a further insight into Patrick's concern for educating the poor through the provision of Sunday schools, often the sole form of education possible for the labouring classes:

'This is a very amusing and instructive tale, written in a pure and plain style. Parents will learn in this little book the advantages of Sunday Schools, while their children will have an example well worthy of the closest imitation. Young women may here especially obtain a knowledge that the path of virtue leads to happiness. We would therefore most cordially recommend this book to all sorts of readers.'

During Patrick's lifetime *The Cottage in the Woods* was published in three different editions and was perhaps his most successful work.

However insignificant, pedestrian or trivial the critics may find Patrick's books, they have an undeniable importance in the story of the Brontë family's literary development. Even their mother had made at least one attempt at literary composition and a respect for literature and an understanding of the discipline of writing permeated the whole of their lives. Whatever their intrinsic worth, Patrick's books were available to his children: they saw them in his study and in shops; they would read them and handle them; but above all, the fact that the books *existed* and that it was *their* Papa's name on the title page was to engage their imagination. At a remarkably early age the Brontë children set out to 'print' their own books, albeit as miniatures and copies of Papa's. As Charlotte tells us, the idea of being authors was as natural to them as walking and one they never forsook.

At Thornton the Brontë's were among friends. Elizabeth Firth, daughter of the patron of the Bell Chapel, recorded her friendship with the Brontë family with methodical care but infuriating brevity. Typical of her diary's notes being:

> *1818 February 12th*
> Expected Mr Brontë to tea, but Mrs B. Poorly.
> *July 30th*
> Emily Jane Brontë born.
> *November 19th*
> Heard of the Queen's death.
> *November 22nd*
> Put on mourning for the Queen.
> *1819 January 8th*
> M., E. and C. Brontë to tea.

The 'M., E. and C. Brontë' in question were only five, four and three years old! Miss Firth is tormentingly silent about her diminutive guests. With equal verbosity on 31 March 1820 she recorded:

> 'Good Friday; no service.
> We sat up expecting the radicals.'

Thus a lady in a house barred and shuttered against a rioting mob recorded the events which were altering the course of history. On 5 April 1820 she confirmed the time of the Brontë's leaving for Haworth:

> *April 5th*
> Took leave of Mr Brontë before leaving home.

On Thursday, 20 April 1820 a covered wagon followed by seven carts set off from Thornton to make the journey north-west by moorland road to Haworth. Patrick left the Bell Chapel to take up his appointment as perpetual curate to the parish of St Michael and All Angels at Haworth.

The events of the three Sundays prior to the Brontë's arrival at Haworth eloquently depict the extraordinary nature of the place to which they came.

Patrick was never vicar of Haworth for the parish was in reality still a part of the parish of Bradford, St Michael's church being a chapel of ease catering for those who could not get into Bradford for services. The appointment therefore was as perpetual curate. This subservience to Bradford was always a cause of friction in Haworth and since 1559 the appointment of a curate had been the occasion of feuding between the Vicar of Bradford, who officially had the right to appoint, and a group of trustees at Haworth who had received a charter from Queen Elizabeth I giving them the power to veto the Vicar of Bradford's choice. Time and again when choosing a curate the trustees and the Vicar of Bradford had found themselves at loggerheads. Patrick's appointment was no exception. On the one hand the Reverend Redhead, who had been assisting at the church during the previous incumbent's illness, was appointed with the support of one or two trustees and the Vicar of Bradford: on the other, Patrick Brontë was the man that the majority of the Haworth trustees wanted to appoint. Throughout a protracted theological/political wrangle Patrick behaved with dignity even to the point of withdrawing in Redhead's favour. But the men of Haworth had made their decision and when Redhead attempted to conduct services scenes ensued worthy of Dickens. Mrs Gaskell, in her *Life of Charlotte Brontë*, gives a lively account of the lengths to which the people of Haworth were prepared to go:

'The first Sunday he (Redhead) officiated, Haworth church was filled even to the aisles; most of the people wearing the wooden clogs of the district. But while Mr Redhead was reading the second lesson, the whole congregation, as by one impulse, began to leave the church, making all the noise they could with clattering and clumping of clogs, till, at length, Mr Redhead and the clerk were the only two left to continue service. This was bad enough, but next Sunday the proceedings were far worse. Then, as before, the church was well filled, but the aisles were left clear; not a creature, not an obstacle was in the way. The reason for this was made evident about the same time in the reading of the service as the disturbances had begun the previous week. A man rode into the church upon an ass, with his face turned towards the tail, and as many old hats piled on his head as he could possibly carry. He began urging his beast round the aisle and the screams, and cries, and laughter of the congregation entirely drowned all sound of Mr Redhead's voice; and, I believe, he was obliged to desist.

'Hitherto they had not proceeded to anything like personal violence; but on the third Sunday they must have been greatly irritated at seeing Mr Redhead determined to brave their will, ride up the village street, accompanied by several gentlemen from Bradford. They

The three-decker pulpit in the old church from which John Wesley and William Grimshaw had preached and inspired the great evangelical revival that made Haworth famous long before the Brontës came to live in the parsonage. The Brontë family pew was at the foot of the pulpit from which Patrick preached during his forty years ministry. The topmost part of the pulpit is now to be seen in the mission church at Stanbury.

put up their horses at the Black Bull – the little inn close upon the churchyard, for the convenience of arvills as well as for other purposes – and went into church. On this the people followed with a chimney sweeper, whom they had employed to clean the chimneys of some outbuildings belonging to the church that very morning, and after-

wards plied with drink till he was in a state of solemn intoxication. They placed him right before the reading-desk, where his blackened face nodded a drunken, stupid assent to all that Mr Redhead said. At last, either prompted by some mischief-maker or from some tipsy impulse, he clambered up the pulpit stairs, and attempted to embrace

An early photograph of the Parsonage at Haworth (The Glebe House) with its flanking graveyard. This is the bare, exposed house as the Brontës found it, before the sheltering trees were planted in the 1870s. Beyond the house stretched the open moorland.

Mr Redhead. Then the profane fun grew fast and furious. They pushed the soot-covered chimney sweeper against Mr Redhead as he tried to escape. They threw both him and his tormentor down on the ground in the churchyard where the soot-bag had been emptied and, though, at last, Mr Redhead escaped into the Black Bull, the doors of which were immediately barred, the people raged without, threatening to stone him and his friends. One of my informants is an old man who was the landlord of the Black Bull at the time, and he stands to it that such was the temper of the irritated mob that Mr Redhead was in danger of losing his life. This man, however, planned an escape for his unpopular inmates. The Black Bull is near the top of the long, steep Haworth street, and at the bottom, close by the bridge, on the road to Keighley, is a turnpike. Giving directions to his hunted guests to steal out at back door (through which, probably, many a ne'er-do-well has escaped from good Mr Grimshaw's horse-whip), the landlord and some of the stable-boys rode the horses belonging to the party from Bradford backwards and forwards before his front door, among the fiercely-expectant crowd. Through some openings between the houses, those on the horses saw Mr Redhead and his friends creeping along behind the streets; and then, striking spurs, they dashed quickly down to the turnpike; the obnoxious clergyman and his friends mounted in haste, and has sped some distance before the people found out that their prey had escaped, and came running to the closed turnpike gate. This was Mr Redhead's last appearance at Haworth for many years.'

To Redhead's credit, he refused to let this experience rankle, and indeed returned to preach at Haworth during Patrick's lifetime.

When Patrick finally arrived in Haworth as the undisputed perpetual curate he was content with his achievement:

'This living is what is here called a Benefice, or Perpetual Curacy. It is mine for life, no-one can take it from me . . . my salary is not large, it is only about 200 a year. But, in addition, I have a good House, which is mine for life, also, and is rent free.'

He had good reason for his satisfaction. The pulpit which he now occupied was famous throughout the length and breadth of the country. Haworth had been the centre of the great Wesleyan revival in Yorkshire and had secured its place in history books long before *Jane Eyre* began bringing sightseers to the parsonage. St Michael and All Angels had been William Grimshaw's church. Here the Wesleys had preached to overflowing congregations, here Grimshaw's own robust ministry had become a legend. Had he not whipped the sinners out of the alehouses and into church? Had he not prayed outside the windows of unbelieving cottagers as they lay dying so that they should 'go to Heaven with the word of God in their lugs' and had he not in the time of frequent typhus epidemics stayed in the parish with his flock, finally himself to die of plague through this strict observance of his duty?

In ascending the steep hill of Main Street, Patrick Brontë was now accepting responsibility for a well known parish, and completing a personal journey from the vicarage of Thomas Tighe in Ireland, where as a boy he had heard talk of the Wesleyan revival, to possession of one of the chief pulpits used in this great religious movement.

With his wife and six children, his book of verses and his unshakeable faith it would seem that all was well with the new curate as he took up residence in the Glebe House, which is now known as the Parsonage.

28

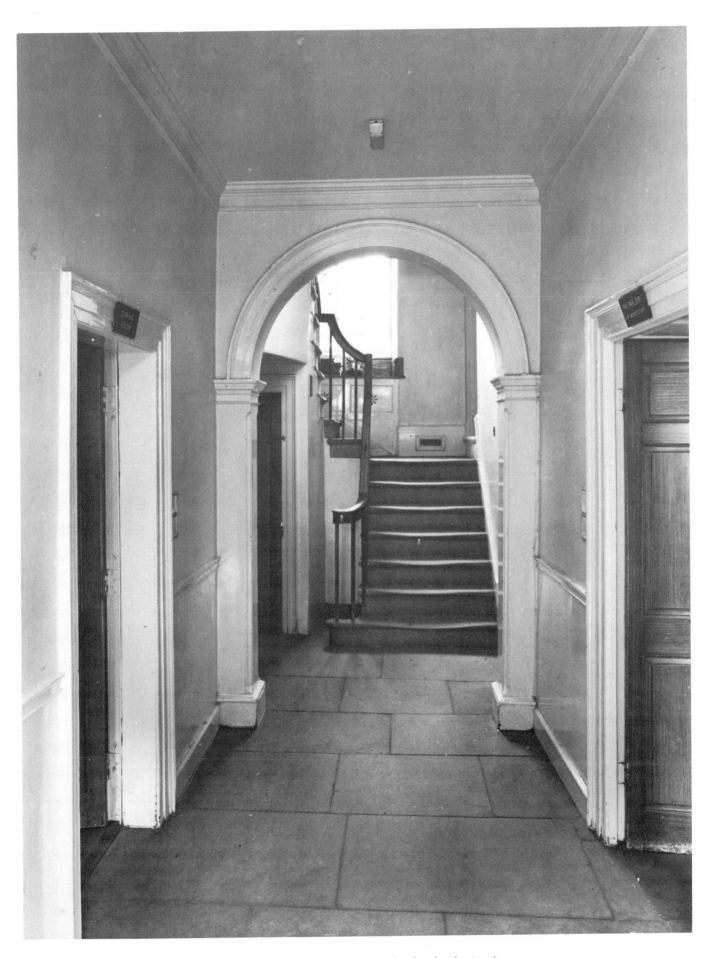

*The central hall of the parsonage as it is today—less damp and
in a better state of repair than the Brontës ever knew it.*

Chapter 4
Haworth

When the Brontë family moved to Haworth they came to the house that was to be their home for the rest of their lives. From childhood to maturity the compact Georgian parsonage influenced each member of the family in a different but equally profound way. Its effect was complex and never static, the way of life that the family developed breeding a peculiar unity and common dependence upon companionship in that one special house. In time this was to become an almost debilitating homesickness, for whenever they were away from home the Brontës' thoughts would turn inevitably towards Haworth, as Charlotte confessed in a letter from her school near Dewsbury:

> I am just going to write because I cannot help it. Wiggins (one of Charlotte's names for her brother Branwell) might indeed talk of scribblemania if he were to see me just now . . . that wind, pouring in impetuous current through the air, sounding wildly, unremittingly from hour to hour, deepening its tone as the night advances, coming not in gusts, but with a rapid gathering stormy swell— that wind I know is heard at this moment far away in the moors of Haworth. Branwell and Emily hear it, and as it sweeps over our house, down the churchyard, and round the old church, they think perhaps of me and Anne.

Here Charlotte describes the features of Haworth that were shared by all the family, that possessed their imaginations in absences and linked them profoundly. She writes of the close companionship; of the howl of the wind; of the church opposite the living room, standing over the sombre churchyard; and she writes of the unshakeable belief that those in the parsonage would be thinking of those elsewhere. Through a variety of circumstances the house came to cast some kind of spell over the children growing up within its grey stone walls. At times it was to seem to them a haven, a paradise to which they could retreat, where they could luxuriate in the relaxed companionship of like minds, at other times it seemed remote, isolated and as set apart from the world as a

prison, holding them enthralled and vulnerable as shy, lonely people.

The story of the Brontës of Haworth is also the story of the parsonage, their home, and we are fortunate in having reliable, clear accounts of its many moods, and the part it played as a background to their happiness and their sorrow.

Beyond the parsonage lay the small town of Haworth and beyond that were the moors, both were to combine to make a unique setting which would dominate and shape the Brontës' developing imaginations. There can be few writers more influenced by the total effect of their circumstances than this Celtic family growing up in Yorkshire. Their response to their environment, to its landscape, its people and their affairs, was part of a continuing dialogue, a constant exchange of impulse and ideas that began when they were very small children and continued until their deaths, shaping their attitudes to life and providing unique experiences which were to fit them for their work as writers.

In 1820, the parish of Haworth was large, covering more than ten thousand acres of high moorland with a population of well over four thousand. A parliamentary inspection of Haworth in 1850 gives a clear picture of the village as the Brontës knew it, and details that we can recognise today:

'The face of the country around Haworth is very hilly and bleak, as there are but few trees to arrest the wintery winds. The village or town of Haworth, as the inhabitants style it, is high up upon the hillside, and is very much exposed to the wind. At a few hundred yards above the village a very extensive tract of moorland commences, which extends far and wide to the south west, with nothing to relieve the unbroken surface of bog and peat, excepting at the end next to Haworth where huge hollows and vast spoil heaps, mark the spots at which it has been very extensively worked for flagstones and ashlar blocks. The Penistone Quarries, as they are called, furnish employment to a considerable number of inhabitants of Haworth, both in quarrying the rock, and in hauling the stone to all parts of the surrounding country.'

Although more than half the parish was uncultivated common land, vast peat bogs and tracts of very poor soil, it is wrong to see Haworth as a remote, isolated, sleepy country village. For many years it had been a busy centre for the woollen industry, being connected with the great sheep farming areas in North Yorkshire and Lancashire. It had a turnpike road and was part of a web of packhorse trails that brought wool for combing and weaving in very large quantities to what was in effect one of the busiest centres of its kind in the whole of Yorkshire. Haworth, already an ancient hamlet in the eighteenth century, played a substantial part in the growth of the wool trade at Halifax and Bradford, and at one time the wool-combers of Haworth, whose cottage workshops can still be seen, processed more wool than their counterparts in Bradford. The Halifax wool exchange had a special room set aside for Haworth trade and long after the introduction of machine combing and weaving, the high quality of Haworth work ensured that trade continued. While the village was surrounded by moors it was also encircled by mills and factories, a feature that Charlotte described: 'The scenery of these hills is not grand, it is not romantic; it is scarcely striking. Long low moors, dark little heaths, shut in valleys where a stream waters here or there a fringe of stunted copse. Mills and scattered cottages chase romance from these valleys, it is only higher up, deep in amongst the ridges of the moors, that Imagination can find rest for the sole of his foot; and even if she finds it there she must be a solitude loving raven, no gentle dove.'

With the mills went a remarkably dense population for so small a hamlet. By 1853, Patrick Brontë's parish included some 7,000, of whom over 2,000 were packed into the tiny town. Haworth was no lonely retreat far from the grim realities of life dependent upon the fickle fortune of trade. The land of the parish was inadequate to support its population, being unsuitable for agriculture, and even the oats for the oatcakes which served for bread came across the Pennines or down from North Yorkshire by pack mule. The life of Haworth depended upon trade, and

---

Haworth in the twentieth century. The stone houses still crowd together at the top of the hill by the rebuilt church and the Black Bull. The long windows of the weavers' cottages are clearly seen, the trees around the church show the extent of the graveyard that undermined the health of the village. The parsonage can be seen opposite the tower of the old church. Beyond the village the stone walls mark off the small fields that the villagers farmed. At the foot of the valley, by the river Worth, are two of the mills, some of the first in Yorkshire to be powered by steam, where the children of the village laboured in the nineteenth century.

Haworth Church and Parsonage.

Published by Smith, Elder & Co, 65 Cornhill, London 1857.

Mrs Gaskell's sketch of the church and parsonage, in which she allowed herself a romantic but telling exaggeration of the desolate prospect facing the parsonage children.

upon an industry that was to see bad times during the Napoleonic wars and the various depressions that accompanied the Industrial Revolution. The village was in many ways a microcosm of greater England where a see-saw of economic boom and depression was to cause considerable social distress and change.

The problems that the country faced, of plague and pollution, of poverty and repressive poor laws, of overcrowding and infant mortality, did not pass Haworth by, on the contrary there is evidence that the small cramped hamlet saw more than its fair share of the human misery that stains the record of progress in the nineteenth century. The Brontë children could not fail to know what life in the village was like; their father was directly concerned with the grim conditions his parishioners endured. The idea that he and they remained aloof from the village is false. The evidence of the parish minutes and all kinds of correspondence show that he was fully involved, often taking the lead, in the affairs of the parish. It was Patrick who read the burial service over the 40 per cent of children in Haworth who died before reaching the age of six, and it was Patrick who had baptised them and married their parents. In forty years of ministry at St Michael's and All Angels, he would have dealings with more than one generation of the families in Haworth, sharing in their joys as well as in their sorrows. Daily and weekly, through the calendar of the church and secular events, he would be at work; schools and churches do not build themselves,

neither do watch committees, nor parish poor-relief meetings organise their own affairs.

The round of church services, geared as they are to the lives of men and women, to births, marriages and deaths, presented the family in the parsonage with first-hand experience of all kinds of people and a great variety of problems. The parsonage was as much a parish office where plans for petitions to parliament were drawn up as it was a home for the Brontë children. The social problems of the people of Haworth, as well as Bishops and Archdeacons, came to the Brontës' front door.

Although trees have softened the outlines of the heavily built stone houses whose roofs are hewn slabs of stone set against powerful winds, the town remains much as it was in 1820, its huddle of buildings sprinkled across the very summit of one of the steepest streets in England. This cobblestone road rises like a wall between houses clinging to each other for support. These houses were the weavers' and the woolcombers' workshops, the long low upstairs windows and the outside stairs bearing witness to the purpose of their design. These were the overcrowded unhealthy homes where charcoal stoves burnt day and night to keep wool the right temperature for processing, and where families slept in unventilated rooms with no means of sanitation. At the top of the hill public houses, general stores and the Post Office still encircle the small cobbled clearing that serves for the village centre. No one who has climbed the hill to reach this 'square' will deny its individuality, the old buildings still asserting their character despite the inevitable trappings that accompany shrines of literary pilgrimage.

The village is, however, changed utterly in one particular since the day that Patrick and his family arrived. Partly due to Patrick's influence and persistence – and the course of history – Haworth is now healthier and sweeter smelling than ever it was in the Brontës' lifetime. Gone are the middens, the privies and the dung-heaps that littered the main streets, clogged the passages between the cramped dwellings, and seeped their disease-laden refuse along open channels down the main street. In common with other 'towns', Haworth in 1820 possessed not one water closet and no drainage system. For many years, through overcrowding, ignorance and by nature of its hill-top setting, Haworth had been particularly susceptible to plague and disease. Its water supply was poor and prone to giving out completely in hot summer months when the typhus epidemics were rife. The villagers' habits were unhealthy in the extreme, many sharing privies and keeping animals close to their own quarters, often cellars below the level of cesspits and drains. The offal of slaughtered animals – many families kept either pigs or donkeys – filled common middens and festered on dung heaps.

Even the parsonage was without proper sanitation, the family of adults and children sharing with their servants a double-seater privy out in the yard. A government inspector's report on conditions in Haworth in 1850 depicts a situation that had not altered much in thirty years:

'Two of the privies used, by a dozen families each are in the public street, not only within view of the houses, but exposed to the gaze of passers by, whilst a third, as though even such a situation were too private, is perched upon an eminence, commanding the whole length of the main street. The cesspit of this privy lies below it, and opens by a small door into the main street; occasionally this door is burst open by the superincumbent weight of night soil and ashes, and they overflow into the public street, and at all times a disgusting effluvium escapes through this door and into the street. Within two yards of this cesspit there is a tap for the supply of water to the neighbouring houses.'

Perhaps here we find good reason for the Brontë children not being seen too frequently in the main street, for the abundant evidence of door scrapers and Aunt Branwell's insistence on wearing pattens to raise her shoes above the ground.

However appalling such conditions may seem to our fastidious noses, they were fairly common in towns throughout the nineteenth century, which makes it all the more significant that a government inspector should find Haworth so exceptional. Invited by a petition organised through a committee which Patrick Brontë chaired, the inspector reported that the mortality rate at Haworth equalled that of the worst slums in London, that the average age at death was at times as low as 19·6 years, with forty-one out of a hundred children dying before their sixth birthday:

'It is lamentable to think that so large an amount of infant mortality should have been taking place year after year unknown and unheeded, the inhabitants of Haworth being quite unaware of it.'

This grim feature of Haworth's history concerned the

Harvesting in the fields. The dual economy of the village saved the inhabitants from the most abject poverty. Although the land was poor it supported some cattle and a few crops. Work in the fields also served to offset the appalling conditions in which the weavers or wool-combers and their families worked and lived.

Brontës directly, Branwell, Emily and Anne all died within the twelve years for which the inspector compiled his figures. But his report was critical of yet another aspect of parish custom, and one that involved the Brontës still more closely: Babbage reported with alarm that the burial ground surrounding the church, and the parsonage, was dangerously over-filled and a constant danger to health.

Edwin Chadwick in his extensive investigations into the sanitary conditions of the country, which led to the first public health act in the 1840s, had established a direct link between the custom of burying the dead in towns and disease:

'Inasmuch as there appear to be no cases in which the emanations from human remains in an advanced stage of decomposition are not of a deleterious nature, so there is no case in which the liability to danger should be incurred either by interment (or by entombment in vaults, which is the most dangerous) amidst the dwellings of the living, it being established as a general conclusion in respect to the physical circumstances of interment, from which no adequate grounds of exception have been established; –

A wool exchange of the early nineteenth century. It was in a similar exchange at Halifax that the Haworth wool was bought and sold, having been brought down from the village by pack-mule train. For many years Haworth wool formed the major part of business at Halifax exchange, while long after the introduction of machinery the hand-weaving and hand-combing of Haworth was still the preferred process for the best quality wool.

PUBLIC HEALTH ACT

(11 & 12 Vict., Cap. 63.)

REPORT

TO THE

GENERAL BOARD OF HEALTH

ON A

PRELIMINARY INQUIRY

INTO THE SEWERAGE, DRAINAGE, AND SUPPLY OF
WATER, AND THE SANITARY CONDITION
OF THE INHABITANTS

OF THE HAMLET OF

HAWORTH,

IN THE WEST RIDING OF THE COUNTY OF YORK.

BY BENJAMIN HERSCHEL BABBAGE, ESQ.

SUPERINTENDING INSPECTOR.

LONDON:
PRINTED BY W. CLOWES & SONS, STAMFORD STREET.
FOR HER MAJESTY'S STATIONERY OFFICE.
1850.

*Title page of a Government Inspector's Report on conditions
in Haworth in 1850.*

That all interments in towns, where bodies decompose, contribute to the mass of atmospheric impurity which is injurious to the public health.'

The parsonage, so Charlotte believed, had not only been built in a graveyard but was also built over graves. Its supply of drinking water, moreover, being a well sunk into that same cemetery. Chadwick in 1843 had also commented on that practice:

'My attention was first directed to this matter in London ten years ago, when a glass of water . . . presented a peculiar film on its surface; . . . after numerous inquiries, I was fully satisfied that the appearance which had attracted my attention arose from the coffins in a church-yard immediately adjoining the well where the water had been drawn. Defective as our information is as to the precise qualities of the various products from drains, church-yards, and other similar places, I think I have seen enough to satisfy me that in all such situations the fluids of the living system imbibe materials which though they

do not always produce great severity of disease, speedily induce a morbid condition, which . . . renders the body more prone to attacks of fever.'

Thus the melancholic cemetery which had seen 1,344 burials in the ten years of the health inspector's survey, a rate on average of two burials a week, was a continual threat to the family's health. Again and again in correspondence and the details of their lives, we read of ill health, of headaches, sore-throats, low fever and weakly constitutions. The bare, overcrowded cemetery at Haworth was a particularly unhealthy one, for added to the usual dangers of an ill drained, over used, small area, there was the custom of covering the graves with great flat stones which ensured that nothing would grow over the graves to assist in decomposition. Babbage, the inspector, was clear in his condemnation:

'This practice is a very bad one as it prevents that access of atmospheric air to the ground which is necessary for promoting decomposition; and, besides, the stones take the place of those grasses and shrubs which, if planted there, would tend to absorb the gases evolved during decomposition, and render the process less likely to contaminate the atmosphere.'

He concluded that all burials in the churchyard should cease and that no further burials should take place in the vaults beneath the church. Both his orders were ignored; only after Patrick Brontë was buried in the family vault in 1861 was the church finally closed for burials.

By that time visitors to the church were adding their experience to Chadwick and Babbage's theories; '. . . the exhalations from the remains of past generations inside the building have long rendered it a most undesirable place in which to worship without being too pungently reminded of the ultimate end of all things.'

It was as much for this reason as any other that Patrick's successor agreed to demolish the church where the Brontës had worshipped and been buried, to cement over the whole floor above the vaults and build the new St Michael's church which we visit today.

The graveyard, now softened by the trees which were planted after the Brontës time, must be seen as a powerful influence in their experience. It was not merely a macabre setting, it was a real menace to their very lives. It is little wonder that Charlotte and Emily could both write of it with such melancholy: the one with clarity, the other with nostalgia, thus typifying the family's ambivalence to their circumstances.

Charlotte:

'There have I sat on the low bedstead, my eyes fixed on the window, through which no other landscape than a monstrous stretch of moorland and a grey church tower rising from the centre of a churchyard so filled with graves that the rank weeds and coarse grass scarce had room to shoot up between the monuments.'

And yet, for all the grim reality of the churchyard setting, Emily could speak for the family, and evoke the spell that the old house could weave:

There is a spot mid barren hills
Where winter howls and drives the rain . . .

. . . the house is old, the trees are bare,
Moonless above bends twilight's dome . . .

. . . the mute bird sitting on the stone,
The dark moss dripping from the wall,
The thorn trees gaunt, the walks o'ergrown
I love them, how I love them all.

Emily's love of Haworth was inclusive, it embraced the harsh physical conditions which appal us, for she saw with a realist's eye. The squalor and menace that so offends today would have been commonplace to the Brontës, and indeed to their contemporaries. The poise and dignity the Brontës sought and found in their striving to transcend the limitations of their environment were the rewards of hard fought battles and life-long campaigns in which physical and mental powers would be stretched to the limit.

In every respect their experience of life is remote from ours; it is only by a great effort of the imagination that we can hope to begin to understand the taut and troubled lives they lived. In medicine, for example, they could hope for little help. Remedies were often desperate, crude, limited and mere expressions of good will on behalf of helpless but sympathetic doctors. They could expect little relief for the agonies of toothache which today we scarcely suffer. Neuralgia, headaches, and slight infections could nag and debilitate them with their depleted diets and weakened resilience for days, weeks and months. The seasons would bring hardships that none could avoid, so that ultimately Charlotte would hope that her dying sister Anne might last a few months until warmer weather when she might have a chance of recovering.

They were vulnerable in many ways that we are not. In common with their contemporaries they suffered childrens ailments that invariably debilitated. Whooping cough and scarlet fever would weaken lungs and constitutions which might never again be sound and robust, but remain vulnerable and susceptible to infection for a lifetime. In this respect their story is no different from many of their contemporaries who survived the vicissitudes of childhood in the early nineteenth century.

But the Brontës were, perhaps, unfortunate in spending virtually all their lives in one of the unhealthiest small towns in England, continually exposed to virulent epidemic diseases and a constant undermining of their constitutions.

Knowing the state of Haworth, the source of the parsonage drinking water and the brief expectancy of life during the period of their youth, it is astonishing, not that they died so young, but that they lived longer than could be expected given the circumstances of their childhood and the trials that they faced.

THE PARSONAGE

To the children the move to Howarth was an adventure and a mystery. They were all too young to understand much that was happening. Maria, the eldest, was only six years old. The long journey across the moors by rough roads and in a covered wagon followed by a string of carts loaded with their belongings, was the farthest the family had ever travelled. To the children none of the drawbacks of Haworth would exist. Even the adults were unaware of the sinister implications of the insanitary overcrowded village. The children only knew that they were going to a new home, to a house where there would be

The churchyard at Haworth in the 1880s.

35

The parlour of the parsonage, with the piano that all the children played, except Charlotte who was too shortsighted. The wallpaper is a reconstruction of a probable pattern, but it should be remembered that it was not until Charlotte was a successful writer that there were any curtains, carpets or wallpaper in the house. Patrick's fear of fire had meant that the windows had remained un-curtained while the children grew up.

new rooms and cellars to explore, a garden to play in with a wilderness of moors waiting beyond. The menace of the cemetery would mean nothing to them; to the small children the parsonage and its little yard would become their world, their brother and sisters their close companions. For some time to come managing the front steps and the stone staircase would preoccupy them above all other concerns.

Despite frequent renovations, additions, and the inevitable patina of veneration acquired by museums, the parsonage as it stands today incorporates the house that the children found on their arrival in 1820. The addition of the north wing by Patrick's successor and the subsequent building behind the house have not altogether altered the original symmetrical and compact house beyond recognition. With the help of Mrs Gaskell's description, and her sketch of the church and parsonage, it is easy to discover the house as the Brontës knew it;

'. . . an oblong stone house, facing down the hill on which the village stands, and with the front door right opposite to the western door of the church, distant about a hundred yards. Of this space twenty yards or so in depth are occupied by the grassy garden, which is scarcely wider than the house. The graveyard goes round house and garden, on all sides but one. The house consists of four rooms on each floor, and is two stories high. When the Brontës took possession, they made the larger parlour, to the left of the entrance, the family sitting-room, while that on the right was appropriated to Mr Brontë as a study. Behind this was the kitchen; behind the former, a sort of flagged store-room. Up-stairs were four bed-chambers of similar size, with the addition of a small apartment over the passage, or "lobby" as we call it in the north. This was to the front, the staircase going up right opposite to the entrance. There is the pleasant old fashion of window seats all through the house; and one can see that the parsonage was built in the days when wood was plentiful, as the massive stair-bannisters, and the wainscots, and the heavy window frames testify.

'This little extra up-stairs room was appropriated to the children. Small as it was, it was not called a nursery;

indeed, it had not the comfort of a fireplace in it; the servants . . . called the room the "children's study".'

In one respect, however, the house and its surroundings have changed beyond recognition. It was not until after the Brontës died that the trees which now dominate the churchyard and the parsonage were planted. The Rev. Wade, who followed Patrick as perpetual curate, made considerable changes to the appearance of the place; he rebuilt the church, leaving only the original tower, added rooms to the house and planted trees, thus incurring the wrath of early Brontë lovers who saw his acts as vandalism. In 1820 no trees at all sheltered the house or screened its living room windows from the newly dug graves. Today, if we are to understand the place the Brontës knew we must, in our imagination, sweep away the trees, shut our ears to the romantically calling rooks and rebuild the small decaying old church in place of the late Victorian building which now dominates the lane. Only then will we visualise the isolated house set four-square against the elements opposite the squat ancient tower.

Patrick and Maria would be pleased with their new house. It was the best that they had ever occupied. Nevertheless it could be a cold and cheerless place, built and paved with stone; it was sparsely furnished with only a few floor coverings and no curtains at all to soften the windows and walls. Through his own poor eyesight and his children's short sightedness Patrick developed an excessive fear of fire which led him to forbid curtains of any kind, a practical eccentricity which would keep the rooms as bleak and draughty as possible.

We know little of the life that Maria established, in the home she managed for her children. There is no reason to believe it was not a happy one. All the children had survived childbirth and must have been comparatively healthy when they came to Haworth. Patrick would find scope for his talents in his parish and they would both share his pride in occupying one of the best-known pulpits in Yorkshire.

But any happiness was to be short-lived. Before they had lived in Haworth twelve months Maria became ill with an incurable stomach cancer. Patrick was stunned; at his time of greatest achievement all that he cared for was now in jeopardy. After Maria's death Patrick wrote to his former Vicar, John Buckworth, at Dewsbury, telling of her suffering:

> My dear wife was taken dangerously ill on the 29th of January last; and, in a little more than seven months afterwards, she died. During every week, and almost every day, of this long, tedious interval, I expected her final removal. For the first three months, I was left nearly quite alone, unless you suppose my six little children, and the nurse and servants, to have been company. Had I been at Dewsbury, I should not have wanted kind friends; had I been at Hartshead, I should have seen them, and others, occasionally; or had I been at Thornton, a family there, who were ever truly kind, would have soothed my sorrows; but I was at Haworth, a stranger in a strange land. It was under these circumstances, after every earthly prop was removed, that I was called on to bear the weight of the greatest load of sorrows, that ever pressed upon me . . . At the earliest opportunity, I called in different medical gentlemen, to visit the beloved sufferer; but all their skill was in vain. Death pursued her unrelentingly. Her constitution was enfeebled, and her frame wasted daily; and after above seven months of more agonising pain than I ever saw anyone endure, she fell asleep in Jesus, and her soul took its flight to the mansions of glory. During many years, she had walked with God; but the great enemy, envying her life of holiness, often disturbed her mind in the last conflict. Still, in general, she had peace and joy in believing; and died, if not triumphantly, at least calmly, and with a holy, yet humble confidence, that Christ was her Saviour, and heaven her eternal home.

During this time all six of the children were also ill with scarlet fever and Patrick felt more keenly his sense of helplessness in his new parish.

This was a testing time for him, the rollicking sprightly young curate, the happy father and proud poet was now oppressed with grief:

> . . . there were seasons when an affectionate, agonizing *something* sickened my whole frame, and which is I think of such a nature as cannot be described, and must be felt in order to be understood.

The optimism of Maria's letters and their plans for their future life now seemed sour with the cruel turn in events. Patrick was desolate:

> And when my dear wife was dead and buried and gone, and when I missed her at every corner and when her memory was hourly raised by the innocent yet distressing prattle of my children, I do assure you my dear Sir, from what I felt, I was happy at the recollection that to sorrow, not as those without hope, was no sin; that our lord himself had wept over his departed friend . . .

Maria's last thoughts had been for her children and there is a tradition that she died saying 'My poor children, my poor children.' With her death on 25 September 1821 one set of circumstances was now complete, the family of small children were thrown upon each others' kindness and companionship, first the young Maria, and later Charlotte, were to be as mothers to the other children. Simultaneously a dependence upon each other and independence from adults began to develop. The scene was now almost set for the unique process of the next twenty years in Haworth parsonage, a process where circumstances and personalities would interact to produce a startling creative energy and imaginative scope. With their father shouldering a lonely burden, the first of a prolonged series of sorrows that dogged him through the rest of his long life, and with their own loss of a mother's care and affection, the whole family came to feel isolated and removed from friends and relatives. Somehow the sorrow at the death of Maria sealed Patrick's solitary nature and ensured a remoteness which accompanied him for the rest of his days and led to his reputation, an unjust one as it happens, as a recluse.

Patrick had himself been ill at various times with acute bronchial trouble which had led to his curious habit of muffling his throat and chest with the scarf which is so prominent a feature of his portraits, and his wife's death led him to share her concern for the children. As long as he lived they had a home, but he knew full well that his house belonged to the church and that, should he die, his children would be homeless in a world that made little provision for orphans. This fear and realistic concern stalked the family for many years. In time it became a sharp spur to the children's drive to be educated and competent to earn their own living.

It is perhaps only natural that a widower with six small children should consider the possibility of remarriage. Patrick made at least two such proposals. The first to his friend, Elizabeth Firth of Thornton, godmother to the children; the second, some two years after Maria's death to his former fiancé of earlier years, Mary Burder: both turned his proposal down. The former kindly but the latter with no little scorn that if she were to marry it would be with a man with a future and not six children at his side.

All too soon the happiness and pride with which Patrick and his beloved Maria had made their way to Haworth had evaporated. Patrick was never quite able to recover from his bereavement, or to find himself as buoyant and contented in his ministry. After a while a satisfactory solution was found for the children's future and the domestic arrangements at the parsonage. Maria's older sister Elizabeth, who had come to Haworth in order to help nurse the dying Maria, agreed to make the parsonage her home, to take the responsibility of bringing up the children and overseeing the running of the household. Always a close friend of Patrick and Maria and a frequent visitor in happier times, Elizabeth Branwell took her place in the parsonage and added her influence to the many others that came together to create the pattern of the Brontë children's childhood.

Chapter 5

Minds cast in the same mould

As Elizabeth Branwell boarded the stage coach in Penzance to begin the long and exhausting journey north to Yorkshire, she could not look forward to her arrival with the pleasure that had lightened her journey for previous visits. Then she had travelled in order to be a godmother at her niece's christening, or to enjoy the social life at Thornton, now she was hurrying to help nurse her desperately ill sister Maria and to share the sadness that surrounded the six small children in the parsonage. The long uncomfortable days in a jolting coach carrying her away from her beloved Cornwall were taking her to a grim bedside and a sad conclusion to a few happy years.

It was an ironic twist of fate that brought Elizabeth to Haworth. At forty-five, the well-educated spinster gentlewoman with a modest but sufficient private income might have expected a reasonably well-ordered and peaceful personal life, instead she was about to be plunged into the very hurly-burly of family affairs which she had expected to forgo. Elizabeth could have looked forward to a life as unencumbered by the inconvenience of children as it was free of the dangers of childbirth and the vicissitudes of matrimony. She would have had her own thoughts about her younger sister's whirlwind courtship and swift marriage to a poor Irish curate. Each year she had received the news of another pregnancy and another birth and would, during the six years, have had ample opportunity to consider the contrast between Maria's experiences and her own more peacefully ordered life.

In coming to Haworth to nurse her dying sister and in ultimately agreeing to live at the parsonage as guardian of her nieces and nephew, Elizabeth was accepting a complete change in her way of life; in doing so, she also found a place in the history of English literature. As Miss Elizabeth Branwell of Penzance, history might well have passed her quietly by; as Aunt Branwell, the presiding genius over domestic matters at Haworth Parsonage, the small maiden lady contributed to the circumstances that nurtured Charlotte, Emily, Anne and Branwell and which, in time, produced their literary works.

By all accounts, Aunt Branwell was a character. Friends of Charlotte who met her later in life noted with a certain awe her delight in arguing fiercely with Patrick, her habit of wearing only silk, that she wore false curls at the front of her old fashioned bonnet and that she took snuff and enjoyed the consternation that this unladylike behaviour caused in company.

Above all, she seems to have lived by a code of doing one's duty, and in this respect her influence in the parsonage was profound. The same sense of obligation that was to bring her to care for her dead sister's children and share in the life of a large family was conveyed in full measure to the children. In their lives and their works a sense of duty, of obligation and concern with moral choices, ebbs and floods as a continuing tide that finds its way into every kind of private and public event.

Patrick would be relieved and grateful that his 'dear sister' was prepared to stand by him and help in bringing up his children. They had previously been on very good terms and all the evidence shows that they were able to share a common view of the priorities that should prevail in the household. Patrick always spoke and wrote with a high regard for Miss Branwell, consulting her and respecting her wishes and opinions in all the matters relating to the children. She thus became very fully a member of the family and not merely a rather sombre and shadowy figure brooding in the best bedroom over the parlour.

In one respect Aunt Branwell obviously—and in a telling way—altered the pattern of life in the parsonage. The presence of a quite 'elderly' maiden lady with her own private bed-sitting room in so small a house established and continually reinforced a highly structured way of life. Her privacy and the need to defer to her presence combined to polarise the domestic affairs of the household and the public life of the parsonage. It emphasised and made distinct the feminine from the masculine and added to the hierarchy of Patrick, the children, and the servants which was quite formally apparent, and which helped in defining the 'little worlds' or domains that sprang up in the compact house. The parsonage was to become a microcosm where a variety of groups or individuals had a right-

Elizabeth Branwell as a young girl. Aunt Branwell came to Haworth to nurse her dying sister Maria and stayed to care for the six small children after her death. Living with the family for twenty years, Aunt Branwell was a good friend to Patrick and a strong influence on the children. To Branwell, the only boy, she was a substitute mother.

which was implanted in the small Brontës' minds, thus nurturing the idea of individuality and a sovereignty of spirit so evident in their mature works. From 1821 to 1842 Aunt Branwell's presence and her personality were effectively part of the parsonage life that enveloped and sustained the family.

As it was illness that brought Aunt Branwell to Haworth, so it was the threat of illness that combined with other factors to shape the course of events over the next few years. Whether or not Patrick was a hypochondriac and self-indulgent in his worries about his health, his illnesses, however slight, were a source of great anxiety. There was little security behind Patrick, his climb to a position in the church and society had achieved much but his stipend of £200 left little room for complacency.

It is hard for us to imagine the precarious nature of the lives people led in the early part of the nineteenth century. We know with hindsight that Patrick was to live for an astonishingly long time; it was the family's part to be vulnerable and a prey to the epidemics and illnesses all too common in their day.

Patrick Brontë was not a rich man, he had no private source of income, no property and no rich relations. His own struggle for education had brought him to Haworth, he now faced the harder struggle of providing for the children and securing for them the means, should the necessity arise of earning their own living. In this, the Aunt was to play an important part.

There is a tradition that the Branwell family had some connection with teaching and that their house in Penzance at one time included some kind of school. Whether Elizabeth had been a governess or not, she became the first teacher of the Brontë children, her bedroom became their classroom. Here they read their lessons, sewed their samplers and learnt to turn collars and cuffs of shirts and dresses. But here too they were encouraged to read and discuss current affairs. Through newspapers and journals, often supposedly inappropriate material for young children, through *Blackwoods, The Lady's Magazine* and all kinds of pamphlets, religious and otherwise, the children were introduced to a wide variety of writing. In this, Aunt Branwell reinforced Patrick's habit of including the children in discussion of events of the times through which they were living, for not only did he maintain an interest in military campaigns, the business of the houses of parliament, the current developments in literature and the arts in general, but he also drew these matters to the children's attention, expecting and encouraging them to become well-informed and able to express opinions founded upon knowledge.

Many commentators have been impressed by this unusual habit, and the older children's ability to discourse at length on affairs of the day became legendary with the servants and acquaintances of the family. In all this, Aunt Branwell shared, adding her personal contribution, of a more 'romantic' and ephemeral nature than Patrick's and providing a feminine approach to the more weighty matters of the day.

On the whole Aunt Branwell remains an enigmatic figure. More than one biographer has wondered why she

ful rôle and position. Such an order, based upon the necessary distinctions of propriety, were in their turn beneficial in the process of education that the children experienced. The clear frontiers and proper distinctions natural to people other than man and wife living in close proximity would be as helpful and conducive to the children's development, as they would at first appear to be restricting. The order of things that meant Papa would keep to his study, Aunt to her room and the servants to the kitchen meant that the children could designate the bedroom their study and be masters of their own territories which included cellars, the peat store, the kitchen (under sufferance), and the moors.

The inhibiting of intimacies that Aunt's presence would imply, and the consequent formality of the arrangements in the house, could provide a powerfully secure home with well-defined patterns for living and behaving. At times this would be a boon and a comfort, at others a stifling constraint. The children early came to know that privacy should be respected and in return were allowed a privacy of their own which is perhaps the most treasured commodity of a growing mind. The Aunt's presence endorsed and amplified the need for discretion and consideration remained at the Parsonage so long after the children had grown up. If all the accounts of her plainings about her long-lost Cornwall are to be believed, it is a wonder she did not shake the dust of Haworth from off her feet at the earliest opportunity. The truth is that, whatever her memories of Penzance, she remained at Haworth, in her own way devoted to her nephew and nieces, leaving them her possessions and her money, and finally, at her own request, being buried beside her sister under the floor of the church at Haworth.

One of her most delightful legacies is her teapot, one of the prize possessions of the Brontë Parsonage Museum. To some its sombre motto:

To me to live is Christ
To die is Gain

smacks of Calvinism and has all manner of sinister implications about a 'religious' bent, and a supposed 'dislike' of children. However this may be the teapot does present a conundrum. The quotation from St Paul emblazoned on its side was also the Rev. Grimshaw of Haworth's favourite text. It was the text painted on the sounding board above the three-decker pulpit from which Grimshaw, Wesley and Patrick Brontë preached, it was painted on Grimshaw's plain wood coffin and preached upon at his funeral. It is the text to be seen today on the splendid candelabra from the old church which now hangs in the Brontë memorial chapel of the new building.

If Aunt Branwell had brought the teapot with her from Cornwall it would be a rare sign of sympathy with the evangelical Grimshaw and one that suggests some kindred feeling for Haworth that we may too readily overlook. Whether the teapot comes before or after her taking up residence at the parsonage, it reminds us that Haworth was celebrated as Grimshaw's parish and pulpit long before it became known as the home of novelists. The self-exiled Cornishwoman may well have known of Grimshaw and Haworth before ever her brother-in-law came to preach in his place or administer Holy Communion from his famous wine flagons. Whatever her reasons for owning the theologically apt but rather morbid teapot it suggests that its owner identified more strongly with some aspects of Yorkshire than we have been led to believe.

Sewing samplers under Aunt Branwell's critical eye, and reading lessons to her and Papa, hardly suffices as an education intended to fit the children to earn their own living. By 1824 it seemed necessary to Patrick that the older children should receive a more formal education than he and his sister-in-law could provide in the parsonage. For a while the older girls attended the school at Crofton, near Wakefield, which their godmother Elizabeth

A sampler sewn by Emily at the age of ten. The Brontë girls' sewing was not the fancy work of leisured ladies but the practical sewing needed in the running of a home for six children, two adults, and servants. The girls were expected to sew, bake, clean and help in all the chores of the household.

So practical was their knowledge and experience that some critics of Charlotte's books were certain that they had been written by a man, for no lady could possibly know how to prepare a fowl for the oven or write with knowledge of such matters.

The Rev. Carus Wilson, founder of the Cowan Bridge School. A man whose harsh view of the 'sinfulness' of small children combined with wealth and great energy to make him an important influence in shaping the nineteenth-century attitude to them. Carus Wilson was Charlotte Brontë's pattern for Mr Brocklehurst as the founder of Lowood in Jane Eyre. *Wilson's supporters saw the fiction as a slander, and mounted a campaign to discredit Charlotte which persisted even after her death.*

Firth had attended but, perhaps through expense, they were soon withdrawn.

Eventually a school was found which seemed particularly suitable. This was the school for the daughters of clergymen which was newly opened at Cowan Bridge near Kirkby Lonsdale, some fifty miles from Haworth. Set on the border of Westmorland and Lancashire, Cowan Bridge school was a semi-charitable institution which provided full board and tuition for the daughters of poor clergymen. It was to cater for orphans and others at a nominal fee of £14 each pupil per year, the balance of the cost of the education to be met from donations and the generosity of sponsors. The school was to be linked with another more senior institution which would train the girls to be governesses: 'so that there is a two-fold advantage conferred on clergymen—a sound and cheap education, and future provision for his daughters' the most likely, if not the sole profession open to them.

Whichever way Patrick and Aunt Branwell looked at the venture, the 'two-fold advantage' would seem sensible and appropriate for his children. Education for girls was not easy to find in the first part of the nineteenth

century. From all accounts, the founder of Cowan Bridge, the Rev. William Carus Wilson, was much respected and admired. The school was well-supported by influential and generally discriminating people and it seemed an ideal opportunity which Patrick and Aunt Branwell could possibly just afford.

Places were found for Maria (10½), Elizabeth (9), Charlotte (8), and Emily who, at 6½, was to be the youngest girl in the school. The four Brontë girls were enrolled among the very first group of pupils. Anne, the baby of the family, and Patrick Branwell, would remain at home, the former because she was as yet too young to be sent away, the latter to continue his studies under his graduate father's supervision. Nothing but optimism surrounded the founder of the school and the father of the girls as the arrangements went ahead for them to take up their places. By November 1824, the four girls were in residence at Cowan Bridge. Maria and Elizabeth were enrolled in July, Charlotte in August and Emily in November. Whooping cough and measles had delayed their start and probably ensured they began their life in the boarding school less robust and fit than the other girls.

The teachers were not impressed with their new pupils, the school registers recording that, on entering, Maria:
'. . . reads tolerably, writes pretty well, ciphers a little, works (needlework) very badly, knows a little Grammar, Geography and History, and has made some progress in reading French, but knows nothing of the language grammatically'.
that her sister Elizabeth
'. . . reads a little, writes pretty well, ciphers none and works very badly, and knows nothing else'.
that Charlotte was,
'. . . altogether clever of her age, but knows nothing systematically'
and that the youngest, Emily,
'. . . works a little, and reads very prettily.'

Thus the teachers noted the arrival of the 'altogether clever' Charlotte who was destined to be at once the school's most distinguished old-girl and incisive critic.

There could hardly have been a greater contrast than that between the house the girls had left and the school to which they had now come. Carus Wilson, the school's founder who personally supervised its affairs was the complete antithesis of their father. Whereas Patrick was poor, of humble origin, Carus Wilson was aristocratic and wealthy. A landowning clergyman, the owner of Casterton Hall, the family's ancestral home in Westmorland, which William Wilberforce 'having never before envied any man . . . felt disposed even to envy'. Wilson moreover was an eminent figure in evangelical and educational circles:
'The Rev. W. Carus Wilson had the singular felicity of embodying, if not anticipating, in his various plans of benevolence, the leading ideas of the age, and his name has long been a household word in every Christian family. In church building, in the diffusion of a cheap Christian literature, and in education, his exertions for half-a-century have earned him the blessings of rich and poor.'

But the 'leading ideas of the age', which Carus Wilson embodied were almost diametrically opposed to those of

Patrick Brontë, the régime he created at Cowan Bridge a stark contrast to the family unity at Haworth. Where Patrick was kindly and, in his own way, fond of small children, often confessing admiration of their 'amusing ways', Carus Wilson, in common with many churchmen and teachers of the day, took a more pessimistic view. Patrick's love of learning, his joy in Wordsworth and readings in Rousseau had endowed him with a sympathetic, supportive view of children, while Carus Wilson's attitude, more typical of Patrick's contemporaries, derived from a zealous regard for correction and the need to offset the sinful bias in children's natures.

The move into the outside world, the exposure to other influences than those of the Parsonage was to prove a shock to the young Brontës: the impact of the confrontation between a stimulating, rather liberal life and the restricted pattern of the routine of the charity school was to have both physical and intellectual repercussions.

Before a year passed the Brontë girls began to fall ill: whether it was the poor conditions at the school or their susceptible constitutions which were the cause, or more probably a combination of both, one by one they faded and sickened. First Maria became so ill with tuberculosis that Patrick was summoned to take her home. Within days she was dead and within weeks Elizabeth was sent home also suffering from consumption. At Elizabeth's death, Patrick went post-haste to withdraw Charlotte and Emily from the school and bring them home. The attempt to find a cheap education for the girls had been a disaster. The Brontës names were removed from the registers and Patrick was refunded a part of their fees.

With Maria's death at eleven years on 6 May 1825 and Elizabeth's at ten years on 15 June 1825 only four children remained in the Parsonage. More dependent upon each other than ever and more united in their isolation, a new pattern was to establish itself in their lives. Their father, after this double blow, which had followed so soon upon the death of his wife, became more distanced from his children, so that the four younger children now began to weave the bonds of affection and companionship they needed to sustain each other in their loneliness and sorrow. Each member of the family responded in his or her own way to the loss of Maria and Elizabeth. Patrick had lost his firstborn and a dear companion, Charlotte, now the eldest child, shouldered a responsibility for her younger brother and sisters, while Branwell, it is said, never fully overcame the loss of Maria, whose serenity in death haunted him throughout his life and inspired some of his most effective verses. The brief experience of the ill-run and altogether inadequate boarding school left Charlotte and Emily shaken and their father more than ever convinced that they would be better off at home. For the next few years, the parsonage was their only school, Patrick and Aunt Branwell their only teachers. The family retrenched and withdrew from the world, outside Haworth, which had dealt them so tragic a blow. Charlotte and Emily resumed their places in the familiar routine and replaced the cheerless misery of Cowan Bridge with the supportive companionship they had so missed during their short exile.

The retreat from Cowan Bridge was perhaps the first occasion when the family withdrew and turned into itself for strength, a response to hardship and sorrow that was to become a familiar feature of the family character as the years passed. Secure at home Charlotte, Branwell, Emily and Anne began to weave 'the web in childhood' that was to envelop their imaginations and determine their personalities. The disastrous attempt to provide a more formal education for the girls ensured in its failure that the children should enjoy the unique education which emanated from their father's love of learning and permeated the parsonage. This eccentric education ultimately proved as stimulating and productive as the alternative under the influence of Carus Wilson had been destructive.

The effect of the time spent at Cowan Bridge was, however, far reaching. The eight-year-old Charlotte would never forget, and Mrs Gaskell believed, never forgive, the 'worrying and the cruelty to which her gentle, patient dying sister had been subjected'. It is not surprising that, when twenty years later Charlotte needed to invent a school for her novel *Jane Eyre* she should draw heavily

A sketch of Mr Brocklehurst, thought to be by Charlotte. At one point Charlotte's publisher asked her to consider providing illustrations for Jane Eyre *herself. She declined, scorning what she termed her 'mere scribblings'. Perhaps she was too modest; this sketch may have been an attempt at just such a set of illustrations.*

upon the memory of her own experiences. In the supposed biography, Charlotte allowed herself to describe Cowan Bridge in embarrassing detail, embarrassing because upon publication, the 'Lowood' of the novel was instantly identified and its founder Rev. Brocklehurst taken for a caricature of Carus Wilson. Had Charlotte's description been as flattering as it was precise all would have been well. As it was, her telling portrayal of 'Lowood'; her devastating attack upon the school's methods and hypocrisy went to the hearts of a public fresh from Dotheboys Hall and Wackforth Squeers maltreatment of his starving urchins in Dickens' *Nicholas Nickleby*, ensuring that Cowan Bridge and Carus Wilson would become as notorious as Currer Bell alias Charlotte Brontë would become renowned. Understandably, Carus Wilson's family and friends rose to his defence, condemning Charlotte for indulging in half-remembered part-truths and allowing herself to attack her former school so forcibly. But it was when Mrs Gaskell, with extraordinary candour, linked the establishments in her biography of Charlotte that the

fiercest uproar broke out.

Mrs Gaskell used all her novelist's skill in cataloguing the incompetence, cruelty and pomposity attached to Cowan Bridge in 1824, relating eye-witness accounts of the scenes which, she claimed, left Charlotte 'forever indignant':

'The dormitory in which Maria slept was a long room, holding a row of narrow little beds on each side, occupied by the pupils; and at the end of this dormitory there was a small bed-chamber opening out of it, appropriated to the use of Miss Scatcherd. Maria's bed stood nearest to the door of this room. One morning, after she had become so seriously unwell as to have had a blister applied to her side (the sore from which was not perfectly healed), when the getting-up bell was heard, poor Maria moaned out that she was so ill, so very ill, she wished she might stop in bed; and some of the girls urged her to do so, and said they would explain it all to Miss Temple, the superintendent. But Miss Scatcherd was close at hand, and her anger would have to be faced before Miss Temple's kind thoughtfulness could interfere; so the sick child began to dress, shivering with cold, as, without leaving her bed, she slowly put on her black worsted stockings over her thin white legs (my informant spoke as if she saw it yet, and her whole face flashed out undying indignation). Just then Miss Scatcherd issued from her room, and, without asking for a word of explanation from the sick and frightened girl, she took her by the arm, on the side to which the blister had been applied, and by one vigorous movement whirled her out into the middle of the floor, abusing her all the time for dirty and untidy habits. There she left her. My informant says, Maria hardly spoke, except to beg some of the more indignant girls to be calm; but, in slow, trembling movements, with many a pause, she went downstairs at last – and was punished for being late.'

Such tales were almost better than *Jane Eyre* itself and Mrs Gaskell's book became the centre of quite a furore. Charlotte never relented or withdrew her account of 'Lowood', being adamant that she did not exaggerate. In a letter to Miss Wooler, in 1848:

> You said Mrs Chapham had some thoughts of sending her daughters to school, and wished to know whether the Clergy Daughters School at Cowan Bridge was an eligible place.
>
> My personal knowledge of that institution is very much out of date, being derived from the experience of twenty years ago; the establishment was at that time in its infancy, and a sad rickety infancy it was. Typhus fever decimated the school periodically, and consumption and scrofula in every variety of form, which bad air and water and bad insufficient diet can generate, preyed on the ill-fated pupils. It would not *then* have been a fit place for any of Mrs Chapham's children.

After Charlotte's death the controversy about the school in *Jane Eyre* and its autobiographical nature became bitter and her husband Arthur Bell Nicholls felt it his 'painful but necessary duty' to defend his wife's reputation. A lengthy and spirited correspondence was conducted in the *Halifax Guardian* of 1857 in which the ex-pupils of the school arranged themselves on one side or the other, swapping reminiscences of their delight or dismay as pupils at the school with, before or after the Brontës, as the case may be.

From all the letters, from both sides, it is clear that Charlotte was right, the infancy was very rickety. Even the most ardent supporters of Carus Wilson admitted that the earliest days of the school were the worst, that bad management, lack of funds and epidemics of various illnesses did indeed cause anxiety and lead to the abandon-

Gaskell described. She was also exposing a popular and particularly unpleasant kind of education to public scrutiny. When little Jane stands indignant before the sombre hectoring pseudo-piety of Mr Brocklehurst, Charlotte is also offering a confrontation between two attitudes to childhood. Brocklehurst represents the kind of corrective training that derives from an unshakeable belief in the wickedness of all children; a primitive, morbid view of teaching that was immensely popular in the nineteenth century. Carus Wilson, Brocklehurst's substantial counterpart in real life, was moreover, one of

ing of the buildings at the stream's édge. It appears that it was a stroke of ill-fortune that took the Brontës to the school at quite the worst moment in its otherwise worthy history.

After three months of letter and counter-letter, Bell Nicholls felt that he had discharged his duty and established the authenticity of Charlotte's account. He wrote his last letter, and concluded: 'Henceforth Charlotte Brontë's assailants may growl and snarl over her grave undisturbed by me.' He kept his word and wrote no more in her defence.

In offering her bitter recreation of the school she knew as a very alert and observant eight-year-old, Charlotte was doing more than being 'the avenging sister' that Mrs

A still from the film of Jane Eyre *which was made in Hollywood and released in 1944, with Joan Fontaine as Jane and the young Orson Welles as Rochester. In this scene Mr Brocklehurst and Mrs Reed, with the evil boy, John, await Jane's entrance. The actor playing Brocklehurst (Henry Daniell) shows a remarkable resemblance to Charlotte's drawing.*

the chief disseminators of this unnatural and perverse belief. His cheap pamphlets, running into as many as 50,000 copies printed in a month, are anthologies of grim cautionary tales where every torment and torture awaits the child who fails to please a vengeful God. This bizarrely named *The Children's Friend*, parodied in *Jane Eyre* as *The Child's Guide*, was edited by Carus Wilson and offers

A sample of the kind of writing that Carus Wilson published in his very successful Childrens Friend, *a journal which aimed to equip the young for life. Among other items are descriptions of amputations of small children's limbs, during which the child smiles and reflects upon Christ's suffering on the cross while her leg is removed, and many deathbed stories of children happier to die and be with their Saviour than to live.*

a view of religious education that was offensive to Charlotte, herself an experienced teacher, and the very opposite of everything that Patrick Brontë believed and taught about children.

In the opening chapters of *Jane Eyre* two worlds met, the one an oppressive world weighed down by a sense of sin and shot through with evil and iniquity: the other a world of honest commonsense and simplicity which reminds us of Wordsworth.

These two worlds, so effectively distilled in the persons of the Rev. Brocklehurst and little ten-year-old Jane, display the contrast between the world of Carus Wilson at Cowan Bridge who believed that God set fire to children to punish them for telling a single lie, and the world of the small children in the parsonage whose father wrote to a newspaper condemning parents' negligence for dressing their children in inflammable night-clothes. The one invoking God as an avenging tormenter, the other using sound practical wisdom to alleviate suffering. Charlotte is her father's daughter when she depicts a solemn catechism from Brocklehurst and a tender assertion of a loving nature in Jane.

Jane, remembering:

'. . . Bessie, as soon as she had dressed her young ladies, used to take herself off to the lively regions of the kitchen and housekeeper's room, generally bearing the candle along with her. I then sat with my doll on my knee until the fire got low, glancing round occasionally to make sure that nothing worse than myself haunted the shadowy room; and when the embers sank to dull red, I undressed hastily, tugging at knots and strings as I best might, and sought shelter from cold and darkness in my crib. To this crib I always took my doll; human beings must love

Much of the Brontë children's education at home came from poring over books and copying what they found. Using illustrations as models they drew their own versions and wrote imitation texts. Such an activity provided rich experience and a fruitful programme of work. Bewick's illustration above is referred to in the first chapter of Jane Eyre. *Jane peruses the book and comments: 'I cannot tell what sentiment haunted the solitary churchyard, with its inscribed headstone; its gate, its two trees, its low horizon, girdled by a broken wall, and its newly risen crescent, attesting the hour of eventide.'*

something, and, in the dearth of worthier objects of affection, I contrived to find a pleasure in loving and cherishing a faded graven image, shabby as a miniature scarecrow. It puzzles me now to remember with what absurd sincerity I doted on this little toy, half fancying it alive and capable of sensation. I could not sleep unless it was folded in my night-gown; and when it lay there nice and warm, I was comparatively happy, believing it to be happy likewise.'

Brocklehurst, examining:

' "Well, Jane Eyre, and are you a good child?"

'Impossible to reply to this in the affirmative – my little world held a contrary opinion – I was silent. Mrs Reed answered for me by an expressive shake of the head, adding soon, "Perhaps the less said on that subject the better, Mr Brocklehurst."

' "Sorry indeed to hear it! she and I must have some talk;" and bending from the perpendicular, he installed his person in the arm-chair opposite Mrs Reed's. "Come here," he said.

'I stepped across the rug; he placed me square and straight before him. What a face he had, now that it was almost on a level with mine! what a great nose! and what a mouth! and what large prominent teeth!

' "No sight so sad as that of a naughty child," he began, "especially a naughty little girl. Do you know where the wicked go after death?"

' "They go to hell," was my ready and orthodox answer.

' "And what is hell? Can you tell me that?"

' "A pit full of fire."

' "And should you like to fall into that pit, and to be burning there forever?"

' "No, sir."

' "What must you do to avoid it?"

'I deliberated a moment; my answer, when it did come, was objectionable: "I must keep in good health, and not die."

' "How can you keep in good health? Children younger than you die daily. I buried a little child of five years old only a day or two since – a good little child, whose soul is now in heaven. It is to be feared the same could not be said of you were you to be called hence."

'Not being in a condition to remove his doubt, I only cast my eyes down on the two large feet planted on the rug, and sighed, wishing myself far enough away.'

Jane Eyre's love for her shabby miniature scarecrow of a doll and the tenderness of Charlotte's description of the little girl, tell us volumes about the kind of life the Brontë family lived in the parsonage. The pets, the toys; the children all derived a security from the affection and bonds of understanding that Patrick and Aunt Branwell sustained. This was the world that the girls had left for the chill confines of Cowan Bridge. The tragic outcome of those few months spent under the influence of ideas more typical of the early nineteenth century meant a return to the warmth and affection and companionship that Patrick Brontë valued so dearly. For the next five years the four children were nurtured in the closeness of each other's company while the memories of death and Cowan Bridge could soften and dissolve.

A drawing, The Winchat, by Emily, aged eleven. Typical of the copied work, which together with studies from life provided practice in drawing. Patrick Brontë took pride in his children's drawings and often described them as 'by my daughter . . .' and signed them himself. Many such are preserved at the Parsonage Museum.

Jane's protest, deriving from her creator's sense of compassion and belief in tenderness, places her alongside Blake's chimney sweep and Kingsley's Tom. It is little wonder that a world bombarded with Carus Wilson's dreadful tales should respond so warmly to Jane Eyre's plight, for Charlotte could celebrate childhood without sentiment or cant, championing the compassionate view of life against the cold.

Further vignettes from Bewick which are described in Jane Eyre. Many such references to books, people and places can be traced to specific equivalents in the Brontës' experience. Their life was their raw material and they made little or no attempt to disguise their sources. The seeking of their originals and exploration of references is for many a beguiling pastime. (Left) 'the broken boat stranded on a desolate coast' from Jane Eyre, Chapter 1. (right) 'the fiend pinning down the thief's pack behind him. I passed over quickly, it was an object of terror'. Branwell's morbid sense of humour made him susceptible to the kind of illustration that Charlotte found disturbing. Many of his scribbled drawings show the Bewick 'fiend'.

Chapter 6

Scribblemania

A direct result of keeping Charlotte, Branwell, Emily and Anne at home together and the product of their close companionship was the phenomenon which Branwell called their 'scribblemania'. Somehow, in the months that followed the grim events of 1825, the children acquired the habit of writing. They began to indulge in an almost spontaneous scribbling of prose and verse which derived from the games they played and led to the production of an astonishing library of small hand-made books. How these young children came to write torrents of words and, in doing so, conduct themselves through a writer's apprenticeship, will always remain something of a mystery. Whether it was by imitation, example and encouragement, or merely by sheer accident, they somehow took to the pen and, through a continuing sharing of ideas, generated a unique energy that drove their imaginations and developed their insight to a most unusual degree.

The earliest of the juvenile writing to survive is a tiny booklet that Charlotte wrote and made as a present for her younger sister Anne at some time during 1824. A simple story beginning 'There was once a little girl and her name was Anne', it is perhaps in itself not unusual, being a rather charming gesture by an elder sister, which is common enough in many families. But in its style, shape, size and the pattern it set, it is most significant. We can now see that, together with Branwell's similar little book of *The Battell of Wch-not-on* it was the first of a series of volumes which was to follow with extraordinary regularity, growing in sophistication and confidence until the sixteen pages of a gentle story told in 125 words becomes the 53,000 words typical of Charlotte's later volumes written in the same manner. The nine-year-old Charlotte and the eight-year-old Branwell, in devising their first little books, had begun a process which was to last for at least the next thirteen years and take them through an extraordinary discipline of invention and composition.

Charlotte's book for Anne bears all the characteristics of the children's later work of this period. The book is written specially for someone, is illustrated and is a conscious attempt to capture a style and atmosphere. For this reason it must claim a special significance in the catalogue of Brontë 'treasures'. Far from being merely things of curiosity and so much dead clutter the astounding library of little books, many of which have survived intact, have direct bearing upon the development of this extraordinary group of children who were to become such influential and effective writers.

Thrown back upon their own resources, encouraged and abetted by their father to the delights, and hard work, involved in composition, they found happiness in a game that they could all share. Many years later, Patrick was to describe this playing and indicate some of the sources for the ideas used; he tells Mrs Gaskell how they formed: 'a little society among themselves with which they seemed contented and happy' and he describes the habit of composition which they were to adopt:

'As soon as they could read and write, Charlotte and her brother and sisters used to invent and act little plays of their own, in which the Duke of Wellington, my daughter Charlotte's hero, was sure to come off the conquering hero–when a dispute would not infrequently arise amongst them regarding the comparative merits of him, Bonaparte, Hannibal, and Caesar. When the argument rose to its height . . . I had sometimes to come in . . . and settle the dispute to the best of my judgement.

'Sometimes they also wrote little works of fiction they called miniature novels. Charlotte got her knowledge of the Duke of Wellington from the newspapers and from what she heard in company and other heroes from Ancient History.'

That Patrick knew what the children were about should come as no surprise; he had purposely taken them to the brink of such an enterprise. By letting them read widely, by helping them understand the importance of writing and above all by involving them in discussions of topical affairs as people capable of understanding them he had ensured that they had plenty of ideas. In the next few years they were to find, and to a large extent perfect, a vehicle to communicate these ideas.

The game of making little books from scraps of paper

Above: A midsummer afternoon with a Methodist preacher, *(possibly Wesley)*, by J. P. de Louthenberg. Patrick Brontë's ministry was one of preaching and teaching and had much in common with the Methodist movement and the work of Wesley and Grimshaw. This kind of preaching had a strong appeal for Yorkshire folk in the eighteenth and nineteenth centuries.

Right: Patrick Brontë in *1825*, five years after his appointment to Haworth. The silk scarf which Patrick always wore derived not from scruples of churchmanship, but from an understandable–in those days– fear of throat and chest infection.

49

Factory children, from The Costumes of Yorkshire. *As children of the parsonage the Brontës escaped the fate of most of those in the village who formed the largest part of the labour force in the local mills. That Charlotte and her sisters were aware of this is clear from their letters: they realised what they were spared. But in her worst moments as a governess Charlotte declared that she would sooner work in a mill than be a teacher.*

that developed so rapidly became a kind of child-industry. While their counterparts, the other children of families in Haworth, were being taken at the same age to the mills and set to work, the children of the parsonage were evolving a very different kind of apprenticeship for themselves, one in which they learnt to weave words instead of wool. Spared the fate of their contemporaries, a bitter fate of toiling in noisy mills for as many as sixteen hours a day, the Brontë children devoted themselves to long hours of writing, looking far beyond the mills of Haworth for their raw material and themes.

The Brontës were aware of the difference between themselves and other children. Charlotte is quite explicit when she writes in 1835 of her childhood and employs the language of the mill to make her point:

> We wove a web in childhood
> A web of sunny air;
> We dug a spring in infancy
> Of water pure and fair;
>
> We sowed in youth a mustard seed
> We cut an almond rod;
> We are now grown up to riper age—
> Are they withered in the sod?
>
> The mustard-seed in distant land
> Bends down a mighty tree,
> The dry unbudding almond wand
> Has touched eternity . . .

The 'webs' of 'cloth' that the Brontë children wove were in time, like the bundles of cloth woven by the other children of the village, to pass along the pack-mule trails, toll roads and eventually the railways to make Haworth as famous for its literature as it once was for its wool. Their weaving was done in the sunny air of the moors and it was words that they spun, delighting in the sheer joy of invention and the satisfaction of finding ways of saying what they meant.

The children played many games, modifying and adapting them with a bewildering confidence, and it is through one of Branwell's books that we know how one such game, and the one that perhaps more directly than any other led to the invention of the little books, came about. Having been on church business in nearby Leeds, Patrick Brontë returned home on the night of 5 June 1826, after the children had gone to bed, with presents for them all. These included a set of ninepins, a toy village and a dancing doll. For Branwell he had brought the now celebrated box of twelve wooden soldiers in response to Branwell's plea that his stock of toy soldiers was becoming rather depleted. The presents were delivered and Branwell faithfully recorded their being discovered next morning by his bed:

'. . . when I first saw them in the morning after they were bought, I carried them to Emily, Charlotte and Anne. They each took up a soldier, gave them names which I consented to, and I gave Charlotte Tweeny (Wellington), to Emily Pare (Parry) and to Anne Trott (Ross) to take care of them though they were to be mine and I have to have the disposal of them as I would—shortly after this I gave them to them as their own . . .'

At some point in the development of the games with the toy soldiers someone, probably Branwell, decided that, like their counterparts in actual life, the heroes should enjoy the benefits of chronicles and journalism, that if the real Duke of Wellington could read his parliamentary speeches as reported in the journals of the day, then so too should their diminutive counterparts. Accordingly, the little books came into being, not merely as writing, but as a kind of intellectual doll's house furniture. The deeds, aspirations and other aspects of the toy soldiers 'lives' were to be recorded in books of a scale in keeping with their heroes' dimensions, designed as miniature replicas of real printed books. They were written in an excrueiatingly small italic hand, almost too small to read, and which must have been extraordinarily difficult to write with a quill pen. They measured as little as 2 inches by $1\frac{1}{2}$ and were later enlarged, to allow more scope for their authors, to $7\frac{1}{2}$ inches by $6\frac{1}{2}$. The soldiers themselves were styled authors, printers and booksellers so that in time the whole enterprise became delicately but thoroughly interwoven with heated correspondence posting from one edition of a journal to the next. Typical of such correspondence, supposedly from Sergeant Bud, a likely pseudonym for a wooden soldier, this appeared in the 1 June edition in Branwell's imitation *Blackwood's Magazine* of 1829 when he was a poised, articulate twelve-year-old:

To the Editor   Glasstown
                                          June 1, 1829

Sir,

I write this to acquaint you of a circumstance which has happened to me and which is of great importance to the world at large. On May 22, 1829 the Chief Genius Tally (Emily) came to me with a small yellow book in her hand. She gave it to me saying that it was the POEMS of that Ossian of whom so much has been said, but whose works could never be got. Upon attentive perusal of the above said works, I found that they were most sublime and excellent. I am engaged in publishing an edition of them, Quarto–3 vols with notes, commentaries etc. I am fully convinced that it is the work of OSSIAN who lived 1000 years ago–and of no other. There is a most intense anxiety prevailing amongst literary men to know its contents. In a short time they shall be gratified for it will be published on the first of July 1829.

I remain

Yours &c, &c

Sergt. Bud. Jun. T. Sc

To the Chief Genius Banny.

By 1830 the early straightforward games had become complex and elaborate, the writing of the little books, originally intended to be toys and part of the soldiers' equipment had become the major part of the games. Gradually the impetus shifted from the soldiers to the more sophisticated game of the writing; it was in this shift that the profoundest implications for the future are to be found. Over the years during which the games developed, the accumulative effect of the writing and the sustained imaginative exercise that the shared fantasy world demanded, provided continuous practice in the handling of words.

The most important single step towards this increasing emphasis upon the little books must be the founding of *The Great Glasstown Confederation* which came about when Branwell re-drew a portion of the map of Africa and apportioned kingdoms to some of the twelve soldiers. With Glasstown came a history, current affairs, celebrities and above all a literature: the occasional journals and

Leeds in the early nineteenth century. This contemporary engraving gives a good impression of a city made, and marred, by the Industrial Revolution. An imposing church stands on the skyline but the swirling river Aire is already filthy with industrial waste. 'Congregations of smoke dark houses clustered round their soot-vomiting mills.' (Charlotte).

books were now to become parts of series which chronicled the times and people of the whole confederation. While telling the story of Glasstown, the children were also discovering a skill and, incidentally, recording their own maturing. Events in Glasstown mirror events in Haworth as the young writers scribble their way into competence

Brigate, Leeds, in 1851, where the family shopped from time to time and where Patrick Brontë bought the toy soldiers that started the writing games that gave the children considerable practice in all kinds of composition.

Above: St John's College, Cambridge, in 1819. Patrick Brontë entered this college as a sizar in 1802, aged twenty-five. He became a prize-winning student in the first class and graduated with the A.B. in 1806.

Right: The Bell Tower Chapel at Thornton where Patrick was the curate in charge and where Charlotte, Emily Jane, Patrick Branwell and Anne were all christened. Today the east wall, the graveyard and the cupola still stand, opposite the church at Thornton built to replace the chapel.

Opposite: The undulating landscape of the Haworth moorland.

and an unusual degree of familiarity with all kinds of ways of writing.

The children absorbed information from every possible source, devouring newspapers, magazines, annuals, children's books and their father's library as source material for their own creations. It is as if, aware of the potential isolation of their circumstances, the whole family went to extreme lengths to be well-informed, as Charlotte records in a fragment entitled the *History of the Year* written on 12 March in 1829:

'While I write this I am in the kitchen of the Parsonage, Haworth; Tabby, the servant, is washing up the breakfast things and Anne, my youngest sister (Maria was my eldest), is kneeling on a chair, looking at some cakes which Tabby has been baking for us. Emily is in the parlour, brushing the carpet, Papa and Branwell are gone to Keighley. Aunt is upstairs in her room, and I am sitting by the table writing this in the kitchen. Keighley is a small town four miles from here. Papa and Branwell are gone for the newspaper, the 'Leeds Intelligencer', a most excellent Tory newspaper, edited by Mr Wood and the proprietor, Mr Heineman. We take two and see three newspapers a week. We take the 'Leeds Intelligencer', Tory, and the 'Leeds Mercury', Whig, edited by Mr Baines, and his brother, son-in-law and his two sons, Edward and Talbot. We see the 'John Bull'; it is a high Tory, very violent. Dr Driver lends us it, as likewise 'Blackwood's Magazine' the most able periodical there is. The editor is Mr Christopher North, an old man seventy four years of age; the 1st of April is his birthday; his company are Timothy Tickler, Morgan O'Doherty, Macrabin Mordecai, Mullion, Warrell, and James Hogg, a man of most extraordinary genius, a Scottish Shepherd.'

A most heartening feature of the juvenile writing is its humour. Obviously the children found a great amount of fun in writing, enjoying the pleasures of parody and savouring nonsense words. Almost everything they came across was absorbed into their writing. Body-snatching, much in evidence in Leeds at the time, ballooning, music festivals and banquets all appear in one guise or another, while poems, songs, national anthems, debates, proclamations and public speeches all have their place. Branwell's bloodthirsty poems occur with obvious and frequent relish:

> His face was haggard, and his sleeve tucked up;
> A knife which reeked with blood was in his hand.
> He trampled upon a victim skinned,
> Who writhed about in dying agonies.

Charlotte seemed to delight in Rabelaisian nonsense words, the new organ in Haworth church being: 'the stupendous organ called rollrogthunderandsqueakand-otheroreimus now glorifying the Cathedral of St North-angerland . . .' The reviving of a swooning poet (Branwell) becomes for Charlotte: 'the application of harts horne, cold water, vinegar, sal-volatile, and sal- everything else', and the musicians that Branwell described playing at a concert included some very rare instruments: 'There are to be five brass bands, each consisting of two trumpets, three bombardones, four Cyclopedes, five Serpents, six Bugles, seven French-horns, eight gongs, nine Kettle-

drums, and ten ramgalongtinas, a new kind of instrument that's never been blown in Africa before.'

Whatever else was happening in the parsonage as the children grew up, a large amount of time was spent in swapping stories, and this spurred them on to attempt more and more ambitious literary exercises. It is little wonder that many years later Charlotte should declare that the first full-length novel she sent to a publisher was by no means her first work, 'as the pen which wrote it had been previously worn a good deal in a practice of some years'. In all, her juvenile writings outweight the work of her maturity in quantity, being many thousands of words more than her four published books.

SCHOOL, AND FRIENDS FOR A LIFETIME

At some time in 1820 Patrick became once more dangerously ill. His severely congested lungs gave cause for alarm and again the family was in jeopardy. As before the illness heralded a change in the course the children's lives were taking, and it was now a matter of some urgency that they should be properly educated and equipped to earn some sort of living.

Charlotte's godparents, the Rev. Thomas and Mrs Atkinson, old friends of Patrick, came to the rescue. They generously offered to finance Charlotte at a new and rather select school for young ladies that had opened recently near their home at Dewsbury. This school took very few pupils at first; there were only ten boarders when Charlotte's name was entered on the register, and it was in every way the opposite of the Clergy Daughters School at Cowan Bridge. Where that had been cheerless, unhealthy and oppressive, Roe Head under Miss Margaret Wooler was cheerful, healthily situated in its own extensive gardens and, in advance of the times, remarkably liberal. As Charlotte had wilted before the severity of the Cowan Bridge régime, so she blossomed at Roe Head. As the one had been a harsh purgatory, so the other was to become remarkably supportive and to provide her with all the blessings of companionship and understanding that she so needed for peace of mind.

Nevertheless, beginning at the school was an ordeal for the fourteen-year-old girl. However kindly and considerate the four Misses Wooler were, however conducive the fine rambling house and spacious the gardens, the fact was that Charlotte was uprooted from the security of home and suddenly bereft of the essential companionship of Branwell, Emily and Anne. The close reciprocal affection upon which this quartet drew for happiness was at Haworth, twenty miles away, and Charlotte was suddenly alone, a small weeping figure amongst girls from very different circumstances from her own. In the long term, however, all was for the best and the choice of this school for Charlotte was inspired.

Her arrival at Roe Head was trying for many reasons. She was delivered to the door of the rather elegant house in the covered wagon that was used for trips to market and her poverty became glaringly apparent almost at once. Other girls noted her drab, faded, old-fashioned clothes and the general plainness of her appearance. To make matters worse Charlotte, though very short-sighted, was

Diary note by Emily and Anne detailing the scene at the Parsonage in 1837.

Above: Some of the little books made and written by the Brontë children. Only examples of Charlotte's and Branwell's have come to light. The books average a mere two inches in height and one and a half inches in width. They are written in an almost microscopic hand.

Left: Charlotte's watercolour of a 'Pine martin' (pine marten).

Opposite: Elizabeth Branwell—the Brontë children's Aunt Branwell—with her old-fashioned bonnet and sides of false curls.

refusing to wear her spectacles, a common enough reaction in adolescent girls, and was consequently almost blind. With very little encouragement she was inclined to find herself extremely ugly and disliked her appearance, and that could only add to her general sense of wretchedness. She became very withdrawn and isolated amidst the self-assured girls already established at Roe Head. But Charlotte was soon to find reassurance and sympathy. At least two girls, themselves new to the school, responded in a kindly way to her plight. Both Ellen Nussey and Mary Taylor befriended Charlotte from her earliest days at Roe Head and established bonds of affection that were to last for the rest of their lives. From strikingly different backgrounds, this trio of schoolgirls were to establish links that survived separation and completely different points of view, and produced an extensive correspondence which has survived in some quantity to provide detailed accounts of the lives of the girls involved. A comfort in those early days at school, Charlotte's friendship with Ellen and Mary was to be a source of strength through many years to come.

'Alexander Percy Esq.', an imaginary character portrayed in a pencil sketch by Branwell. Alexander Percy appears in both Charlotte and Branwell's many stories.

The organ which Patrick Brontë had built in the church as part of the improvements he accomplished during his ministry. Branwell played the organ for services from time to time, and it appears in Charlotte's juvenile writing as: 'The stupendous organ called rollroarthunderandsqueekandotheroreimus'.

The ultimate indignity that Charlotte suffered on arrival at the school arose from her teachers' assessment of her ability. For Charlotte, already secretly the author of a great many books, was placed amongst the junior girls. The eccentric education that she had assembled in the parsonage left huge gaps and appeared sadly inadequate against the more orthodox learning and accomplishments expected in a school system. It is to Miss Wooler's credit that she soon spotted Charlotte's quality and allowed her to join her more 'schooled' but no more intelligent peers in the senior group. Once given her head and established in this class, Charlotte, as her father many years before in Cambridge, quickly found her academic feet and won several prizes for the year's work.

Roe Head proved the ideal setting for Charlotte and an appropriate form of education for her nature and inclinations. Still an odd little figure, unable to play ball games through her near-blindness, having to hold books within inches of her nose to read at all, Charlotte found warmth, understanding and even love amongst the girls and teachers. She remained loyal to the memory of her experiences there and obviously owed much to the example and instruction she received from Margaret Wooler, who, in 1850, twenty years later, was still among Charlotte's closest friends.

Miss Wooler's influence upon Charlotte, and thereby upon the other children of the parsonage, can hardly be overestimated. She was an able teacher and one who encouraged conversation and discussion in comparatively relaxed surroundings as part of the process of education. In some ways, though in a warmer and womanly fashion, Margaret Wooler continued Patrick Brontë's habit of discourse and debate with young children. All the pupils of Roe Head remembered with great affection her habit of walking in the evenings with girls at each arm, discussing the work of the day. These perambulations, outside the constrictions of timetable and exercise-learning, were invaluable–a mutual respect and enjoyment of learning could take the place of more formal work. Charlotte was so taken with the practice that she, Emily and Anne adopted it for themselves. As Miss Wooler had walked with her pupils talking and discussing all manner of topics so Charlotte, Emily and Anne made it their custom to walk together of an evening around the parlour table of the parsonage recounting the stories they were writing, and sharing the events of the day. This custom was to continue until Emily and Anne died and Charlotte, the sole surviving child, came to walk alone around the room where once she had walked in the warmth of her sisters' company.

Charlotte's time as a pupil at Roe Head was short. By July 1831 she was back home devoting herself to teaching her younger sisters. Of all the things she could transmit, there was one, and perhaps the most important, that she could not share. For at Roe Head Charlotte had faced life away from the parsonage and had succeeded. Despite her profound homesickness she had stood on her own feet and found her own way into new relationships and a society of some kind. She was the only one of the four ever to achieve this kind of equilibrium. Her nature prevented her from being at ease in company; but at least she had stood the test of coping with others and finding an ability to maintain her independence. Her success amongst her schoolfellows was real and would give her a confidence that the others would never possess. The respect she commanded and the endorsement of her ability afforded by Miss Wooler and the school prizes would add to her self-esteem and provide some measure of antidote to the natural reserve and introspection that could at times be crippling to the point of debilitation. The friendships she had established were as important as the subjects she had learnt; the time at Roe Head was to prove a step forward and be a source of strength in the years ahead.

Charlotte's pencil drawing of Roe Head School where she, Emily and Anne were pupils, and where she later taught. It was here that she met Ellen Nussey, who was to become her lifelong friend and correspondent.

There were several ways in which Charlotte's time at Roe Head was well spent. Along with the other girls she left with all the necessary accomplishments for becoming a governess, for joining the ranks of that relatively new kind of teacher, the lady who lived with a family as if in limbo, being neither a servant nor a guest but a paid employee whose duties were often ill-defined. Nevertheless, however isolated the role of governess might be, it was a means of earning a living. It was natural, therefore, that Charlotte should spend the next few years passing on her knowledge to her sisters in the hope, soon to be realised, that they too might become self-sufficient or at least employable. Thus in a letter to Ellen Nussey she described her days back home:

> You ask me to give you a description of the manner in which I have passed every day since I left school; this is soon done, as an account of one day is an account of all. In the morning from 9 o'clock to half past 12, I instruct my sisters and

The medal that Charlotte won at Miss Wooler's school at Roe Head. Like her father she proved a prizewinning scholar. She was proud that she was invited to teach at the school where she herself had been a pupil.

*Above left: Branwell's first little book showing his toy soldiers
in action.*

Above right: A page from Charlotte's first book.

Opposite: Charlotte's water colour depicting The Bay of
Glasstown, *the chief city of the imaginary land created in the
little books. The painting clearly shows the influence of John
Martin, and belies Charlotte's scorn for her own artistic
ability.*

draw, then we walk till dinner, after dinner I sew till teatime, and after tea I either read, write, do a little Fancy work, or draw, as I please. Thus in one delightful, though somewhat monotonous course, my life is passed . . .

Writing to Ellen Nussey was yet another outcome of the Roe Head experience and one for which generations have shown gratitude. On Charlotte leaving school Ellen had suggested that they should each write a monthly letter in order to maintain their friendship. The ensuing correspondence was to last twenty-five years, to produce well over 400 letters from Charlotte, and provide one of the most fascinating and, for various reasons, frustrating records of a great writer's development as a person. For Charlotte's relationship with Ellen, as indicated above, stops short of sharing any insight into the true nature of the activities in hand. Ellen is told that Charlotte 'draws' and that she sometimes 'writes', but she is not told what it is that Charlotte draws or writes; on the contrary the secret of the many volumes that now absorbed Charlotte and kept her pen busy was never revealed to Ellen. The writing remained the secret of the parsonage, as the repository of the childrens' collective fantasies it was not to be violated by publication. It is ironic that Charlotte never revealed her secret and that she was content to camouflage her real involvement beneath a passing reference.

Throughout her entire correspondence with Ellen,

A view of Conway Castle, from the pencil sketch by Charlotte.

Charlotte maintains a reserve which speaks volumes but will always leave us with doubts. Even at the time of her great success as Currer Bell, the author of the best-selling *Jane Eyre*, Charlotte coolly affirms that she has been engaged upon some writing, and it is not until very late that she revealed to Ellen that she was indeed that Mr Bell, who, incidentally, had found little favour with Ellen through his lack of religious sentiment. But Ellen was to prove a true friend and soon after her first letter, a letter which Charlotte had not really expected to materialise, came an invitation for her to stay at Rydings, the Nussey home near Birstall. In the autumn of 1832 the visit was made, the first of many, and Branwell accompanied his sister in the two-wheeled gig that made the journey from

Haworth. Branwell was transported by the house and its setting. In her reminiscences of Charlotte, Ellen describes his 'wild ecstasy with everything', his delight for Charlotte and his insistence that 'if she were not intensely happy' in the 'Paradise' where he was leaving her then she never would be!

The house that provoked this not unusual enthusiasm from the volatile and sensitive Branwell, did indeed impress Charlotte. With its battlements, its rockery and ancient trees set in parkland, Rydings was to serve as a model for aspects of Mr Rochester's Thornfield Hall in *Jane Eyre*. Branwell's paean of praise for Ellen's house was matched by his sister's quiet but meticulous observation, a quality often remarked upon in the shy girl. Charlotte protested that she first became interested in character when she was five; clearly, she was equally early in noting places, atmosphere and the influence of environment. In common with many writers Charlotte drew extensively upon her own experience; perhaps uncommonly she took little pains to disguise her models, a feature of her writing that has delighted many a tourist and literary detective from the first day of publication of her novels to the present. Her friends, their relatives, and the houses of her friends are all woven into Charlotte's fictional fabric. She re-created people so well, and evoked places so accurately that an early recreation was found in seeking one's neighbours and their houses in the latest of Mr Currer Bell's, alias Charlotte Brontë's works. In the event the identifications, as of Cowan Bridge School, were not always pleasing. Charlotte's other close schoolfriend, Mary Taylor, also invited her home and eventually she too found the Red House at Gomersal, her childhood home, enshrined in *Shirley* as Briarmains, while her father, Joshua Taylor, was to appear in two stories as Hiram Yorks in *Shirley* and Yorke Hudson in *The Professor*.

Joshua Taylor delighted Charlotte, his robust Yorkshire accent, his Radical views and his non-conformity all appealed to her, while his family business, a nearby mill with a history of Luddite troubles, was to provide her with material for a whole novel. Bankrupted during the depressions following the Napoleonic Wars, Taylor battled to pay his debts and, unlike the Nussey family, maintain some standards of culture and concern with topical affairs. He travelled much, speaking French and Italian, and was a rare mixture of matter-of-fact cloth manufacturer and a man of some culture. His house was hung with paintings, filled with books and albums of engravings so that Charlotte, who had under her father developed a fondness for drawings and paintings, was in her element. He must have been a kindly man for he not only introduced Charlotte to French literature but over many years saw to it that she could borrow any of his latest acquisitions. This lively household played an important part in Charlotte's growth and her intellectual development. This was the enriching experience that Branwell, Emily and Anne would miss, leaving them curiously independent and free, yet at the same time vulnerable and insecure in company. Charlotte warmly acknowledged the friendship and society which she was offered at the Red House, confessing, 'the society of the

Taylors is one of the most rousing pleasures I have ever known'.

Certainly her friendship with Mary, which was to last until Mary emigrated to New Zealand to run a provisions store, played a large part in fostering her own interests, reinforcing the priorities which she had been encouraged to adopt at Haworth Parsonage. The premium that Joshua Taylor placed upon art and culture would be in full accord with Charlotte's inclinations, and the enrichment she found in the house with the stained glass windows, celebrating her father's heroes Milton and Shakespeare, would never fail her.

In her school, Charlotte was favoured; in her friends and their families she found an identity and a welcome that would do much to help her accommodate her own reticence and shyness.

But if Charlotte returned to Haworth with riches from Roe Head, she was met on her return by an almost equal share of enthusiasm and cheerfulness. Papa was fully recovered and all were in good health. The family now began the most happy and busy years of their lives; the ten years from 1832 to 1842 saw the children mature and a great many of Patrick Brontë's plans come to fruition. He involved his children in all his affairs at every stage, thereby indirectly ensuring that their apparent isolation was offset by their occupation with the life of the village and through newspapers, journals and literature with the affairs of the world beyond. The young Branwell had long owned an illustrated description of London which he had annotated with his own comments, a sign of at least a theoretical understanding that a world awaited them beyond the boundaries of their father's parish. Charlotte was able to add her augmented talents to the intellectual life of the parsonage. Like her father she had now read and discussed Milton and Shakespeare as well as some of the more forbidding grammar books so commonly in use. The talents for which she won her prizes at Roe Head, her memory, her love of poetry and her quick creative mind were all reapplied to the imaginative ferment of the parsonage. Moving towards her own most productive years she was now well-equipped to act as a catalyst against her lively brother and sisters' minds. The joy of returning and the pleasures of a few years together served to help them weave their web of friendship more closely, so that their dependence as small children would grow with them towards maturity. Back home, Charlotte was able to endorse her earlier beliefs:

My home is humble and unattractive to strangers, but to me it contains what I shall find nowhere else in the world – the profound, the intense affection which brothers and sisters feel for each other when their minds are cast in the same mould, their ideas drawn from the same source – when they have clung to each other from childhood, and when disputes have never sprung up to divide them . . .

Pencil drawing by Anne Brontë.

Top: Emily's painting of Hero, her tame merlin.

*Above: The moor ablaze with heather. A momentary
transformation that occurs once a year.*

64

Chapter 7

The Family at Home

Patrick Branwell Brontë, 'Brany' as the girls called him, will always remain the enigma of the Brontë family. We just do not know enough about the ill-fated boy of such remarkable and uneven talents. Almost everything about him lies beneath a question mark. From his earliest days until his death at thirty-one in 1848 the story of his life is one of great promise and yet profound disillusion. He has been seen as excessively melancholic; as a boy and man possessed by a religious mania; as a man haunted by the memory of his dead sister Maria, and as a genius manqué who broke his father's heart. Whether he was, as some believe, an epileptic (hence his being kept at home rather than sent away to school); or whether he was simply spoiled beyond reason by his doting sisters and indulgent father, the upshot of his education and life was drunkenness, addiction to drugs and a total inability to organise his own affairs.

Against this pitiful tale of ability wasted and resolve unravelled so reminiscent of a Victorian tract about vice, must be set the accounts of his good looks, his charm, his wit, his poetry—he was the first of the Brontë children to see one of his poems in print—his musical talents and his ability to draw and paint in oils and write a creditable translation of Horace's Odes. Branwell, as he was called at home to distinguish his name from his father's 'Patrick', was loved deeply by all the other members of the family. He spurred the girls on in their games and, from his lessons with his father, continuously added ideas from literature and the classics.

In particular, Charlotte and Branwell were on good terms. The eldest child and the only boy were well-matched, Charlotte's advantage in age balancing Branwell's boyish energy. The closeness of their companionship enabled them to sustain a sparkling intellectual rivalry in which they aided and abetted each other. Together they were to amplify each other's talents; apart they pined for the stimulus and excitement of the other's company. It was to Branwell that Charlotte addressed her letters home for he was the one to whom she found she had

most to say, and once, while she was at Roe Head, Branwell walked a round trip of forty miles to visit her. While Charlotte was away at school Branwell had been deprived of his nearest and closest companion. In the inventing of the little books they had worked together, while Emily and Anne had gradually evolved their own games. On her return Charlotte found her brother challenging, he was living through a time of great inventiveness but also one of asserting his manhood. As well as continuing to share all kinds of games with Charlotte, he now sought the company of other youths, having developed a passion for the highly disreputable sport of boxing.

While continuing to cram notebooks with poems and fragments of prose, Branwell also practised the fine art of pugilism in the back room of a public house. Poring over the latest edition of *Blackwoods* or *Frazers*, he would set them aside for *Bell's Life in London*, the sporting journal lent him by Thomas Sugden, the landlord of the Black Bull. With this encouragement Branwell's early delight in battle and legends of valour now turned to a limited practical experience and the accounts of celebrated matches fought up and down the country. The same powers of memory that provided his great fund of knowledge of political matters now served to supply an equal store of boxing stories; the legends of Tom Spring and Ben Gregson taking their place alongside the legends of antiquity. While Charlotte was being introduced to the sheltered influence of a girls school, where considerable care and thought was involved, her brother was having to find his place amongst the far less equal youths and young men of Haworth Boxing Club. Such unequal acquaintanceships seldom prove conducive to alert minds, and it is perhaps part of Branwell's tragedy that outside the family, beyond 'those girls', he could not find in Haworth the companionship he so desperately needed.

Boxing, however, along with shooting, he was able to share with others; his interest, once aroused, remained with him. The sport may have appealed to him because of his stature. A small, sharp-featured youth with his father's Celtic red hair, he was by all accounts a rather quaint figure with a wild, impetuous nature. For whatever reason, Branwell was beginning to take a road along which Charlotte could not follow, and which in time would leave the once close pair remote from each other.

There was much that the children shared before things began to take a turn for the worse with Branwell, and it was the years after Charlotte's return from Roe Head that were to be the happiest and richest for them all. During this time, as the children grew up and established their separate identities, the parsonage must have hummed with creative activity. This is the period when Patrick Brontë paid his subscription to the Keighley Mechanics Institute and the library of that institution became available to him and his family. Charlotte, Branwell, Emily and Anne were busy developing other talents which would compliment their writing and add to their artistic insight.

The earliest of Branwell's little books, like those of Charlotte, show his wish to draw and paint. From their father's interest in art and his patient descriptions of paintings which accompanied his talk about Cambridge and London, the parsonage children all assumed that art was important. As they absorbed a love of literature, finding poetry as natural a form of expression as conversation, so they never questioned the necessity for painting and drawing. In the world of Glasstown and their fantasy games, artists were afforded considerable respect, being highly valued members of the imagined society.

But Patrick did more than pay lip service to the idea that the children should be able to appreciate paintings; he twice set aside money for them to have painting and drawing lessons. For a while a painter from Keighley came to teach them and later when their talents and interest had developed, Patrick paid William Robinson, a well-known Leeds portrait painter who could number the Duke of Wellington as one of his sitters, two guineas a lesson, which indicates his seriousness about the undertaking (four pounds could represent the rent for a cottage for a year in those days).

Clearly the notion that Branwell had real talent and could train as a painter was taken seriously and it is wrong to dismiss these lessons as perfunctory, or the fond indulgence of minor accomplishments. The lessons given by Robinson were intended to develop the skill and provide some technique for children who had already proved a determination to draw by scribbling on almost anything that came to hand. There are those who claim the pencil drawings on the plaster walls of the children's study above the front hall of the parsonage as theirs; while the evidence of schoolbooks covered in elaborate drawings and designs bears more authentic witness. Patrick had a love of painting, keeping engravings in the parsonage, and it was his ambition that Branwell should become a painter. To this end, Branwell's studies were serious and he alone was taught to paint in oils. For a time a bedroom became his studio and he made a very real attempt to become a portrait painter. The evidence of the work which has survived show that he achieved many of the skills necessary and did paint some effective portraits. Continuing to read in *Blackwoods*, both he and Charlotte became well-informed about painting, each drawing up lists of paintings they particularly liked and wished to see, so that when eventually they got to London they would know exactly where to go to fulfil some of their early wishes. In time Charlotte was able to do this, drawing great pleasure from visits to art galleries in London, Edinburgh and Brussels as well as Leeds. For Branwell such visits were to have a very different effect, filling him with as much dismay at his own shortcomings as offering any pleasure.

In learning to draw and paint the children, as was their habit, set themselves arduous tasks, copying engravings with precise and minute pencil strokes to imitate steel etching. The resulting sketches are breathtaking in their detail and alarming for the damage that such close work must have wrought upon already weak eyes. The predilection for the tiny, for detail, for almost microscopic design is a puzzling motif of all the children's work. In their writing as well as their drawing it is the closest details that are observed and that make the descriptive writing so compelling. Charlotte's detailed memory of places, of the smallest intricacies of dress and appearance must derive at least in part from the exercises in reproducing engravings that she set herself. Scorning the results in later years as pointless, she nevertheless benefited from the precision and care with which she accomplished these tasks. Copying from Bewick's *Book of Birds*, or from woodcuts in their father's guide to the *Gardens and Menagerie of the Zoological Society*, or drawing their own pets from life, there is a distinctive style and competence common to their work which cannot be dismissed as the afternoon pastime of bored young ladies.

Patrick cherished his children's work and time and again one finds his signature at the back of a sketch stating that 'this picture is by my daughter Charlotte' or whoever. Many of these pictures are preserved and they must form a companion study for any reading of the juvenile writings since many of the scenes, people and places drawn and painted have their source in the worlds of Glasstown, Angria or Gondal which the children invented. The architecture of Glasstown is itself depicted by Charlotte in one of the most successful of her paintings. A view of Glasstown, it is clearly derived from the engravings by Martin which hung, as they still do today, in Patrick Brontë's study. Once again it is clear that the children were able to analyse and extract with extraordinary skill the elements that they needed for their own creations.

Whether it be the creating of a word picture, or the designing of a landscape or scene, they seemed to have the rare knack of abstracting the features they required and of reassembling them in a new order to satisfy the purpose in hand. In creating verse and prose as well as in the visual arts they developed advanced skills of composition which arose from an extensive experience in imitation and adaptation. It is difficult to believe that this was a taught skill, it having all the signs of a collective inspiration that generated its own impetus.

The results of the drawing lessons are everywhere apparent today in the parsonage museum. It is hard to realize that our impression of what the girls looked like, of many of the places referred to in their lives, of the animals

Above left: Tennyson, whose work also impressed itself upon the children. With their father's interest in poetry and literature the children accepted verse-making and learning as a natural and necessary part of life. Poetry formed for them the highest form of expression; throughout their childhood and into maturity they competed with each other as versifiers.

Above right: Walter Scott, from the portrait by Landseer. He was one of the Brontë family's heroes and a major influence, and Charlotte made a literary pilgrimage to Scott's home at Abbotsford. Landseer was one of the family's favourite painters, and one from whom they derived inspiration, both Charlotte and Branwell writing a poem based upon his The Shepherd's Chief Mourner.

and pets that they owned, all derive from their own paintings and drawings. It is odd that so many believe Branwell to be a failed portrait painter while his oil-portraits of his sisters hang in the National Portrait Gallery.

Painting and drawing were but one aspect of the multi-faceted talents nurtured in Haworth parsonage. Alongside the art lessons went music lessons. All but Charlotte, to whom eyesight again proved a handicap, learnt to play the pianoforte while Branwell also played the flute and organ. Emily and Anne, in particular, were to become more than competent performers as the music they played and the reminiscences of contemporaries bear witness.

The most striking feature of their music making must have been the delight and pleasure that accompanied it.

We know that Handel was Branwell's favourite composer, and it is hard to imagine too solemn an atmosphere where the sparkling robust music of Handel is being enjoyed. It is obvious from the songs, duets and sonatas that the girls played and sang that the parsonage must have resounded to laughter and enjoyment through the years that the young girls were acquiring these accomplishments. Music is not entirely a melancholic affair, neither was the music they owned and played always in a minor key.

EMILY JANE

While Branwell was learning to box and Charlotte was away at school, Emily Jane, the fifth child, was pursuing her own education and discovering an artistic vision that was to beome the most distinct and powerful talent nurtured in Haworth parsonage. It was also the most baffling, there being no obvious clues to her thinking or to the inner life that produced *Wuthering Heights*, the novel that, more than any other work coming from the parsonage, carried the name of Haworth round the world. The emergence of Emily's singular artistic vision was gradual and at one with the other children's developments. At first, together with Anne, she merely added to the more sophisticated games that Branwell and Charlotte organised, accepting rôles allotted, and taking her lead from her elders. But with Charlotte's departure for Roe Head in 1831, Emily and Anne found a new impetus to their story telling, founding their own kingdom of Gondal to explore while Branwell and Charlotte continued to develop Angria. With Branwell preoccupied with writing the *History of the Young Men* and his explorations of Haworth, the two girls quickly established their new game along more fanciful lines than Charlotte and Branwell's dominance had permitted. Where Glasstown and Angria were the settings for political intrigue and military campaigns, Gondal, born of readings in Byron, was in every respect more poetic, its scenery more obviously romantic and its people the typical outlaws, bandits, exiles and prisoners of Byron's narratives. This invention

Self portrait of William Robinson, the portrait painter of Leeds who became the Brontë children's drawing master. It was he who taught Branwell to paint in oils.

captivated Anne and Emily, becoming a source of great pleasure and a refuge for the next twenty years.

Emily's sisterly affection for Anne, a binding closeness that all who visited the parsonage bore witness to, indicates the ambiguity of her personality; while totally absorbed in the life of the family, drawing her strength and inspiration from the same sources, she nevertheless retained an almost complete privacy, keeping her own counsel and proving enigmatic even to her sisters.

By far the chief ingredients in Emily's home-made curriculum were the influence of the moorland landscape upon her; the view of life that her father offered; and the activities undertaken in the parsonage kitchen under the sharp eye and keen tongue of Tabby, the widow Tabitha Aykroyd, who came as cook and servant to the parsonage in 1825 and stayed for over thirty years.

Tabby was a native-born Yorkshire woman, who brought to her kitchen all the local yarns, gossip, fairy stories and superstitions common to any northern village at the time. A homely, loving, kindly woman, Tabby more than balanced the austere gentility of Aunt Branwell, thereby captivating the children and earning their unquestioning affection. It was Tabby who offered a constant check to the children's flights of fancy, who brought plain common sense to bear upon their problems, and above all who provided their authentic link with Haworth, its history and people. For Emily, Tabby also provided the model for Nelly Dean, the narrator of *Wuthering Heights*.

Emily's affection for Tabby appears in her diary notes where she deftly portrays the scene in the kitchen:

'November the 24 1834 Monday
Emily Jane Brontë
Anne Brontë

I fed Rainbow, Diamond Snowflake Jasper pheasant (alias) this morning Branwell went down to Mr Driver's and brought news that Sir Robert Peel was going to be invited to stand for Leeds.

Anne and I have been peeling apples for Charlotte to make us an apple pudding and for Aunt nuts and apples Charlotte said she made puddings perfectly and she was of a quick but limited intellect. Tabby said just now Come Anne pilloputate (i.e. pill a putato) Aunt has come into the kitchen just now and said where are your feet Anne Anne answered On the floor Aunt papa opened the parlour door and gave Branwell a letter saying here Branwell read this and show it to your Aunt and Charlotte The Gondals are discovering the interior of Gaaldine Sally Mosley is washing in the back kitchen.

It is past Twelve O'clock Anne and I have not tidied ourselves, done our bedwork or done our lessons and we want to go out to play we are going to have for Dinner Boiled Beef, Turnips, Potatoes and Applepudding. The Kitchen is in a very untidy state Anne and I have not done our music exercises which consists of B major Tabby said on my putting a pen in her face Ya pitter pattering there instead of pilling a potate I answered O Dear, O Dear, O dear I will directly with that I get up, take a knife and begin pilling (finished) pilling the potatoes Papa going to walk Mr Sunderland expected

An engraving of John Martin's The Fall of Babylon, *a copy of which hung in the parsonage. Charlotte drew upon Martin's style and subjects both in her writing and in her painting.*

Anne and I say I wonder what we shall be like and what we shall be and where we shall be if all goes on well in the year 1874 in which year I shall be in my 54th year

Anne will be going in her 55th year Branwell will be going in his 58th year Ande Charlotte in her 57th year hoping we shall all be well at that time we close our paper.'

It was from her lifelong familiarity with Tabby that Emily acquired her acute ear for dialect and an intricate knowledge of the folklore of Haworth but it was from Papa that she derived her profound love of its high moorland setting.

Emily took after her father. Branwell suffered the indignity of watching his younger sister outgrow him until she was almost as tall as Papa. This physical affinity, which was also distinctive, for Charlotte and Anne took after their petite mother—their dresses, gloves and shoes being too small for an average twentieth-century teenager to wear—serves to emphasise the individuality of this fifth child. Of the four daughters, only Emily Jane was given two names at christening and somehow she remains at all times significantly separate from the other children. She it was who shared in Patrick's eccentricity and wilful disregard for convention. If she wished to summon her dog she whistled it to her in a most unladylike manner; if she needed to warn Branwell to leave the parlour of the Black Bull, the slim young lady would fearlessly flout convention and go down to the public house and do so. It can be no surprise, therefore, to be told that she would join her father in the yard at the rear of the parsonage to be taught to fire the pistols which he kept in the house for protection.

But eccentricity on one side, Patrick's love of nature was profound and was passed on to all his children in some degree; but in full measure to Emily who added her especial perception to the delight he took in his moorland parish.

Patrick was brought up and educated with the poetry of Wordsworth. For him, Nature was the divine instructress from whom all, children, men and women alike could learn. To this end the great expanse of moor, stretching uncompromisingly from horizon to horizon, a still sea of heather filled with its secret life of wild birds and animals, displayed God's handiwork. It was to Patrick Brontë, as it was to Wordsworth, the natural schoolroom for growing minds. All the Brontë children were devoted to the vastness of the moors but it was to Emily the breath of life itself, as Charlotte recorded:

'My sister Emily loved the moors. Flowers brighter than the rose bloomed in the blackest of the heath for her; out of a sullen hollow in a livid hillside her mind could make an Eden. She found in the bleak solitude many and dear delights; and not the least and best loved—was liberty.'

And yet this was no swooning superficial romanticism. With Milton, Patrick taught that it is the mind of man that makes an Eden, or indeed a Hell, of a place, and it was his continuing belief that his children could also share this enlightened view. So effective was his teaching that Emily not only endorsed his attitude but enshrined it in so fine a piece of writing that the moorland parish and the nature of its landscape would reach a universal audience.

Charlotte's pencil sketch of Bolton Abbey, Yorkshire.

One instance of Patrick's concern that events in nature should be studied, and that man and environment are interwoven in a common fate, sheds considerable light on the origins of Emily's involvement with the moors and indicates the atmosphere in which the children were reared. On Thursday, 2 September 1824, in the evening, while the very young Emily, Branwell and Anne were being taken walking on the moors, the marsh at Crow Hill erupted during a thunderstorm precipitating a great flood of water, mud and boulders down the moors. Patrick's anxiety for the children caused him to watch the course of the storm when 'the clouds were copper coloured, gloomy, and lowering; the atmosphere was strongly electrified, and unusually close', so that he not only preached a sermon about the phenomenon, but wrote a detailed account of the scene of the devastation for the *Leeds Mercury* and followed that account with a long blank verse description intended to be used as a Sunday School prize for children. In all, three versions of the event were published by Patrick and were likely to be known by the children who were among those very close to the scene of the eruption.

Patrick's descriptions show his concern that his parishioners and their children should understand the causes of the landslide, and they provide a splendid example of a curate of the church taking seriously his task of teacher. In his sermon preached at Haworth on the Sunday following, he does not merely moralise nor meditate solely on God's wrath as evidenced in the storm, but goes to considerable lengths to present as objective, full and accurate an account as possible:

'You all know, that on the second day of this month of September, and in this present year of our Lord one thousand eight hundred and twenty-four, at about six o'clock in the afternoon, two portions of the Moors in the neighbourhood sunk several yards, during a heavy storm of thunder, lightning and rain, and issued forth a mighty volume of mud and water, that spread alarm, astonishment, and danger, along its course of many miles.

'Previously to the issuing forth of this flood, as I learn from some who reside near the place, there was a very considerable tremour of the neighbouring parts, and I was able myself to perceive something of the kind, though at the distance of four miles. This circumstance, which was not noticed by many who live much nearer, requires some explanation, which I shall give you in a few words. As the day was exceedingly fine, I had sent my little children, who were indisposed, accompanied by the servants, to take an airing on the common, and as they stayed rather longer than I expected, I went to an upper chamber to look out for their return. The heavens over the moors were blackening fast. I heard muttering of distant thunder, and saw the frequent flashing of the lightning. Though, ten minutes before, there was scarcely a breath of air stirring; the gale freshened rapidly and carried along with it clouds of dust and stubble; and by this time, some large drops of rain, clearly announced an approaching heavy shower. My little family had escaped to a place of shelter, but I did not know it. I consequently watched every movement of the coming tempest with a painful degree of interest. The house was perfectly still. Under these circumstances, I heard a deep, distant explosion, something resembling, yet something differing from thunder, and I perceived a gentle tremour in the chamber in which I was standing, and in the glass of the window just before me, which, at the time, made an extraordinary impression on my mind; and which, I have no manner of doubt now, was the effect of an Earthquake at the place of eruption. This was a solemn visitation of Providence, which, by the help of God, I shall endeavour to improve.'

Patrick continues with a discussion of 'How and for what reason Earthquakes are produced' concluding that such events should put us all in mind of our inadequacies. Not surprisingly for an evangelically minded curate of the established church Patrick's warning to his flock is unambiguous:

'Thus we often find it to be in daily life. When some grievous calamity befals a neighbourhood, or unexpected and sudden death hurries away an individual of consequence, a few are only impressed as they ought to be with the solemn occurrence: the greater part continued to indulge in their bad passions and practices, utterly regardless of every warning, and not considering the awful reckoning they will be brought to for these things on the last day.

'Let us pray earnestly for divine grace, that we may be enabled to act differently, and to walk by faith in Christ Jesus. We have just seen something of the mighty power of God: he has unsheathed his sword, and brandished it over our heads, but still the blow is suspended in mercy— it has not yet fallen upon us. As well might he have shaken and sunk all Haworth, as those parts of the uninhabited moors on which the bolts of his vengeance have fallen.'

By far the most important feature of Patrick's reporting and reflecting upon this incident, and the one of greatest significance for appreciating the way he educated his children, is the manner in which he retold the events in verse. The preface to this book for children speaks volumes in its tone and understanding, being much in advance of Carus Wilson's and other contemporary ideas about education:

To My
YOUNG READERS

Through the merciful providence of God, and the interposition of kind friends, you are now, as I suppose, in the first class in your Sunday-school, and, consequently are able to read considerably well. This is one reason why I have not been careful to select for you the easiest words and phrases, judging it proper that you should have a dictionary, and be able to find out in it the meaning of such phrases and words as you do not clearly understand. This talent of reading which you possess, will prove a blessing or a curse, just according to the use you make of it. If you read the scriptures and other good books only, your souls will be edified and comforted; but if you read every tract that is put into your hands by cunning and designing people, or eagerly search out for, and peruse such tracts and books as you know before to be bad, then you are sure to be corrupted and misled, and your talent of reading will become a source of sin and misery to yourselves and others . . . The phenomenon I am about to speak of, was of an extraordinary nature. During the time of a tremendous storm of thunder, lightning, and rain, a part of the moors in my chapelry, at the time specified in the title-page, sunk into two wide cavities; the larger of

Charlotte's pencil drawing for a design for a plate border.

which measured three hundred yards in length, above two hundred in breadth, and was five or six yards deep. From these cavities ran deep rivers, which uniting at the distance of a hundred yards, formed a vast volume of mud and water, varying from thirty to sixty yards in breadth, and from five to six in depth; uprooting trees, damaging, or altogether overthrowing solid stone bridges, stopping mills, and occasionally overwhelming fields of corn, all along its course of ten or fifteen miles. Now, the grand First Cause of this, and every other phenomenon, is God, whose instruments all are the elements, to execute his various purposes of infinite justice or mercy. Nevertheless, as to second causes, we may fairly reason thus:—

The moor in which this phenomenon took place, had, for years past, been rather soft and swampy; so that even during the summer season, it required a little precaution in the traveller, to go over it dryshod. It shook also to the tread, and contained several small oozing springs. At the distance of about half a mile, there were eminences also of a marshy nature. Under the surface of the ground, in all probability, a watery and muddy reservoir, or number of reservoirs, communicating with each other, may have

been forming for many ages. On the day of the phenomenon, there were heavy rains, much lightning and thunder, and unusually great heat. These reservoirs may have been overcharged by the water that descended immediately upon them, and by that which oozed into them, from the neighbouring eminences. The extraordinary heat also, must have produced considerable expansion, which, in conjunction with the tremour occasioned by the loud thunder, may have caused the surface of the ground to shake and rend, and open a passage for the struggling elements. Whether this may be called the disruption of a bog, or an earthquake, is of no great consequence, either as it relates to the interest it may excite, or the effects it has produced.

The gentle tone, the clarity and the real desire to communicate some understanding of the events to the children, all speak of a rare talent for dealing with the young. It is inconceivable that such a man should withhold these qualities from his own children, who were in time all to teach at the Sunday School where this small book would be available as a prize.

The poem, possibly Patrick Brontë's best, serves its purpose and indicates the impetus that his own writing must have given to Emily, Charlotte, Anne and Branwell:

Top Withens, near Haworth. Many believe that Emily chose this location as the setting for Wuthering Heights.

November the 24 1834 Monday

Emily Jane Bronte
Anne Bronte

I fed Rainbow, Diamond Snowflake Jasper pheasant (alias) this morning Branwell went down to Mr Drivers and brought news that Sir Robert peel was going to be invited to stand for leeds Anne and I have been peeling Apples for Charlotte to make us an apple pudding and for Aunts and and charlott's C[harlotte] said she made puddings perfectly and she is a quick but limited Intellect Taby said just now Come Anne pillopatate (i.e. pill a potato) Aunt has come into the Kitchen just now and said where are your feet Anne Anne answered on the floor Aunt papa opened the parlour Door and gave Branwell a letter saying here Branwell read this and show it to your Aunt and Charlotte — The Gondals are discovering the interior of Gaaldine Sally mosley is washing in the back Kitchen

A diary paper of 1834.

THE

PHENOMENON

OR,

AN ACCOUNT IN VERSE.

OF THE

Extraordinary Disruption of a Bog,

Which took place in the Moors of Haworth,

ON THE 2ND DAY OF SEPTEMBER, 1824:

BY THE

REV. PATRICK BRONTË, A.B.,

Incumbent of Haworth, near Keighley,

The title page of Patrick Brontë's pamphlet on the so-called 'Earthquake on the Moors'. The booklet was intended as a Sunday School prize book and contains what is probably Patrick's best verse.

Now kawing rooks on rapid pinions move,
For their lov'd home, the safe sequester'd grove;
Far inland scream the frighten'd sea-gulls loud,
High the blue heron sails along the cloud;
The humming bees, sagacious, homewards fly,
The conscious heifer snuffs the tempest nigh:
But, see! the hazy sun has reached the west,
The murmuring trees proclaim the coming blast.
Fast dusty whirlwinds drive along the plain,
The gusty tempest gives the slacken'd rein;
Low bend the trees, the lofty steeples rock,
And firmest fabrics own the sullen shock.
Condensing fast, the black'ning clouds o'erspread
The low'ring sky: the frequent lightning red,
With quivering glance, the streaming clouds do
                                                sunder,
And rumbles deep, and long, and loud, the thunder!
　The tempest gathering from the murky west,
Rests on the peak, and forms a horrid crest.
Down pour the heavy clouds their copious streams,

Quick shoots the lightning's fiercely vivid gleams;
And loud and louder peals the crashing thunder;
The mountains shake as they would rend asunder
But, see! the solid ground, like ocean driven,
With mighty force by the four winds of heaven,
In strange commotion rolls its earthy tide—
Whilst the riven mountain from its rugged side,
A muddy torrent issues, dark and deep,
That foaming, thunders down the trembling steep!
As high on Alpine hills, for ages past,
The falling snows, pil'd by the stifl'ning blast,
Rise a huge mountain on the dazzled eye,
Jut o'er their base, far curling in the sky;
Till, by their weight, these mighty masses fail,
And breaking, thunder down the trembling vale;
Bury whole towns in everlasting snow,
And chill with horror pale, the world below.
So, rocks on rocks, pil'd by the foaming flood,
All its vast force with trembling base withstood;
Till the indignant waves collecting fast,
Form'd a dark lake, urged by the incumbent blast;
And push'd at once, with wide resistless sway,
The mighty mass, 'midst thund'ring sounds, away;
Shook all the neighbouring hills, and thrill'd with
                                                fear,
The peasant's heart, and stunn'd his listening ear!

Patrick Brontë's exposition of the causes of the 'earthquake' on the moors, his concern to provide an easily comprehensible version of the events, for the common parishioners and for their children, presents a clear picture of a sensitive, gentle and committed clergyman. Without a hint of condescension he fulfilled a duty, accepting a responsibility derived from his own education and a cool understanding of his responsibilities. The attitudes, the tone and poise of his writing, all suggest that his teaching, of which these publications are examples, was habitual and instinctive. We can, therefore, be sure that he was as gentle and informative at home as he was in his pulpit and publications.

During the 1830s he published at least two more such expositions, one upon *Haley's Comet* and the other entitled *On the signs of the time* in which he attempted a survey of the progress achieved during the first part of the nineteenth century. Close to such a man, the Brontë children assumed an unquestioning curiosity and confidence. Phenomena should be observed, considered and commented upon. Such a habit, linked with an obsessive desire to scribble could scarcely fail to produce children with a creative artist's ambitions.

Emily's affinity with her father was an affinity with his philosophy and his love of poetry. His days at St John's, Cambridge, Wordsworth's college, had left their mark, and were to commit Emily and the other children of the parsonage to Wordsworth's romantic vision. The idyllic and superficial, the industrial and the society of man failed to move her. With Wordsworth and through her father's example, she developed a thorough poetical philosophy which pervades *Wuthering Heights* and is the constant theme of much of her verse:

Often rebuked, yet always back returning
    To those first feelings that were born with me,
And leaving busy chase of wealth and learning
    For idle dreams of things which cannot be:

Today, I will seek not the shadowy region:
    Its unsustaining vastness waxes drear;
And visions rising, legion after legion,
    Bring the unreal world too strangely near.

I'll walk, but not in old heroic traces,
    And not in paths of high morality,
And not among the half distinguished faces,
    The clouded forms of long-past history

I'll walk where my own nature would be leading:
    It vexes me to chose another guide:
Where the grey flocks in ferny glens are feeding;
    Where the wild wind blows on the mountain-side.

What have those lovely mountains worth revealing?
    More glory and more grief than I can tell:
The earth that wakes *one* human heart to feeling
    Can centre both the worlds of Heaven and Hell.

As the father so the daughter, with the additional scope of an even more compelling and distinct imagination. In Emily, Patrick's belief that he could look 'by faith through Nature, to Nature's God' found a ready response. Whatever the contemporary feelings about attendance at church might be, Emily could embrace Wordsworth's creed and share her father's view:

Let others seek its beams divine
    In cell or cloister drear;
But I have found a fairer shrine
    And happier worship here.

An early photograph of the Haworth churchyard and Sunday School. The low building is the Sunday School which Patrick had built and where he and all the children taught from time to time. Charlotte was appointed the school's first superintendent on her return from Roe Head. The house at the end of the school was John Brown's. He was Branwell's close friend and drinking companion.

Wordworth, from the portrait by Haydon. His poetry and philosophy profoundly influenced Patrick and, in turn, his children and their writing.

75

Chapter 8

The World beyond Haworth

In 1835 Charlotte was invited to return to Roe Head—and Miss Wooler—as a teacher. The school had now expanded and a post was available. Charlotte accepted and it was agreed that, as part of her payment one of her sisters could attend as a pupil. Thus, when Charlotte, the prize-winning student returned she was accompanied by Emily, making her first attempt to live away from Haworth since Cowan Bridge when she was very young.

At seventeen Emily proved no better equipped to survive away from home than were her sisters some ten years earlier. Her stay at Roe Head lasted less than three months, during which time Charlotte, becoming seriously concerned for her health, diagnosed acute homesickness and a love of the moorland vastnesses as her complaint:

'Liberty was the breath of Emily's nostrils: without it she perished. The change from her own home to a school, and from her own very noiseless, very secluded, but unrestricted and inartificial mode of life, to one of disciplined routine (though under the kindliest auspices) was what she failed in enduring. Her nature proved here too strong for her fortitude. Every morning when she woke, the vision of home and the moors rushed on her, and darkened and saddened the day that lay before her. Nobody knew what ailed her but me—I knew only too well. In this struggle her health was quickly broken; her white faced, attenuated form, and failing strength threatened rapid decline. I felt

in my heart she would die, if she did not go home, and with this conviction obtained her recall.'

And so Emily returned home to her pets, her liberty, her poems and her moors, to the life of 'absolute retirement of a village parsonage' which suited her so well, and which through her own determination proved a more than adequate education.

At this time, being tall, Emily had a striking appearance, she had a 'lithesome graceful figure', a pale complexion and grey-blue eyes which, through her intense reserve, seldom met a stranger's gaze. In company she spoke little, but liberated amidst her family or on the moors she could command the day. Ellen Nussey, perhaps over fondly recalling her in those years noted the reserve, which she found impenetrable, but found her 'intensely loveable': 'One of her rare expressive looks was something to remember through life, there was such a depth of soul and feeling, and yet such a shyness of revealing herself.'

Ellen thus exemplifies the difficulty we face in trying to understand Emily. Even Charlotte confessed that after a lifetime she never knew what Emily was feeling. The tall girl must always remain mysterious and yet tantalisingly so. Her intensity of feeling, so fundamental to her poetry and so evident in *Wuthering Heights* is nowhere chronicled or explained, the reserve Ellen noted has ensured that her privacy has remained intact.

Emily's retreat from the outside world was not the only admission of defeat before a new experience that occurred to the family in the late thirties. Branwell's progress as a painter had seemed so promising that his painting teacher, Robinson, had made arrangements for him to travel to London to seek admission to the schools at the Royal Academy in Somerset House. William Robinson had himself been taught there and could provide him with

Queen Victoria and Family in Scotland, from the painting by Landseer. Emily named a pet goose Victoria and its companion Adelaide. The Princess Victoria figured in many of Emily's writings, and when Charlotte was in Brussels at the time of Victoria's state visit she sent a detailed account of the Queen's activities to Emily at home in Haworth.

letters of introduction. So the boy who had pored over his illustrated guide to London, marking off the buildings he wished to see and those he deplored and considered 'execrable', was equipped with a map drawn by his father and sent by stagecoach to London. All the hopes of the family rode with him, it long having been their idea that Branwell would one day be a famous artist. In the event their hopes were dashed and their ambitions for him thwarted. For Branwell never presented himself at the Royal Academy. He reached London all right and visited most of the public buildings and institutions of which he had read; but for some reason the small, overstimulated young man (he was eighteen at the time) was overwhelmed by his experience. There is no way of knowing what happened to him, or what the cause of his taking flight may have been, there was no sister or companion with him to record the event or note his reactions. Branwell never wrote home to confirm his arrival in 'that great Babylon' and was never able to confide the truth about his experiences to anyone. The nearest description we have is unreliable, being part of an invention of Branwell's in one of his stories, describing a hypothetical visit to St Paul's which may well bear some resemblance to his own ill-fated excursion. Branwell tells of a visitor so overcome by the scale of the dome of St Paul's that he scarcely dare enter the building. His whole description is of a man transported and fuddled through oversensitivity who ultimately takes refuge in 'squibs of rum' and lapses into aimless meandering about London to no real purpose whatsoever. But Branwell, unlike his fictitious counterpart, did discover a purpose of sorts. A fellow Yorkshireman met him at Tom Spring's parlour and tells how the excitable Branwell, fresh from the conducive amiability of Sugden's Black Bull at Haworth, seemed to make himself at home in the ex-boxer's tavern in Holborn.

Tom Spring was one of Branwell's heroes and it is highly probable that the smoke-filled atmosphere of the sporting men's parlour with its necessary and ubiquitous alcohol overwhelmed Branwell as powerfully as he claims the hero of his story was overawed by Wren's masterpiece. The outcome of the episode was an ignominious return to Haworth to face a perplexed, saddened father and a confused Aunt. He had spent, or lost, all the money that they had got together to finance his stay in London, failed to present himself at the Royal Academy and invented some cock-and-bull story of being set upon by thieves as a way of explaining his penniless condition. We do not know whether his story was convincing, or if it was believed. With hindsight, this signal failure of nerve and the attempt to avoid the truth of the situation is significant; it may not have been the first of such evasions, it was destined not to be the last. Nowhere is the event referred to in any of the family writing; nevertheless, it must have been a bitter and bewildering conclusion to the years of hope and encouragement that had preceded the introduction to the world outside. Within a short space of time both Emily and Branwell had tested their wings and found them wanting. Were they perhaps *too well* prepared for the life of the artist? Perhaps Patrick had aroused them too effectively to a sensitive awareness of their surroundings.

Be this as it may, the effect for Emily was to allow her back to the security upon which she thrived. For Branwell and his masculine pride, the recovery was never so simple nor permanently effective.

DEAR, GENTLE ANNE

The stature of Emily as a major novelist, the near melodrama of Branwell's notorious decline, and the abundance of biographical material relating to Charlotte, all tend to obscure the story of their younger sister, the 'Dear, gentle Anne' who, despite their challenging talents, nevertheless made her own way in life.

Brought up entirely by Aunt Branwell, her mother having died when she was only eight months old, Anne's early life differed from that of the other children. She slept in her aunt's room and came into closer contact with her Methodism, which may have had something to do with her 'religious' turn of mind as she matured.

Plaster relief, Head of Branwell Brontë *by Branwell's friend Leyland, whose work is still to be seen in York Minster.*

We know little of her early life except that Branwell teased her for lisping and Charlotte wrote her a little book. But we do know that by thirteen she was strikingly pretty. A miniature portrait painted by Charlotte confirms Ellen Nussey's description:

'Anne–was quite different in appearance from the others. She was her aunt's favourite. Her hair was a very pretty light brown and fell on her neck in graceful curls. She had lovely violet-blue eyes, fine pencilled eyebrows, and a clear, almost transparent complexion.'

Always 'little Anne', the baby of the family, she attracted all the other children's affection so that she appeared passive to a fault. Charlotte found her painfully shy and feared that strangers might imagine she had a speech impediment. But Charlotte was habitually harsh in her judgements of her brother and sisters and the evidence of Anne's writing and her ability to stay in employment as a governess with the Robinson family for five years suggest that she was quite capable of doing herself justice when the need arose. Anne has rested in the shadow of her talented sisters for a long time, removed from this shade she is seen to have her own artistic vision and to have lived her own life in her own way. In the bustle of the quartet of artists maturing within the close walls of the old parsonage, it is easy to miss her own distinct voice. It is nevertheless there, as *Agnes Grey* and *The Tenant of Wildfell Hall* bear witness.

It was with Emily that Anne related most thoroughly. Ellen Nussey found that they were as 'twins—inseparable companions, and in the very closest sympathy, which never had any interruption'. But if it was this close companionship for which Emily had pined at Roe Head, her return home was bound to prove a disappointment, for with Emily's return from school, Anne was at once dispatched to take up the place that she had vacated. Despite her delicate constitution Anne was to succeed where Emily had failed. In all, she remained at Roe Head for two and a half years, establishing an ability to survive away from Haworth that was to serve her well.

The Royal Academy in London, after Thomas Malton. To which Branwell came but lacked the courage to enter.

Surprisingly little is known of Anne's life at the school. Charlotte was wretchedly busy and in despair at having to work so hard for so little reward. She now found teaching a drudgery and counting her income soon discovered that after clothing herself and Anne there was nothing left, though she had hoped to be able to save something. In January 1838 Anne was taken ill at school and Charlotte—understandably in the light of her earlier experience—became alarmed. In a letter to Ellen she described what happened:

Anne continued wretchedly ill—neither the pain nor the difficulty of breathing left her—and how could I feel otherwise than very miserable? I looked upon her case in a different light to what I could wish or expect any disinterested person to view it in. Miss Wooler thought me a fool, and by way of proving her opinion treated me with marked coldness. We came to a little *éclaircissement* one evening. I told her one or two rather plain truths, which set her a-crying, and the next day unknown to me, she wrote to papa telling him that I had reproached her bitterly—taken her severely to task, etc. etc. Papa sent for us the day after he had received her letter.

In time the rift was healed but Charlotte had resolved, one of her 'firm resolutions', that she would 'quit Miss Wooler and her concerns for ever', and so quit she did a

78

few months later. Charlotte was unrepentant. Anne's health improved at home and Charlotte thought it rather weak of Miss Wooler to 'cry for two days and two nights' and owned she 'should have respected her far more if she had turned me out'.

LITERARY ASPIRATIONS

The next few years saw several sorties from the parsonage out into the world beyond Haworth. All were short and, in the long term, unsatisfactory as a means of earning a living. The girls had little choice but to go as governesses while Branwell could toy with the idea of choosing whether to be a painter or a poet. Both Branwell and Charlotte sought advice about their literary ambitions. Charlotte wrote to Southey, the poet laureate, confessing her lifelong wish to become a writer only to be admonished and warned that so unfeminine a career was hardly likely to be suitable:

> Literature cannot be the business of a woman's life, and it ought not to be. The more she is engaged in her proper duties, the less leisure she will have for it, even as an accomplishment and a recreation.

Charlotte was mildly incensed by Southey's pompous masculine reply. She knew only too well the burden of responsibilities that life offered. Had she not accepted her duties as the eldest child and did she not have to watch over her sisters' health, even to the extent of fighting battles on their behalf to save their lives? Southey could hardly have known to whom he wrote so patronisingly of 'the vicissitudes of life'. Charlotte wrote again, particularly stung by the sombre Southey's warning that 'the daydreams in which you habitually indulge are likely to induce a distempered state of mind' for here he had touched a tender nerve, her daydreams of Angria being her sole means of surviving as a governess. Already Charlotte could write with some style, and a fighting spirit;

You do not forbid me to write; you do not say

A detail from Branwell's sketch book, which clearly demonstrates his ability to draw in pencil. Could the head be that of the dead Aunt Branwell, whom Branwell so loved and at whose deathbed he watched in grief?

that what I write is utterly destitute of merit. You only warn me against the folly of neglecting real duties for the sake of imaginative pleasures; of writing for the love of fame; for the selfish excitement of emulation. You kindly allow me to write poetry for its own sake, provided I have undone nothing which I ought to do, in order to

A page from Branwell's sketch book.

79

pursue that single, absorbing, exquisite gratification. I am afraid, sir, you think me very foolish. I know the first letter I wrote to you was all senseless trash from beginning to end; but I am not altogether the idle, dreaming being it would seem to denote.

With great temerity and confidence Charlotte defended herself. Yes, she had always sought to discharge her feminine duty, but, she continued, 'I don't always succeed, for sometimes when I'm teaching or sewing I would rather be reading or writing; but I try to deny myself.'

It is tempting to wonder what would have happened to *Jane Eyre* and *Wuthering Heights* if the daughters of the parsonage had always disciplined themselves merely to teach and to sew in keeping with the female condition the elderly poet recommended.

But Southey answered in a kindlier fashion to Char-

Sir,–Read what I write
And would to Heaven you would believe in me, for then you would attend to and act upon it!
. . . Now, Sir, to you I appear writing with conceited assurance: but *I am not*; for I know myself so far as to believe my own originality, and on that ground to desire admittance into your ranks . . .
. . . I *know* that I am not one of the wretched writers of the day. I know that I possess strength to assist you beyond some of your own contributors . . .

With the plea 'Condemn not unheard' Branwell persisted against absolute silence from the editor of the magazine he valued so highly, but to no avail. He was equally unsuccessful with Wordsworth who confessed that Branwell's letter was offensive to him. Looking at this letter, very different in tone from those sent to *Blackwood's*, it

Patrick Brontë's sketch map, drawn for Branwell to help him find his lodgings, the Chapter Coffee House near St Paul's Cathedral.

lotte's spirited reply, flatteringly signing himself her sincere friend, while once again warning her of over-excitement.

Branwell did not fare as well as his sister. His letters to the editor of *Blackwood's Magazine* offering his services as a writer were without exception unanswered. Rightly or wrongly, they were received and treated as curiosities, as the near ravings of an unbalanced mind. Certainly they are odd:

seems a pity that Wordsworth was not able to encourage Branwell in some small way.

Sir,
I most earnestly entreat you to read and pass judgement upon what I have sent you because from the day of my birth to this the nineteenth year of my life I have lived among secluded hills, where I could neither know what I was or what I could do. I read for the same reason that I ate or drank, because it was a real craving of nature. I wrote on the same principle as I spoke–out of the impulse and feelings of the mind . . .

As it was, Wordsworth's silence only aggravated Branwell's sense of inadequacy and defeat. At best a vain, erratic and mercurial person, Branwell found it hard to organise his affairs and his letter to Wordsworth shows a restraint and control which must have given him some trouble. One wonders whether a kinder response from the poet might have shone as a hopeful gleam in Branwell's Cowper-like gloom. Inadvertently, Wordsworth added to Branwell's torments of self-doubt, providing yet another rejection to the unfortunate young man's burden.

Nursing his impatience, perhaps even content with the now predictable response to his efforts, Branwell turned again to painting as a way of earning a living. Aunt Branwell paid for him to resume lessons with Robinson at the artist's studio in Leeds and Branwell attempted to revive the talent that had taken him once to the doors of the Royal Academy. This time he was reasonably successful and the temperament that denied him a place at the Royal Academy must have been held in check, for his paintings of this period show that he made a serious attempt to master the techniques of portrait painting. The well-known triple portrait of the Brontë girls dates from this time of renewed effort, as does the fragment of battered canvas which portrays Emily. Both of these paintings, now hung in the National Portrait Gallery, pose problems. In the triple portrait a fourth painted-out figure, probably Branwell himself, broods in the most dominant position on the canvas, and the portrait of Emily would seem to have been cut from a larger canvas which has been lost. It is widely believed that Branwell painted several such portraits of the family and Mrs Gaskell, who saw them while Charlotte was still alive, vouched that they were good likenesses.

The work of this period is impressive; clearly Branwell could paint. He was quite an accomplished draughtsman, as his sketchbook shows, which suggests that the family's belief in his talent and their ambition for him was not altogether ill-founded.

Branwell made sufficient progress to set himself up as a portrait painter in Bradford. Through William Morgan, his father's old friend, he found lodgings and received his first commissions, painting several portraits which were considered competent by the people who paid for them. Bradford seemed to suit Branwell. There was a small circle of intellectuals and fellow-artists whose company he enjoyed and he was able to make some firm friendships, notably with the sculptor Leyland who was to remain sympathetic to Branwell through thick and thin. But soon he had come to the end of his commissioned portraits and it became clear to him that he would not be able to support himself any longer as a portrait painter. Again Branwell found himself offering the world a talent which it did not seem to require.

Portrait painting, a profession that had enjoyed a long history, was, at the moment when Branwell sought to join its ranks, on the point of suffering its biggest set-back.

The daguerrotype was becoming available and within a few years the photographer was to oust the professional painter for all but the very rich. Soon the walls of the very merchants whom Branwell hoped to paint would bear the chemically produced and well posed 'likenesses' of the early photograph. Branwell might have fared better had he been a chemist and adopted photography as his profession.

This was Branwell's constant problem. Like his sister's dresses, he was always slightly old fashioned and out of step with progress. The education that his father provided unfortunately fitted him for little that was relevant in the rapidly changing world of the 1830s. Patrick Brontë had perhaps been too indulgent in allowing his own love of literature and the classics to dominate Branwell's learning. It had always been his ambition that his son should be either a poet or a painter. No attempt was made to equip him with a formal education and train him for any

The Chapter Coffee House where Patrick stayed in London at the time of his ordination, and to which Branwell, Charlotte, Emily and Anne were to come in turn. It seems that this was the only place in London that the family knew where to go for lodgings.

INTERIOR OF TOM SPRING'S PARLOUR.

Tom Spring's Parlour. A retired pugilist, Spring was renowned in London and even talked of in Haworth. It is believed that Branwell bolted to this refuge when he came to London to present himself at the Royal Academy, and that it was here that he revelled in the company and the drinking that Tom Spring's Parlour offered, spending his money and losing his resolve to be a painter.

profession. In this, and the terrible effect it was to have on the growing boy, the father is not altogether blameless. Branwell's education was entirely intellectual and fundamentally of an old order that was rapidly passing.

Tragically for Branwell, his father was educated at a time when society was at a watershed; all Patrick's experience was of a world before engineering, before the drift to factories and large cities, and before Darwin's *Voyage of the Beagle*. By the time Branwell came to face life as a young man the world of the homilies and the rural society that his father knew and loved was no more. In this way Branwell became trapped by circumstances and a victim of the remoteness of Haworth parsonage.

All the experiences that gave his sisters strength, that gave them a single-minded determination to concentrate their energy and drive themselves to undertake and complete large scale works of art, had an opposite effect

upon the solitary boy. Everything that toughened the girls and made them resilient and resourceful seemed ultimately to weaken him. The limited means on which they lived ensured that the daughters of the house helped with household chores and were expected to help with all the sewing 'work' of the house. When Branwell set off for London or Bradford it was the girls who had spent long hours finishing the cuffs, collars and frills of his shirts. While he would be translating Horace in his father's study, they would be preparing and cooking food. Branwell could happily pursue his own interests knowing that Southey, the poet laureate, endorsed his belief that 'freedom' fell to the male while 'duty' kept the girls busy about the house.

The family knew very well the seat of Branwell's difficulty, as indeed he came to know it himself. He was ill-equipped by nature and his upbringing to cope with the world as he found it. Charlotte recreates and defines just such a problem for a young man in her novel *The Professor* when the plain-speaking Mr Hunsden assesses the difficulties that beset an impoverished intellectual in the 1830s:

'"Now if you'd only an estate and a mansion, and a park, and a title, how you could play the exclusive, maintain the rights of your class, train your tenantry in habits of respect to the peerage, oppose at every step the advancing power of the people, support your rotten order, and be ready for its sake to wade knee-deep in churls' blood; as it is, you've no power; you can do nothing; you're wrecked and stranded on the shores of commerce; forced into collision with practical men, with whom you cannot cope, for *you'll never be a tradesman* . . .

'"You'll make nothing by trade," continued he; "nothing more than the crust of dry bread and the draught of fair water on which you now live; your only chance of getting a competency lies in marrying a rich widow, or running away with an heiress."

Here indeed is Branwell's problem. To be painting in oils in Bradford, the boom town of industrialisation, was to be stranded on the shores of commerce. Branwell was the impoverished intellectual par excellence, his wit, his Latin and Greek puns, his love of poetry, and above all his complete lack of money left him ill-suited for the practical bustling world in which he had to live. As Hunsden, and through him Charlotte, aptly concluded:

'"You think perhaps you look intelligent and polished; carry your intellect and refinement to market, and tell me in a private note what price is bid for them."'

Wyon's wax medallion of the poet, Robert Southey, to whom Charlotte wrote seeking advice about her wish to become a writer. Southey gave her a short answer: writing, he thought, was not a woman's work. The young Charlotte replied in a spirited letter that she knew the world's opinion—but that nevertheless she intended to do what she could to write as well as be a woman.

In 1840 Branwell did in fact take his intellect to market when, after a short time in Broughton as tutor in a family, he applied for and obtained a post as a railway clerk at Sowerby Bridge. Here was the poet turned porter in a bid to heave himself into the vigorous developments of his day, for this was the time of railway-mania when fortunes were being made as line after line was projected, planned and built. Soon Branwell was promoted to a small station of his own when the Calder Valley line was inaugurated. He was to be clerk in charge of Luddendon Foot station, a position from which he could expect promotion. But the keeping of ledgers, the checking of freight charges and the return of empty wagons at this none too busy station held little to occupy Branwell's teeming brain. In time he began to scrawl poetry in his ledger, ornament his accounts with cartoons and landscapes and generally neglect his duties. Again Branwell seemed fated. Being the first clerk at Luddendon, there was no station house in which he could live. Consequently he took lodgings in the village and spent much of his time at the Lord Nelson Inn where there was good company, cheap ale, and, perhaps surprisingly, quite a substantial lending library. As time passed so he became lax about his duties, indulging in what he himself called 'Grovelling Carelessness' until, inevitably, the company for whom he worked found things not quite in order. Branwell, it appears, while in no way being himself dishonest, had not kept as keen a watch on the station porter as he should. There was a deficit in the books and the young Mr Brontë was held responsible. After only a year he was dismissed from his post, unable to account for the £11-1s-7d missing from the company's funds. Moreover, the audit of the Luddendon Books had revealed his doodlings and quite erratic book-keeping. Branwell's days of drinking and neglecting his work had finally brought him into public disgrace. Confessing his folly in retrospect he later wrote harshly of his time at Luddendon:

> I would rather give my hand than undergo again the grovelling carelessness, the malignant yet cold debauchery, the determination to find how far mind could carry body without being chucked into hell, which too often marked my conduct, when there, lost as I was to all I really liked . . .

Branwell's dismissal was a serious affair for it sent him back to the parsonage with an even greater sense of failure than before. He later came to describe himself as more firmly aground than the ship the *Great Britain*, so thoroughly had he found himself, in Charlotte's words 'stranded on the shores of commerce'. He had indeed been found wanting. The man whom Francis Grundy, a fellow railway clerk, described as; 'Poor, brilliant, gay, moody, moping, wildly exciteable, miserable Brontë' a friend in whom he had found 'wit, brilliance, attractiveness, eagerness for excitement' was forced to retire in disgrace to the home where a stern rule of honesty and rectitude was upheld. Dismissed from his post Branwell had no alternative but to return to Haworth. At twenty-five he was still wholly dependent upon his father and unable to avoid admitting the cause of his dismissal. Not surprisingly on his return home he fell ill, thoroughly demoralised and

Mr and Mrs Kirby, painted by Branwell Brontë. Branwell, in high hopes of a successful career, set himself up as a portrait painter in Bradford in 1837. Mr Isaac Kirby, a 'Porter & Ale Merchant', was Branwell's landlord.

wretchedly depressed. Writing to Grundy he took stock of his situation:

> I cannot avoid . . . scribbling a few lines to you while I sit here alone–all the household being at Church–the sole occupant of an ancient parsonage, among lonely hills, which probably will never hear the whistle of an engine till I am in my grave.
>
> . . . After experiencing, since my return home, extreme pain and illness, with mental depression worse than either, I have at length acquired health and strength and soundness of mind, far superior I trust, to anything shown by that miserable wreck you used to know under my name. I can now speak cheerfully and enjoy the company of another without stimulus of six glasses of whiskey; I can write, think and act with some apparent approach to resolution, and I only want a motive for exertion to be happier than I have been for years. But I feel my recovery from almost insanity to be retarded by having nothing to listen to except the wind moaning among old chimneys and older ash trees and nothing to look at except heathery hills walked over when life had all to hope for and nothing to regret with me–no one to speak to except crabbed old Greeks and Romans who have been dust the last five thousand years. And yet this quiet life, from its contrast, makes the year passed at Luddendon Foot appear like a nightmare. . . .

During that 'nightmare', through the help of friends,

Branwell had published poems in the *Halifax Guardian*. Thus being the first of the Brontë children to have any work published. Typically his themes are morbid and biographical as the following, written in August 1841, shows:

Brearly Hill Aug 8–1841

Oh Thou, whose beams were most withdrawn
    When should have risen my morning sun,
Who, frowning most at earliest dawn,
    Foretold the storm through which 't would run;

Great God! when hour on hour has passed
    In an unsmiling storm away,
No sound but bleak December's blast
No sighs but tempests, through my day,

Branwell's pencil sketch of the church at Broughton where he was a tutor for a while. In time his drinking worried his employers; thinking that he would be a bad influence upon his charges, they dismissed him.

At length, in twilight's dark decline,
  Roll back the clouds that mark Thy frown,
Give but a single silver line–
  One sunblink, as the day goes down.

My prayer is earnest, for my breast
  No more can buffet with these storms;
I must have one short space of rest
  Ere I go home to dust and worms;

I must a single gleam of light
  Amid increasing darkness see,
Ere I, resigned to churchyard night,
  Bid day farewell eternally!

My body is oppressed with pain,
  My mind is prostrate 'neath despair–
Nor mind nor body may again
  Do more than call Thy wrath to spare,

Both void of power to fight or flee,
  To bear or to avert Thy eye,
With sunken heart, with suppliant knee,
  Implore a peaceful hour to die.

When I look back on former life,
  I scarcely know what I have been
So swift the change from strife to strife
  That passes o'er the 'wildering scene.

I only feel that every power–
  And Thou hadst given much to me–
Was spent upon the present hour,
  Was never turned, my God, to Thee;

That what I did to make me blest
  Sooner or later changed to pain;
That still I laughed at peace and rest
  So neither must behold again.

The Railway Juggernaut, *upon which Branwell climbed
when he became a deputy station master, first at Sowerby
Bridge and then as a clerk in charge of Luddenden Foot
Station. From a contemporary cartoon.*

Chapter 9

Governesses

While Branwell was making ill-fated attempts to face up to life away from Haworth, his sisters were trying to reconcile themselves to being governesses. As he came to loathe his own carelessness, they unequivocally hated teaching. In letters and novels they compile a chorus of complaint in which they all shared: teaching was a drudgery that dissipated their energies and exhausted them. Charlotte is quite explicit about the problem facing them all:

> I am miserable when I allow myself to dwell on the necessity of spending my life as a governess. The chief requisite for that station seems to me to be the power of taking things easily as they come, and of making oneself comfortable and at home wherever we may chance to be–qualities in which all our family are singularly deficient. I know I cannot live with a person like Mrs Sidgwick, [her employer] but I hope all women are not like her; and my motto is 'try again'.

But the foundation of Miss Wooler's teaching, which was reinforced by Aunt Branwell and Papa, was 'the bending of our inclinations to our duty', a lesson Charlotte took to heart and made the basis for her quite astonishing stamina. Charlotte could never seek her pleasure while a duty remained unfulfilled, but she nevertheless cried aloud in complaint as she felt her spirits flagging.

'Winning their bread amongst strangers' as Charlotte described earning a living was always irksome to her, but we should not make the mistake of concluding that it was her charges, and children in general, that Charlotte disliked. The evidence is to the contrary. Charlotte was capable of warm affection for children, it being 'indulged' and 'spoiled' children whom she found troublesome. At a time of spring-cleaning, while she was governess with the White family at Upperwood House, Rawdon, she confesses a response to a small child that corresponds with her compassionate view of children in her fiction:

> May 4th, 1841
> During the last three weeks that hideous operation called a 'thorough clean' has been going on in the house. It is now nearly completed, for which I thank my stars, as during its progress I have fulfilled the twofold character of nurse and governess, while the nurse has been transmuted into cook and nursemaid . . .
> . . . Somehow, I have managed to get a good deal more control over the children lately–this makes my life a good deal easier; also by dint of nursing the fat baby, it has got to know me and be fond of me. I suspect myself of growing rather fond of it.

Again, in a letter to Ellen Nussey many years later, when she rather wryly considers herself a real 'old maid' she betrays a gentle humour when writing of a baby:

> I don't know what that dear Mrs Taylor will make of her little one in the end, between port wine and calomel, and Mr B. and Mr A. I should not like to be in its socks. Yet I think it will live . . . ;

The fondness which Charlotte found herself able to confess makes doubly tragic her death after her marriage, for not only did this kindly woman die so soon after her wedding, but the woman who could write of Mrs Taylor's little one's socks also died pregnant, denied not only the comfort of a husband but also the possible joy of her own child.

'The inevitable evils of being a governess' never paled as far as Charlotte was concerned. Her sympathies were extended to her sisters whom she saw as trapped in some kind of slavery, and throughout her life she continued to feel for anyone unfortunate enough to need to become that social nonentity, a governess. The famous tale is told of the small child who evinced some affection for Charlotte, whose 'I love 'oo Miss Brontë' was met with the proper reply 'Love a Governess? Really!' Perhaps it was in reaction that whenever possible in society Charlotte sought out any governess she could and passed the time with her rather than with the grander people present.

But all the Brontë girls, despite their loathing for their station, enjoyed teaching promising pupils. In advice to her publisher, when his daughters were thinking of becoming teachers, Charlotte, while remaining consistent in her attitude to governesses offers good advice to anyone contemplating the teaching profession:

> The young teacher's chief anxiety, when she sets out in life, always is to know a great deal; her chief fear that she should not know enough. Brief experience will, in most instances, show her that this anxiety has been misdirected. She will rarely be found ignorant by her pupils . . . But on her patience, on her self-control, the requirement will be enormous; on her animal spirits (and woe be to her if these fail!) the pressure will be immense.

Health, strength and cheerfulness are Charlotte's ingredients for success in teaching.

The time the sisters spent in other people's houses caring for their children, all too aware of their dependence upon work to make their way, was also a time for observation and the accumulation of experience. Together with the life they led in Haworth, the trials of the Brontë sisters as teachers and governesses were to provide a profound source of ideas and stimulus for their writing. Without the anguish Charlotte felt at Roe Head, hedged round 'by stupid asses' of girls; without the bitter embarrassment of accepting a role as a nonentity in other people's drawing-rooms, Charlotte could never have realised the telling portrait of Jane Eyre, nor Anne her counterpart in Agnes Grey. While Emily's imagination fed upon the moors, their elemental mysteries and open landscape, so her sisters bore their burden in society, drawing a great strength from the enforced silence of their situations. Both Charlotte and Anne recorded their experiences as governesses and drew upon their suffering as inspiration. Isolated from each other they lived through their imaginations and continued to develop and refine their creative genius.

Surprisingly, Anne seems to have fared better than either of her sisters, remaining with one family, the

---

Law Hill School where Emily taught for a while in conditions that Charlotte believed amounted to slavery.

Robinsons of Thorp Green Hall, near to York, for as long as four years, the longest that any of the children remained in continuous employment. A letter of Charlotte's uncharacteristically praises Anne for her coolness and competence, which rather suggests that the quiet 'gentle Anne' may have been altogether misrepresented:

> You [Ellen Nussey] and Anne are a pair for marvellous philosophic powers of endurance; no spoilt dinners, scorched linen, dirtied carpets, torn soft-covers, squealing brats, cross husbands, would ever discompose either of you.

We know too little of Anne to be able to judge her, but here, her sister's admiration seems sincere.

Someone was, however, able to 'discompose' Anne, and that was one of her father's many curates, one William Weightman M.A., an 'excellent classical scholar' from Durham University who arrived in Haworth in 1839 and managed to alter, almost completely for a brief spell, the pattern of life in the parsonage.

CURATES

Patrick Brontë's curates were several, and mostly treated with profound contempt by his children. Clergymen were altogether too frequently a part of their life to have any charm or attraction for the lively youngsters who watched them come and go. They were to Charlotte, who was always ready to fix people with a neat phrase, 'a self-seeking, vain empty race' and people who counted for nought and were not worth discussing. That is, until Mr Weightman arrived, when amid the flurry of giggles and contempt afforded all of his kind by the three girls and the arrogant, assured Branwell, the auburn-haired, blue-eyed, vivacious new curate caused as much consternation as he was meant to endure. For William Weightman was more than equal to Charlotte's scorn and her sister's teasing. Instead of withering beneath their onslaughts, he quickly established himself as the favourite curate of all, leading the Brontë sisters as merry a dance as they had led others before him.

Weightman had much to commend him. He was as vital and extroverted in his behaviour as the Brontë's were introspective, he was jovial and cheerful; but above all he was a flirt. Charlotte's letters to Ellen at this time are sparkling with the fun and innuendo to be expected in marriageable young ladies correspondence but which had hitherto been sadly missing from Charlotte's. Letter after letter chronicles his latest apparent 'conquest' and tells that he is 'treading' on young ladies' feet as often as ever in the parsonage.

The year of 1840 had become, through the presence of Willy Weightman, something of a landmark in the Brontë biography. It is easy to believe that this scholarly young man with his apparently uncomplicated view of courtship and the 'nobleness of life' it implied came as a tonic to a household where people took themselves all too seriously. Certainly all the evidence indicates a levity and happiness which is hard to find at other times in the parsonage's history. Weightman not only delighted the girls, he also impressed their father. Here was a young clergyman after his own heart, and moreover a fit, indeed an admirable,

The view, from the back windows of Law Hill School, of the Shibden Valley. It is believed that this landscape, together with some of the houses in the area, helped Emily shape the story for Wuthering Heights.

companion for Branwell, who was quick to be on good terms with a young man who could match him in his knowledge of the classics, shoot game on the moors, and talk of his latest 'conquests' as well as his sermon on Sunday.

With their customary wicked wit the girls christened Weightman Miss Celia Amelia and ever after referred to him by that sex and epithet. And so Miss Celia Amelia became a force to be reckoned with and the provider of much to talk about in those times when 'we curl our hair'.

Among his conquests Weightman could number Papa's profound admiration, Branwell's devotion as a friend, Charlotte's fascinated if wry interest, Ellen Nussey's 'concern' and above all, the gentle Anne's quiet, speechless admiration. How good it would be to record the longevity of this hopeful and beneficial addition to the Haworth landscape. Here in one man was the help Patrick Brontë needed, the companion Branwell sought, and the young man who could set the sisters' hearts beating. What matter if his 'carrying on' and keeping the girls out late infuriated Aunt Branwell, or that he played fast and loose with the affections of all the ladies he met.

But longevity was not common in Haworth in 1840. Too-frequent outbreaks of cholera and the annual drought in summer saw to that. In the epidemic of 1842, through the humane fulfilling of his duty in attending the sick of the parish, Weightman died of cholera, watched and prayed over by Patrick and Branwell, father and son grieving over the same companion and friend.

Patrick preached a fine sermon in praise of his young curate which was printed as a memorial. In it he exemplified Weightman's qualities and demonstrated his own prevailing belief in a ministry for the humblest:
'In his preaching, and practising, he was, as every clergyman ought to be, neither distant nor austere, timid nor obtrusive, nor bigoted, exclusive nor dogmatical. He was affable but not familiar; open, but not too confiding. He thought it better, and more scriptural, to make the love of God, rather than the fear of Hell, the ruling motive for obedience . . .

'Agreeable in person and manners, and constitutionally cheerful, his first introduction was prepossessing. But what he gained at first, he did not lose afterwards . . .

'When I stated to him that it would be desirable he should descend to the level of the lowest and most illiterate of his audiences, without departing from the pure and dignified simplicity of the scriptures, he would good-naturedly promise to do so—and in this respect,

88

there evidently was a gradual, but sure improvement. As it ought to be with every incumbent, and his clerical coadjutor, we were always like father and son . . .'

Typically for Patrick Brontë and his fierce belief in the life of this world rather than of the hereafter, the memorial sermon sought to praise Weightman's life, and not to demonstrate the more popular deathbed conversion of the Calvinist tradition. Patrick's words are startlingly fresh and ahead of his time, belonging more to the compassion of Jane Eyre's love for Rochester than the prevailing attitudes of his fellow clergy:

'Don't ask how a man died, ask how he lived. But after all, I do not, and never did consider, the transactions of a dying bed as exclusively a safe criterion to judge of a man's character. If we would know whether a man has died in the Lord, we ought, in the first instance to ask, has he lived in the Lord?'

Anne was to leave her own memorial to Celia Amelia. Charlotte had noticed her behaviour in church with Weightman and it is popularly believed that she nursed an unspoken love for the dashing curate:

He sits opposite Anne at Church, sighing softly and looking out of the corners of his eyes to win her attention – and Anne is so quiet, her look so downcast – they are a picture.

Many of her poems would serve as an epitaph for just such an unpublished affection for the 'handsome, cheery, and good tempered' young man who made eyes at her in church:

Yes, thou art gone, and never more
Thy sunny smile shall gladden me
But I may pass the old church door
And pace the floor that covers thee . . .

May stand upon the cold, damp stone
And think that, frozen, lies below
The lightest heart that I have ever known,
The kindest I shall ever know.

A Reminiscence 1844

But Weightman's best memorial is his response to learning that neither Charlotte, Emily nor Anne had ever received a Valentine. For 14 February 1840, he trudged the ten miles to Bradford to send them a Valentine poem each and thereby remedy the sad deficiency. So able a tease deserved the affection that the whole family, and the parish afforded the young man who died at twenty-six.

Even Charlotte, the arch-critic of curates, conceded that her 'revered friend' Willy Weightman was 'bonny, pleasant, light-hearted, good-tempered, generous, careless, fickle and unclerical', and of his successor she pronounced:

'Mr Weightman was worth 200 Mr Smiths tied in a bunch.'

Keighley Mechanics Institute, where William Weightman, one of Patrick's curates, lectured and where Patrick himself spoke on 'The Influence of Circumstances'. All his life Patrick supported the Mechanics Institute Movement, being a firm believer in popular education. He was active in establishing the Haworth Branch, which at one stage had to institute a fines system for overdue borrowings of copies of Jane Eyre.

THIS MONUMENT
WAS ERECTED BY THE INHABITANTS,
IN MEMORY OF THE LATE
WILLIAM WEIGHTMAN, M.A.
WHO DIED SEPTᴿ 6ᵀᴴ 1842, AGED 26 YEARS
AND WAS BURIED IN THIS CHURCH
ON THE 10ᵀᴴ OF THE SAME MONTH.
HE WAS THREE YEARS CURATE OF HAWORTH,
AND BY THE CONGREGATION, AND PARISHIONERS
IN GENERAL, WAS GREATLY RESPECTED,
FOR HIS ORTHODOX PRINCIPLES,
ACTIVE ZEAL, MORAL HABITS, LEARNING,
MILDNESS, AND AFFABILITY:
HIS USEFUL LABOURS WILL LONG BE
GRATEFULLY REMEMBERED,
BY THE MEMBERS OF THE CONGREGATION;
AND SUNDAY SCHOOL TEACHERS,
AND SCHOLARS.

The memorial in Haworth Church to William Weightman, the curate who brought sunshine into the lives of all the family. His tragic early death was a bitter blow to Branwell, who had at last found a true friend; and the cause of grief to Anne, who was in love with him.

Chapter 10

Brussels

Before Willy Weightman's death added its weight to the blows that the Brontës' confidence was to take, Charlotte and Emily had hatched a plan in keeping with the young man's optimism and cheerfulness. Aunt Branwell, Papa and the three girls hit upon the idea of opening a school. As the Misses Wooler had succeeded at Roe Head, so might the Misses Brontë. Originating from Charlotte, always the organiser, the project gathered momentum until it clearly preoccupied all the girls and grew to be their most urgent concern. They were encouraged from all quarters and once again Aunt Branwell agreed to back their scheme from her own income. At this point letters from Charlotte's old school friend Mary Taylor were to tip the balance for the school further still and enlarge the scope of the project. Mary's father having recently died, the family had dispersed and Mary, with her brother Joe, found herself in Brussels. Her letters so glowed with delights of that city and so moved the enslaved Charlotte that a plan formed itself in her mind and became one of her clear, firm resolves.

Mary's description of the cathedrals of Brussels, of the pictures she had seen and of the advantages of study and travel abroad enthralled Charlotte; 'I hardly know what swelled to my throat as I read her letter', and she realised, not for the first time, her sense of frustration at talents wasted, of 'faculties unexercised' and of an urgent need to learn, to know and to see. At first she saw these feelings as 'rebellious and absurd emotions' which were 'acutely painful' but soon, with more encouragement from Mary Taylor and support from Mr and Mrs White, her employers, whose fat baby she had so effectively nursed, Charlotte saw the sense of going to a finishing school on the continent as a way of acquiring the accomplishments that would be expected of ladies establishing their own school. Time spent abroad, she calculated, would ensure the success of their venture. Thus armed she screwed up courage to write from Upperwood House in Rawdon, where she was employed as governess, to Aunt Branwell. In a splendidly tactful, practical and gracious letter she approached the now aging Aunt whose patience and generosity had many

times come to their aid. Charlotte outlined her plan in detail. She would go to Brussels, where she knew 'the facilities for education are equal and superior to any other place in Europe' to improve her knowledge of French, 'improve greatly in Italian' and even get a 'dash of German', languages being so important in education. With precise details of costs, and the suggestion that Emily should accompany her, she concluded:

> . . . I feel certain, while I am writing, that you will see the propriety of what I say; you always like to use your money to the best advantage, you are not fond of making shabby purchases; when you do confer a favour, it is often done in style; and depend on it, £50 or £100 thus laid out would be well-employed. Of course, I know no other friend in the world to whom I could apply on this subject except yourself. I feel an absolute conviction that, if this advantage were allowed us, it would be the making of us for life.

Then, in a masterly touch–Charlotte never wrote with greater effect in her life–she demonstrated the continuity of the Brontë endeavour, showing herself to be truly her father's daughter:

> Papa will perhaps think it a wild and ambitious scheme; but who ever rose in the world without ambition? When he left Ireland to go to Cambridge University, he was as ambitious as I am now. I want us all to go on. I know we have talents, and I want them to be turned to account. I look to you, aunt, to help us. I think you will not refuse. I know if you consent, it shall not be my fault if you ever repent your kindness.

The Aunt did not refuse the eloquent request, and once again the true friend whom Patrick had come to regard with affection as long ago as 1812 offered real help just when it was needed.

Plans were spurred on by Charlotte's enthusiasm, letters flew back and forth, she had promised Ellen that she would make good use of Mr Hill's new penny post, and the great project was under way. After some hesitation an appropriate school was found, the Pensionnat Heger in Rue d'Isabelle in Brussels under the supervision of a young couple, Monsieur Heger, thirty-three, and his wife who was thirty-eight. The school was run along 'domestic lines', being based upon the family life of the Hegers, and enjoyed a good reputation. Charlotte's letter of application was kindly received and arrangements were made for both she and Emily to join the school forthwith.

Patrick accompanied his daughters to Belgium in February 1842, staying with them in London at the Chapter Coffee House where he had lodged at the time of his ordination and to which he had earlier sent Branwell on his fruitless journey to the Royal Academy. In many ways the scheme was a success. There is a sense in which the time at the 'finishing school' did provide a 'finish' to their education. Their horizons broadened and their knowledge of other literature increased. Emily was able to study the piano with a professor and they both coped with learning and teaching in French. Monsieur Heger was a fine teacher and the standards of the domestic arrangements were high. Charlotte was able to write home to Ellen Nussey that she and Emily had done well and 'got into a very good school—and are considerably comfortable'. Despite their isolation as the only Protestants in a Catholic school, the difference in country and religion

A nineteenth-century engraving of the port of London, from which the Brontës sailed.

making 'a broad line of demarcation', Charlotte claimed that she was 'never unhappy!' Her present life, being a schoolgirl again at the ripe age of twenty-six, was 'so delightful, so congenial to my own nature, compared with that of a governess'. Emily, it appears, had to work 'like a horse' in order to improve her French, but both she and Charlotte seemed cheerful with this chance to learn at the feet of a 'professor of rhetoric, a man of power as to mind'.

The impact that Brussels made upon Charlotte was lasting and deep. The Pensionnat Heger, its director, his wife, its gardens, its history and its pupils are all recreated in her novels *The Professor* and *Villette* with the same precision that Cowan Bridge was remade in *Jane Eyre*. The atmosphere of the long dormitory and the close over-supervised school is powerfully evoked. Once again she observed every smallest detail of place and character and employed them in her own creations. Both Emily and Charlotte were respected pupils and the project seemed to be fulfilling its purpose. However, in the October of 1842, the year they had taken up their studies with Monsieur Heger and only a month after Weightman's death, Aunt Branwell fell ill, and was watched over by an agonised Branwell:

Oct 25th 1842

I have had a long attendance at the death-bed of the Rev. William Weightman, one of my dearest friends, and now I am attending at the death bed of my aunt, who has been for twenty years as my mother.

Elizabeth Branwell was dying from an acute blockage in her stomach and Branwell, the only one of the children at home, sat with her 'witnessing such agonising suffering as I would not wish my worst enemy to endure'. He confessed that when Elizabeth Branwell died he had 'lost the guide and director of all happy days' connected with his childhood.

Although Emily and Charlotte were summoned back

An advertisement for 'Cheap Travelling' in an age when few people ever left their native heath. Emily and Charlotte travelled to Brussels with their father, making the crossing to Ostend by paddle-steamer.

A photograph of the gardens at the rear of Le Pensionnat Heger, taken during the 1840s. This was the school in Brussels that Emily and Charlotte attended as pupils with money that their aunt provided, and where Charlotte was later to become a teacher.

from Brussels their Aunt was dead and buried before they reached England. In her will she left each of the girls a small income and various of her personal effects, many of which are to be seen at the parsonage museum:

'. . . Should I die at Haworth, I request that my remains may be deposited in the church in that place as near as convenient to the remains of my dear sister . . . My Indian workbox, I leave to my niece, Charlotte Brontë; my workbox with a china top I leave to my niece Emily Jane Brontë together with my ivory fan; my Japan dressing-box I leave to my nephew, Patrick Branwell Brontë; to my niece Anne Brontë, I leave my watch with all that belongs with it; as also my eyeglass and its chain, my rings, silver spoons, books, clothes etc. etc. I leave to be divided between my above named three nieces . . .'

With Aunt dead and no longer clattering about the parsonage in her wooden pattens, or dispensing the servants' ration of home-brewed ale, someone would need to take over the running of the household. It would be surprising if Emily had found it a hard decision to make. She would remain and Charlotte could return to Brussels, they had both left Monsieur Heger's school with a pleasing record of progress and a warm invitation to return as teachers; Emily of piano and Charlotte of English, and Anne could continue as governess with the Robinson family.

This was the plan that they followed. Anne, somehow, had managed to procure Branwell a post as tutor with her own employers and in January 1843 Emily was left alone at home with her father, Tabby and Martha, the servants, and her pets.

The Family Heger, *from a painting by Ange François in 1848, a few years after the Brontë sisters knew them. Constantine, presenting the bespectacled profile, was the teacher with whom Charlotte became infatuated.*

92

Chapter 11

The Time of Failure

Charlotte pondered long over Monsieur Heger's suggestion that she should return to teach at the Pensionnat in Brussels. Unlike Emily, she had been reluctant to leave the Rue d'Isabelle and the atmosphere of learning at the school. Charlotte consulted her conscience and then, for the first and, she afterwards claimed, only, time in her life, ignored it. Such was her determination to return to the one place where her mind had taken wings after the restrictions of being a governess, that this small, normally timid lady made her way unchaperoned from Haworth to London, thence to Ostend and Brussels where she was warmly welcomed by the Hegers. It was agreed that she should teach in return for her keep and that she should receive a small salary. The Hegers offered to share as much of their home with her as possible in order that she should not feel alienated as the only English person in the school. She was to use their sitting room and be, to all intents and purposes, as one of the family.

All seemed set fair. As part of her 'contract' Charlotte was to teach Monsieur Heger English, a task which enlivened her day and, if the truth were told, was the real reason for her return and the cause of her twinge of conscience. For Charlotte, the English Protestant clergyman's daughter, was deeply attached to her Catholic Professor. His mind, his conversation, his consideration for his assistant governess all conspired to sweep her off her feet. Her lessons with her 'master' gave her the pleasure of spending time with the man for whom she had made her lonely journey from Haworth.

But, in time, inevitably in so close a family, Madame Heger sensed Charlotte's infatuation for her husband. He was thirty-three and Charlotte was twenty-seven, and she feared lest a more embarrassing situation were to arise. Consequently she engineered the ending of the private lessons which had brought Charlotte so much contentment and saw to it that the professor and the former pupil had little opportunity to meet. This deprivation, coupled with the effort of teaching which she had already found a strain, made Charlotte bitterly unhappy. Once again, as at Roe Head, she found that the pleasures of being a pupil in a school did not readily transfer to those who teach. With reluctant pupils whom she must teach in French Charlotte found that lessons were a torment, and without the constant reassurance of time spent with Monsieur Heger she became more and more depressed. Her exclusion from the former closeness with the Hegers left her isolated and lonely. Soon she was writing pitifully to Emily and Branwell complaining of her 'Robinson-Crusoe-like condition', confessing that she

Constantine Heger in later life, from a portrait by Joseph Gerard. His refusal to answer any of Charlotte's letters after her return to England caused her a deep and lasting distress. Charlotte became abject and physically ill, pleading with her former teacher for any small crumb of comfort.

93

had grown increasingly 'misanthropic and sour' for 'want of companionship'.

Charlotte's committment to Monsieur Heger, the excitement of his teaching which had so bowled her over and made Brussels so delightful a city, had all now turned against her. Succumbing to the family malaise she was overwhelmed by nostalgia, by a need to be back in Haworth. She now began to loathe Brussels as much as she had once adored it, openly confessing 'I do so wish to go home'.

But Charlotte's despair was never simple homesickness. She had so set herself to benefit from her return to Brussels that she was reluctant to abandon her decision too readily. Moreover, she was now clearly in love with her former teacher. Only he could brighten her day, his absence from her leaving her wretched and in despair. Without his considerate and flattering attention she lived a wretched 'easeful stagnant life'. She now found that her enthusiasm for writing had left her, that she could not settle to read or to paint. For a year she battled on in great anguish but with a desperate resolve to stay close to Monsieur Heger, the only man who had ever moved her in a manner remotely similar to that of her heroes in the early writings. Charlotte was an affectionate woman whose reserve imprisoned her in solitude and silence. At length her 'homesickness' as she called the mental struggle which she was undergoing led her to return to Haworth, the desired haven where Emily had chosen to remain:

Brussels 1 Oct. 1843

> Dear E.J.–This is Sunday morning. They are at their idolatrous *messe*, and I am here–i.e.–in the refectoire–I should like uncommonly to be in the dining room at home, or in the kitchen, or in the back-kitchen–I should like, even, to be cutting up the hash, with the Clerk and some registry people at the other table, and you standing by, watching that I put enough flour and not too much pepper, and, above all, that I save the best piece of the leg of mutton for Tiger and Keeper (parsonage pets), the first of which personages would be jumping about the dish and carving knife, and the latter standing like a devouring flame on the kitchen floor . . .
>
> . . . tell me whether Papa really wants me very much to come home, and whether you do likewise. I have an idea that I should be of no use there–a sort of aged person upon the parish. I pray, with heart and soul, that all may continue well at Haworth; above all in our grey, half-inhabited house. God bless the walls thereof!

For Charlotte, life in Brussels was dreary and her relationship with the Hegers increasingly strained. She was convinced that the other teachers were set to spy upon her and in this as in everything she blamed her idol's wife. At length, after a scene, perhaps reminiscent of that with Miss Wooler, Charlotte resolved that she had no alternative but to leave Brussels. In December of 1843 she wrote to Emily asking for more money to be sent to help her pay her way home. With a heavy heart she prepared to return to Haworth confiding in Emily that her

Ellen Nussey in later life. From the time of their first meeting at Roe Head School, Charlotte and Ellen kept up a regular correspondence to which we owe much that we know of Charlotte's life and the family's comings and goings.

spirits were low and her mind 'a trifle shaken'. The low spirits were to persist for many months after her return to the parsonage and were to preoccupy her waking thoughts for a long time.

Charlotte's retreat from Brussels is uncharacteristic. She had reached out with confidence, perhaps hastily, for a joy which she believed was possible, and now, in a manner more in keeping with Branwell's personality, she was hastening home to lick her wounds. In time, the experience would strengthen her; as it was, it left her desolate and, for a while, aimless.

Much of her anguish is recreated in *The Professor* and *Villette*, where her own conflict and misery are seen alongside descriptions of the immediately recognisable school where she had experienced so much joy mingled with bitterness. The mature young woman who, as an adolescent, had allowed herself to daydream and write of love and romance, now found herself having to nurse an aching heart, to pine remote from the object of her affection and to pester the postman daily for a letter with a Belgian postmark. For two years Charlotte nursed the pain while pouring out her misery in letters to the man who so possessed her thoughts, letters which were so explicit that Mrs Gaskell found it impossible to admit them in her biography of Charlotte, it being left to later biographers to demonstrate the true cause of Charlotte's wretchedness and the embarrassment of the position in which Madame Heger had found herself with the English governess.

From all accounts Monsieur Heger conducted himself with dignity and no little sympathy for Charlotte, perhaps little aware of the infatuation which he fed when he made presents of books to his younger admirer.

For Charlotte, however, it was his behaviour after she

had left Brussels that caused her the most pain. As she left, they had agreed to correspond, their parting having been amicably conducted. But Charlotte allowed herself to write of her feelings with some frankness, which provoked a rebuke from Heger and in time, too frequently for her peace of mind, ensured that her letters, which were seen by Madame Heger, remained unanswered.

Charlotte's letters to Heger grow in intensity and in sheer panic at the thought, confirmed by the long silences when she received no reply nor any indication that her letters had been delivered, that she must live without any contact with the 'master' to whom she owed so much:

> All I know is, that I cannot, that I will not, resign myself to lose wholly the friendship of my master. I would rather suffer the greatest physical pain than always have my heart lacerated by smarting regrets. If my master withdraws his friendship from me entirely I shall be altogether without hope; if he gives me a little–just a little–I shall be satisfied–happy; I shall have a reason for living on, for working.

After a few replies, infrequent and formal, Heger's letters stopped altogether. Bewildered and beside herself, Charlotte continued to write, sending letters by friends as well as by post, but to no avail.

Eventually, Charlotte was able to tell her anguish in verse, her ability to write helping her, perhaps, to come to terms with her suffering:

> Unloved–I love; unwept–I weep;
> Grief I restrain–hope I repress:
> Vain is the anguish–fixed and deep:
> Vainer, desires and dreams of bliss–
>
> My love awakes no love again,
> My tears collect and fall unfelt;
> My sorrow touches none with pain,
> My humble hopes to nothing melt.
>
> For me the universe is dumb,
> Stone-deaf and blank, and wholly blind
> Life I must bound, existence sum
> In the strait limits of one mind;
>
> That mind my own. Oh! narrow cell;
> Dark–imageless–a living tomb!
> There must I sleep, there wake and dwell
> Content with palsy, pain and gloom!

By November 1845 she could still write of her need for contact with her 'beloved':

> When day by day I await a letter and when day by day disappointment comes to fling me back into overwhelming sorrow . . .–I lose appetite and sleep–I pine away.

A fragment of one of Charlotte's last letters to Heger, confessing her love and consequent misery. It is believed that the letter was torn up and thrown away, and that it was Madame Heger who extracted the pieces from the waste-paper basket and sewed them together in order to know the content of Charlotte's letters. Perhaps it was Madame Heger who forbade any reply?

The tablet over the door of the Sunday School in the lane by the parsonage.

Despite Heger's advice that she should forsake her ambition to be a writer, advice moreover which Charlotte took very seriously, her love for her teacher, her 'professor', was to become the informing experience behind her greatest creations. Jane Eyre's secret love for Rochester, untold and seemingly unnoticed owes much to the bitterness that gripped Charlotte's heart when she returned from Brussels and was then denied the sustaining comfort of correspondence.

'Buried Away from the World'

Charlotte's return from Brussels in January 1844 marked the end of her serious attempts to live and work away from Haworth. She found her father, now sixty-six, both ageing and rapidly losing his sight. Her own unhappiness was not the sole concern and anxiety in the parsonage. Together with Emily she remained at home, realising day by day that her father depended upon her increasingly, until the time came when she resigned herself to placing her ambitions second to her duty as a daughter. Apart from a few brief visits she never again left Haworth and even after her marriage returned to live in the parsonage to care for her father.

Her father's eyesight, which had always been poor, was deteriorating rapidly. Increasingly he had to rely upon his curates, none of whom were as competent or pleasing to him as Willy Weightman. It was a relief, therefore, when Arthur Bell Nicholls, who was appointed in the following August, turned out to be a capable man well able to carry a large part of the parish business on his shoulders.

The 1840s were the mid-point of Patrick Brontë's ministry, since he came to Haworth in 1820 he had been active in every sphere of parish life and the evidence of his energy was all around him. He had built the Sunday Schools in the lane leading from the church to the parsonage, he had installed an organ in the church, hung a peal of bells, and made any number of minor improvements. By 1850 two new churches would be consecrated to serve the outlying parts of the parish: St Mary's at Oxenhope, a

splendid replica of a Norman parish church; and the little mission church at Stanbury, where Patrick's pulpit, from the old church of St Michael's in Haworth, is still in use today. In secular matters he had been equally busy. Lecturing to the Conservative Club in the White Lion; speaking from election platforms at the time of the Reform Agitations; president of the Temperance Society; a supporter of the Mechanics Institute; 't'parson' was a well known figure noted for his high principles and outspoken fearless manner.

We have some idea of the man that Charlotte and Emily looked after from just two examples of his involvement in the private and public affairs of his parishioners. The one a report in the London *Times* of a public meeting which he held, the other a letter he sent to the Editor of the *Leeds Mercury* about children's clothes catching fire. Both indicate the energy of the man and the extraordinary compassion which he showed and encouraged. A return to Haworth parsonage was by no means a retreat from reality.

The Times for Monday, 27 February 1837 carried a full report of Patrick Brontë's outspoken attack on the New Poor Law Act, an act which many up and down the country found harsh and a cruel imposition upon those who already suffered from poverty and lack of work. At a public meeting which he chaired – held at the Sunday School which he had built – Patrick organised a petition to Parliament for the repeal of the Act. True to the spirit of his *Cottage Poems*, he was zealous on behalf of the poor and the common work-people of his parish, who, despite being warned off by their employers, the 'liberal manufacturers' who owned the Haworth Mills, turned out to support their parson in such numbers that the meeting had to be conducted in the open air.

Patrick's address was reported in full in *The Times* and the following extracts serve to demonstrate the swingeing attack which he delivered against legislation which he profoundly believed to be evil:
'. . . now the old bill, though not a perfect one, was sufficient for our wants, and like John Bull himself it was generous as well as testy, shaking a cudgel over our heads at times, but closing the punishment with shaking of hands over a quart of ale; while the new bill was a nose-hewing, finger-lopping quack, a legal deformity, hunch-backed, and one-handed, though that one hand grasped the trenchant dagger . . . This poor law was termed a remedy for the poor but in that sense a man might take a strong dose of opium for a remedy while in the cholic, and then, as now, the remedy would prove worse than the disease. Then again, 'guardian of the poor' seemed a pretty name, and the guardians of Haworth were all honest men, – but there's many a pretty name for an ugly thing, and three honest men would possess no power but to do mischief.

'Guardians were in the situation of the fox guarding the goose. Supposing the fox gives his ward a loving pinch by the neck, the poor goose might complain, but the fox assures it that all is for its good, though the pinch might end in worrying. However, he hoped that in the case before him, the geese would soon turn to eagles triumph-

Top: Charlotte's painting of Flossie, Anne's King Charles spaniel.

Above: Charlotte's miniature of her sister Anne.

Right: Branwell's portrait of his friend John Brown, the sexton at Haworth.

*The board to celebrate the ringing of the first peal of the bells
which Patrick had installed in the tower.*

ing, with talons clinched in their prostrate enemy, and he could assure them that Yorkshire and Lancashire united, would prove more than a match for all opposition to their welfare. He entreated them to rouse themselves, for their laws, and bodies, and souls, were equally concerned in that matter—and country too, for if dear times and general distress should come on, starvation, deprived of relief, would break into open rebellion; but the time for healthy action was now or never, and if Englishmen only exerted themselves they would in the end come off more than conquerors.'

It is little wonder that the meeting closed with three cheers for its chairman, or that his daughters in their writings could defend the underdog with similar eloquence.

But public meetings were only one aspect of his involvement in parishioners affairs. His ability to move a crowd was matched by an ability to sustain a cool argument on behalf of the smallest members of his parish. In a letter entitled 'Cremation', published in the *Leeds Mercury* in the March following Charlotte's return from Brussels, he offered some sound advice for parents:

'. . . though I have been a subscriber to your paper for more than thirty years, I can remember only one article in it respecting the misconduct of parents in regard to the death of children, in consequence of their clothes catching fire. How, with your critical acumen, this important case could have been overlooked by you, I can hardly conjecture. I know that you have admonished mothers to stay at home with their children; but when a little village gossip is afloat, you might as well tell mankind to chain the sunbeams, in a cloudless summer day. You know, and those less knowing than you are must be conscious that all garments of linen, or cotton, are particularly inflammable, and that clothes of woollen, or silk, are much less so, and cannot be ignited at all without the most careless and wanton neglect. Hence it is evident that if women and children were, in general or always, to have their garments of silk or wool, there would be little or no danger of their losing their lives by accidental ignition. You may, and perhaps some of your readers may, think me to be trivial. Well, I cannot help it; nor do I wish to write or state my sentiment otherwise. I like to talk plainly and openly, and I may say faithfully; and then I leave the consequences to the Supreme Disposer of events, and the Controller of all hearts. I have been at Haworth for more than twenty years, and during that long interval of time, as far as I can remember, I have performed the funeral service over ninety or a hundred children, who were burnt to death in consequence of their clothes having taken fire, and on inquiry in every case I have found that the poor sufferers had been clothed in either cotton or linen. Believing this to be an important lesson, and by giving it to the world, in all its simplicity, I shall be amply gratified should I be the means of saving only one life in this our state of probation.

'I remain, Gentlemen, your most obedient servant, Patrick Brontë.'

Such an enlightened understanding of the beguiling nature of 'village gossip' must be compared with the popular belief that it was God who set children's clothes alight in order to teach them a lesson!

In returning to Haworth Charlotte was once again accepting a place in the pattern of life in the parsonage, a life dominated by the church calendar and a routine of services and parish meetings. Having tasted freedom she now found Haworth 'a lonely, quiet spot, buried away from the world'. She had returned from Brussels determined to revive her plan for establishing a school; she now had the money left her by Aunt Branwell and the qualifications, from Monsieur Heger. But her father's condition spoke plainly, as she confided in Ellen Nussey:

> . . . I cannot permit myself to enter upon life – to touch the object which seems now within my reach, and which I have been so long straining to attain. You will ask me why. It is on Papa's account; he is now, as you know, getting old, and it grieves me to tell you that he is losing his sight. I have felt for some months that I ought not to be away from him; and I feel now that it would be too selfish to leave him (at least as long as Branwell and Anne are absent) in order to pursue selfish interests of my own. With the help of God I will try to deny myself in this matter and to wait.

Charlotte was now a little ashamed of herself. She no longer regarded herself as young. She would be twenty-eight soon after she wrote the above letter, and she was sure that she should be out earning a living. But she felt it her duty to restrain that feeling, and, being Charlotte, restrain it she did. Nevertheless the isolation of Haworth after life in Brussels made her feel 'buried away from the world', despite the various local activities of the parish in which, through her father, she would become involved.

The bells which Patrick installed, and which now hang silent for lack of funds to allow renovation. The bells that tolled for each of the family in turn are now to be replaced by a tape-recording.

Above: Branwell's portrait of Emily.

Opposite: The Brontë sisters, painted by their brother Branwell, c. 1825. From left to right are Anne, Emily and Charlotte, with a painted-out space in the background which probably once held a self-portrait of Branwell himself.

Chapter 12

Branwell

While in Brussels, Charlotte had been relieved to have news that Branwell was making a success of his post as tutor to Edmund Robinson at Thorp Green Hall. On her return home she heard that both he and Anne were 'wondrously valued in their situations'. But her relief that he seemed at last to be making something of his life was short-lived. Late one night in July 1845, on returning from a visit to friends, Charlotte was greeted with the news that Branwell was home, ill, a not uncommon occurrence which did not, at first, cause her any alarm. But on learning the cause of his present illness Charlotte's peace of mind was shattered and she realised that the entire family were about to be subjected to the most difficult times.

> He had last Thursday received a note from Mr Robinson sternly dismissing him, intimating that he had discovered his proceedings, which he characterised as bad beyond expression, and charging him on pain of exposure to break off instantly and for ever all communication with every member of his family.

In Branwell's words (in a letter to J. B. Leyland), Lydia Robinson, his employer's wife, and he had exchanged 'declarations of more than ordinary feeling';

> This lady (though her husband detested me) showed me a degree of kindness which, when I was deeply grieved one day at her husband's conduct, ripened into declarations of more than ordinary feelings. My admiration of her mental and personal attractions, my knowledge of her unselfish sincerity, her sweet temper and unwearied care for others although she is seventeen years my senior, all combined to an attachment on my part, and led to reciprocations which I had little looked for. During nearly three years I had daily 'troubled pleasure soon chastised by fear'. Three months since, I received a furious letter from my employer, threatening to shoot me if I returned from my vacation . . .

Thus Charlotte's grief at having to leave Monsieur

Silhouette of Patrick Branwell Brontë, always called Branwell or Brany, in the family.

Heger was matched by Branwell's more violent and passionate depression at severance from Lydia Robinson. Charlotte's impulsive overriding of her conscience which had taken her back to Brussels cost her, in her own estimation, two years peace of mind. Branwell's three years 'attachment', without the intervening safeguard of a Madame Heger to keep the affair within reasonable limits, was to lead to an equal period of utter torment. Without Charlotte's ferocious will-power Branwell had led himself, or tumbled into, a pit (a common theme in his scribbled drawings), from which he would never be able to climb.

In short, if we are to believe Branwell (though hyperbole and wild exaggeration were as common as nouns and verbs in his vocabulary), he had become involved in a long and passionate affair with his employer's wife, by all accounts an indulged and indulgent woman. Whether Branwell's account is to be trusted or not, the effect of

The Black Bull in an early photograph. Fully modernised, the inn has retained its exterior intact, flanking the little opening at the top of the hill that serves as the centre of Haworth. It was to the Bull that Branwell frequently made his way in an attempt to find some relief from his melancholy, and it was here that he established a reputation for his fine conversation and social ease.

whatever passed between the tutor and the lady of the house was his sudden dismissal in disgrace and the complete mental and physical breakdown that accompanied it. But where the details of what actually happened at Thorp Green Hall may never be made known, the unrelieved misery that Branwell's dismissal brought to the parsonage is all too clearly written in the story of the Brontës' lives. Whether, as some believe, Branwell really had been in love with Lydia Robinson and she with him as he protested; or whether he simply wallowed in a fantasy of self pity and remorse, the outcome was the same.

The man who confessed 'I have been in truth too much petted through my life' and resigned himself to being a 'thoroughly old man – mentally and bodily' at twenty-eight, took to drinking away what money he had, resorted to drugs when he could get them, and began a steady decline that led to a gradual wasting away from which he eventually died – no other cause of death being recorded. To the romantic critic he was the only Brontë to die of a broken heart, to Emily he was a poor hopeless being, to himself he was an 'utter wreck', a martyr awaiting execution, a man preparing to be hanged.

All of Branwell's morbid fantasies had finally found a cause upon which they could settle. His melancholy now became macabre, his scribbled drawings tormented depictions of devils and himself, chained to a stake in anguish. His 'lacerated nerves', his 'roasting daily and nightly over a slow fire' troubled by 'almost killing cares'

drove him to all kinds of excess and those who had to care for him were pushed to the point of despair.

Charlotte's 'we have had sad work with Branwell' was to become a daily fact through the course of a depression that totally disabled Branwell for the whole of the next three years. Years during which his sister and almost totally blind father had to cope with fits, drunkenness, drugged stupors and the weariness of waiting upon the unpredictable ravings of a mind 'possessed' and shackled in a 'constant and unavoidable depression of mind and body'.

In lucid moments Branwell pitied his family, in particular his father, 'the poor old man who does what he can', but on the whole he convinced himself that they rejected and despised him: 'the quietude of my home, and the inability to make my family aware of the nature of most of my sufferings makes me write:

Home thoughts are not, with me
    Bright as of yore.
Joys are forgot by me,
    Taught to deplore.'

Like Charlotte, he now found the peace of Haworth stifling; once again, as after his dismissal from Luddenden Foot, he found himself imprisoned in the remoteness of the parsonage, or, to use his own image, aground and stuck fast out of the tide of men's affairs. The whole weight of his previous failures must now have borne down upon him. His whole history was of hopes dashed, of ambitions thwarted and trust betrayed. The boy who fled London

A view of Luddenden showing the Lord Nelson Inn (the white buildings at the left) where Branwell resorted while clerk in charge at Luddenden Foot. The photograph shows clearly the mountainous nature of many of the Yorkshire villages, with the stone houses and their heavy paved roofs set against the force of the wind. Although the Lord Nelson housed a lending library, not unusual for inns of the day, Branwell spent much of his time drinking heavily and he looked back on his time there with shame and regret. While at Luddenden he wrote some of his best poetry, some of which was published in a Halifax newspaper.

St. Paul's Cathedral.

The Bank of England.

Keeper from life April 24th 1838 — Emily Jane Brontë

Above: Emily's watercolour of Keeper, the family house dog of whom she was particularly fond. Keeper, the legend tells, followed Emily's coffin to its grave and howled for many nights at her bedroom door.

Opposite top: Leech Finders. A reminder of the state of medicine in the nineteenth century, from George Walker's The Costumes of Yorkshire. Patrick Brontë endured an operation for cataract without the blessing of anaesthesia, and the operation was followed by the application of leeches to his temples for 'blood-letting'.

Opposite bottom: A page from A Description of London owned by Branwell from an early age, which bears what are supposedly his comments on the merits of the buildings shown.

1844.

Thorp Green, a sketch by Branwell of the house where he and Anne were employed by the Rev. and Mrs Robinson.

was now accustomed to accept disgrace. Once again 'a grovelling carelessness' or the 'more than ordinary feeling' of his attachment had betrayed him. This he called 'the undercurrent of distress which bore my bark to a whirlpool, despite the surface waves of life that seemed floating me to peace'. His need for affection, a need shared by the whole family, had beguiled him as it had also beguiled his less passionate but equally feeling sister, Charlotte.

History has been harsh in judging Branwell. For want of any accurate information he has been too simply styled a reprobate, a drunkard and a rake. Equally, Charlotte's view of her brother's wretchedness has been unsympathetically drawn. Fresh from her own heart-ache, filled with anxiety for her father, she saw the reality of Branwell's condition. Where once she felt that she should leave Haworth to 'brave the rough realities of the world' she now found enough of them within the walls of her own home. Her refusal to invite Ellen to stay while 'he is at home' and her realistic 'Branwell offers no prospect of hope–he professes to be too ill to think of seeking for employment–he makes comfort scant at home . . .' are undisguised admissions of the truth of the situation rather than out-of-hand condemnations of a sinner. The reality was that Haworth parsonage was a small house, with one sitting room. Charlotte's admission, which must have cost her much in heartache, that at times it was impossible for

anyone to be in the same room as Branwell, must be seen as part of three years spent in helping, and cleaning up after a frequently drunk and sick man who at least once had managed to set his bedclothes afire. Nursing and caring for someone in Branwell's condition with only the most primitive forms of sanitation and no hot and cold running water must have been a nightmare. The three girls and the servants obviously did much and saw only too clearly how thoroughly Branwell was destroying himself.

After a while, for his own safety, his bed was moved into his father's room, where, Charlotte recorded in 1848: 'Papa is harassed day and night: he' (Branwell) 'is always sick; has two or three times fallen down in fits; what will be the ultimate end, God knows.'

For a while, early in his illness, Branwell was able to sustain himself by believing that with Mr Robinson's death Lydia would speed to his side. A sonnet written when he had been sent to Wales with John Brown, his father's sexton, in an attempt to lift his spirits, tells how vain the attempt was to clear his mind of its infatuation:

Penmaenmawr

I knew a flower, whose leaves were meant to bloom
Till Death should snatch it to adorn a tomb,
Now, blanching 'neath the blight of hopeless grief,
With never blooming, and yet living leaf:
A flower on which my mind would wish to shine,
If but one beam could break from mind like mine.
I had an ear which could on accents dwell
That might as well say 'perish' as 'farewell!'

The Misses Brontë's Establishment

FOR

THE BOARD AND EDUCATION

OF A LIMITED NUMBER OF

YOUNG LADIES,

THE PARSONAGE, HAWORTH,

NEAR BRADFORD.

Terms.

	£.	s.	d.
BOARD AND EDUCATION, including Writing, Arithmetic, History, Grammar, Geography, and Needle Work, per Annum, ...	35	0	0
French, German, Latin — each per Quarter, ...	1	1	0
Music, Drawing — each per Quarter, ...	1	1	0
Use of Piano Forte, per Quarter, ...	0	5	0
Washing, per Quarter, ...	0	15	0

Each Young Lady to be provided with One Pair of Sheets, Pillow Cases, Four Towels, a Dessert and Tea-spoon.

A Quarter's Notice, or a Quarter's Board, is required previous to the Removal of a Pupil.

An eye which saw, far off, a tender form,
Beaten, unsheltered, by afflictions storm;
An arm–a lip–that trembled to embrace
My angel's gentle breast and sorrowing face;
A mind that clung to Ouse's fertile side
With toiling–objectless–on Menai's tide.
But in the event, when Mr Robinson died and Branwell daily expected to be summoned to his 'beloved's side', the coachman from Thorp Green arrived in Haworth with

The prospectus for the proposed Brontë school. Not one application was received. Charlotte said later that she quite understood why no one would wish to send a child to school in so desolate a place. She confessed that she was content to have tried the experiment and was not at all startled by the outcome. It is interesting to conjecture where any pupils were to have been boarded in an already rather crowded house had the response been other than it was.

Above: The pathway to the waterfall beyond Haworth Parsonage.

Opposite: Elizabeth Gaskell, the distinguished novelist who became Charlotte's close friend in the last five years of her life. She was Charlotte's first biographer. By George Richmond, 1851.

contrary news, confirming that Mrs Robinson must never see him again. This Branwell took as his 'finishing stroke', a letter from the Robinson's family doctor, who had been a good friend to Branwell, left him 'stunned into marble':

> I have this morning received a long, kind and faithful letter from the medical gentleman who attended Mr R. in his last illness and who has since had an interview with one whom I can never forget.
>
> . . . When he mentioned my name—she stared at him and fainted. When she recovered she in tears dwelt on her inextinguishable love for me— her horror at having been the first to delude me into wretchedness, and her agony at having been the cause of the death of her husband, who, in his last hours, bitterly repented of his treatment of her.
>
> Her sensitive mind was totally wrecked. She wandered into talking of entering a nunnery; and the Doctor fairly debars me from hope in the future.
>
> It's hard work for me, dear Sir; I would bear it but my health is so bad that the body seems as if it could not bear the mental shock . . .
>
> May God bless her, but I wish I had never known her!
>
> My appetite is lost; my nights are dreadful, and having nothing to do makes me dwell on past scenes—on her own self, her voice, her person, her thoughts, till I could be glad if God would take me. In the next world I could not be worse than I am in this.

Branwell managed to convince himself, wrongly as the facts show, that Mr Robinson had altered his will in order to ensure that Lydia, should she ever again see him, would be cut off from her inheritance. No such alteration exists in the will and before long Mrs Robinson had re-married well, and, as far as we know, never gave Branwell another thought until she found herself readily identified in Mrs Gaskell's life of Charlotte as the mature lady who seduced Charlotte Brontë's younger brother and, thus libelled, sought and obtained an unconditional apology from the celebrated authoress.

By 1847 Branwell was lost in the grip of self-pity and remorse mingled with arrogance and sincerity, he had once entertained proud hopes and now was pitifully cast down:

> I had reason to hope that ere very long I should be the husband of a Lady whom I loved best in the world, and with whom, in more than competence, I might live at leisure to try and make myself a name in the world of posterity, without being pestered by the small but countless botherments, which like mosquitoes sting in the world of workday toil . . .

Eloquent in his fantasies of sorrow and sensitivity, Branwell parades his misery, in his letters to Leyland, with all the trappings of forlorn heroes in a gothic novel and repining with a terrifying intensity. Nothing is admitted as an aid or comfort:

> Noble writings, works of art, music or poetry now instead of rousing my imagination, cause a whirlwind of blighting sorrow that sweeps over my mind with unspeakable dreariness, and if I sit down and try to unite all ideas that used to come clothed in sunlight now press round me in funeral black, for nearly every pleasurable excitement that I used to know has changed to insipidity or pain.

While Branwell was in this torment, the village witnessing his decline as his clothes came to hang from his wasted frame and he took to restless aimless wandering in his misery, the family tried to cope as best they could. While he confessed himself unable to take refuge in writing, various attempts to write novels were left unfinished, his sisters increasingly found comfort in their writing and in sharing their compositions in their nightly walks around the dining room table. All this they kept a secret from their brother, now excluding him from their company as much as once they had seen him as their most prized and inventive leader.

It is almost unbelievable that Charlotte's *Jane Eyre*, Emily's *Wuthering Heights* and Anne's *Agnes Grey* were all written during the worst times of Branwell's illness. The refuge which he found himself denied must have served them as a means of comfort and escape.

Branwell's dismissal had effectively also ended Anne's career. She returned to Haworth having witnessed 'some very unpleasant and undreamt of experience of human nature' but seems, after five years away from home, to have quickly readjusted to the former life of close companionship and the shared primary need to write. For Anne, as for Charlotte and Emily, writing was a continuous part of life:

'We had very early cherished the dream of becoming authors. This dream, never relinquished, even when distance and absorbing tasks occupied us, now suddenly acquired strength and consistency; it took the character of a resolve.'

In the midst of all this distress, living with a drunkard and drug-addict they maintained a belief in their dream, and what is more, after all their attempts to set up a school failed, they set out to launch themselves upon the world as authors.

The scheme for a school, which even went as far as the production of advertisements which were sent out to friends and distributed quite widely, foundered in no uncertain manner. After weeks of planning and waiting, not one pupil or parent came forward. Charlotte considered the experience valuable and suggested that no parent, seeing the parsonage set inside a graveyard would have dreamt of leaving a child there for a moment. The 'Misses Brontës School' therefore, got no farther than it's brief prospectus, which must have been all to the good with the parsonage as cramped and fully occupied as it was. As Charlotte philosophically concluded, it was a scheme she wished to attempt and having done so she was content. It was, however, by no means the first of the Brontë ventures to founder and was, alas, not to be the last.

Chapter 13
Currer, Ellis and Acton Bell

Currer Bell

Ellis Bell

Acton Bell

The disaster that returned Anne and Branwell so un-expectedly to Haworth when Charlotte and Emily were already established with their father, began the final and most complete time of unity and common experience the family were to experience. The grief at Branwell's condition, the constant anxiety for Papa's health, wove a new web between the inhabitants of the parsonage. As Branwell suggested, the web of sunshine woven in their common childhood was now overlaid by one of more sombre tones. Under the burden of suffering which they all bore, each of them found their own courage and way of enduring. Charlotte reached out to Ellen Nussey and trod a clear path of duty; Anne wrote, exploring her deep and disturbed religious beliefs; Emily, the practical, capable no-nonsense young woman, became a legend for her devotion to Branwell and also for the closeness of her privacy, writing and hiding her poems, offering no dis-cussion of her innermost feelings. With Branwell en-tranced by his own plight, the young women formed a team, a team of writers and a team that strove to keep some kind of world together for their ailing father and themselves. In the one they were doomed to failure, in the other, their writing, they could have little idea of the success that awaited their effort. But success was still some way away in 1845.

Following the salutary experience of not being able to open their school, a now famous chance-find of Charlotte's was to set the parsonage daughters off on a completely different enterprise:

'One day, in the autumn of 1845, I accidentally lighted on a MS volume of verse in my sister Emily's handwriting. Of course I was not surprised, knowing that she could and did write verse. I looked it over, and something more than surprise seized me—a deep conviction that these were not common effusions, not at all like the poetry women generally write.'

The discovery of these poems left Charlotte in a quandary. Emily would not take kindly to the news that the poems had been found, let alone read, for Emily, in Charlotte's words, was not a person who welcomed any intrusion into her privacy. Not even those nearest to her could intrude 'unlicensed' with impunity. As expected 'it took hours to reconcile her to the discovery' and, once that was achieved, 'days to persuade her that such poems merited publication'. While the battle raged with Char-lotte refusing to wilt before Emily's fury, Anne 'quietly produced some of her own compositions' and suggested that perhaps Charlotte would care to read these as well.

The outcome of the whole affair was the decision to gather the best of the poems together and to attempt to get them printed. The poems assembled, the three young women thought it best that they adopt pseudonyms and 'veiled their own names under those of Currer, Ellis and Acton Bell'. The need for the subterfuge was their sex, a 'vague impression that authoresses are liable to be looked on with prejudice' and the belief that the poems which they offered were somehow not 'feminine'. The poems were printed at their own expense; the money they each had inherited from their Aunt, which enabled them to live at home, making it possible for them to undertake the financing of the venture. Amidst great excitement a publisher was found, Aylott and Jones of London, and by the end of May 1846 the blue volume of *Poems by Currer, Ellis and Acton Bell* was launched. After a month and two favourable reviews, one in the *Athenaeum*, the other the *Dublin University Magazine*, and *one* request for the poets' autograph, the grand total of two copies had been sold. Once again the Brontë resilience kept disillusion at bay. Charlotte cheerfully concluded 'As was to be expected, neither we nor our poems were at all wanted'. But she adds: 'Ill-success failed to crush us; the mere effort to succeed had given a wonderful zest to existence . . . We each set to work on a prose tale.'

The prose tales were *Wuthering Heights* which Ellis (Emily) set to work on, *Agnes Grey*, Acton (Anne), and *The Professor*, Currer (Charlotte)

The little excursion into publishing and the sad response seemed not to have distressed the 'authors Bell' too much. They kept their identity secret and busied themselves with major writing projects. Now, the long apprenticeship was

Charlotte Brontë in 1850, by George Richmond.

to bear fruit and the writers' workshop which met in the evening in the parlour was nearing its most productive and astonishing period.

In retrospect Charlotte stood by her first reaction to Emily's poems, at their best she was sure they were unusual. The world has since agreed. Branwell knew nothing of his sisters' activities, they thought it best to go ahead without him. Whether some part in the book would have helped him we shall never know. Yet another failure would hardly have invoked the mild response from him that it did from Charlotte.

Before there was much time to mope over the singularly silent reception of their poems, Papa's blindness had reached the point where Charlotte felt something should be done. She had heard of operations for cataract and somehow the daughters were able to persuade their father, now nearing his seventieth birthday, to risk an operation knowing that if it failed he would be permanently blind.

Emily and Charlotte made 'a pilgrimage' to Manchester and found Dr William James Wilson M.R.C.S., a Leeds man who was honorary surgeon at the Manchester Infirmary, who asked that Patrick be brought to Manchester for an examination. He would judge 'if the cataract were ripe' and operate if it were; if not, Charlotte adds in a letter to Ellen Nussey 'papa must remain in darkness a little while longer'.

Charlotte and her father took lodgings in Boundary Street, Manchester, on 21 August, preparing to go to the hospital. Mr Wilson judged the cataract ripe for operating and on 25 August it was performed, without anaesthesia as with all operations of the time, and with Charlotte to hold her father's hand.

> The operation is over; it took place yesterday. Mr Wilson performed it; two other surgeons assisted. Mr Wilson says he considered it quite successful; but papa cannot yet see anything . . . Papa displayed extraordinary patience and firmness; the surgeons seemed surprised. I was in the room all the time, as it was his wish that I should be there . . .

Patrick's own account of the operation in his notebook is a fit companion to the letter from his stoic daughter, and indicates a lifelong interest which Patrick had in medicine. Since his days at Cambridge, where he had studied some medicine, he kept copious notes about all kinds of medical knowledge. Such a practice was no mere eccentricity. Such a compilation of knowledge would serve a conscientious parson well in his parish and Patrick was by no means alone in collecting all manner of helpful recipes for tried and effective remedies.

'Cataract. In Augt. 1846–Mr Wilson, Surgeon,–72 Mosley St. Manchester, operated for cataract in one of my eyes– the left one. He informed me, and others, also, that, generally, they do not operate on both eyes–for fear of inflammation, which would destroy the sight. Belladonna, a virulent poison, prepared from the deadly nightshade, was first applied, twice, in order to expand the pupil–this occasioned very acute pain, for only about five seconds–The feeling, under the operation–which lasted fifteen minutes was of a burning nature–but not intolerable–as I have read is generally the case in surgical operations. My lens was extracted so that cataract can never return in that eye–I was confined on my back a month in a dark room, with bandages over my eyes for the greater part of the time and had a careful nurse, to attend me both night and day–I was bled with 8 leeches, at one time, and 6, on another, (these caused but little pain) in order to prevent inflammation–Through Divine Mercy, and the skill of the Surgeon, as well as my dear Charlotte's attention, and the assiduity of the nurse– after a year of (nearly total blindness) blindness–I was so far restored in sight, as to be able to read, and write, and find my way, without a guide–The operation is critical,

---

Facsimile of poem by Emily in a small notebook. It was a similar notebook of poems that Charlotte found and read, thereby invoking Emily's wrath for a breach of her jealously guarded privacy. Despite the anger Charlotte's 'impertinance' caused she was convinced that Emily's poems were no ordinary verse and set about getting them a publisher. The imitation print, in a crabbed and minute italic, is common to all the little books that the children made. They all persisted in dual writing styles, a flowing longhand and the minute print. The similarity of the print and the ease with which it can be copied has led over the years to great confusion over which piece of writing belonged to which member of the family. A scholars' nightmare and a forger's delight.

and ought not to be ventured on, without due precaution. P.B. Leeches must be put on the temples, and not on the eyelids–B. Darkly coloured glasses should be worn in a strong light–B. Mr Wilson charged me only £10–I believe he often charges £20 or £30. The whole expenses, however, amounted to nearly £50–as I had to take three rooms at £1-3-0, per week and to board myself besides . . . the nurse was paid 15s per week and boarded besides at Mr Balls. Mr Redscar, Surgeon, was the assistant, on whose proper management of the eye, during the operation, much depends.

'Before the operation, for about a year, I could neither see to read, or write, or walk without a guide.'

Charlotte found her father's convalescence tedious. Never flinching from her duty she nevertheless longed to be back home and released from the bedside. While Papa was imprisoned, first in his bandages and then in the darkened room, Charlotte was agonised by toothache which left her stupified. In a great effort of will she drove herself to write. The work she began, which was intended to take her mind off her pain and boredom was *Jane Eyre*.

By mid-September Charlotte and Patrick were back at Haworth. All had gone well and by November he was able to conduct all the Sunday Services himself and no

The title page of the Poems *by Currer, Ellis and Acton Bell, of which but two copies were ever sold in this edition.*

POEMS

BY

CURRER, ELLIS, AND ACTON

BELL.

LONDON:
AYLOTT AND JONES, 8, PATERNOSTER-ROW.

1846.

longer needed to be led by the hand. Thanks to Charlotte's powers of persuasion, Patrick's courage, and the surgeons skill, his sight was restored and remained adequate until he died fifteen years later.

Emily and Anne had cared for Branwell while Charlotte and Papa had been in Manchester. Their task was not an easy one, and by the time the family were back together things had not improved. The success of the operation which had given them all courage providing a 'joyful change' and being 'a continual subject for gratitude' was perhaps only marred by the sad sight that Branwell presented to his father's restored vision. There was no respite in his decline and the reserves of courage that the family drew upon were yet to be drained more fully. While Papa gradually resumed his fuller function in the parish, Branwell continued to wallow in self-pity, making it more and more impossible for himself ever to contemplate employment.

Astonishingly, throughout this period, the sisters maintained their evening ritual of walking in the parlour, discussing the writing they were each doing, reading extracts to each other and planning new chapters. The dream of authorship was so powerful that it dominated their lives, drawing them away from their distress and providing an alternative world where they could create patterns of health and justice, thereby protecting themselves against despair.

By the time that Charlotte took her father to Manchester the 'prose tales' with which the sisters occupied themselves after the failure of their book of poems had become three manuscripts which were already posting from one publisher to another seeking acceptance. The completion of these works, *Wuthering Heights*, *The Professor* and *Agnes Grey*, was an astonishing, almost defiant gesture. Against all the odds, the dream and the discipline had triumphed, all that now remained was for a publisher to recognise the worth of the very different but equally competent manuscripts.

With the invention of what an American critic came to call 'Bell & Co.' a strange ambiguity crept into Charlotte's life. The secrecy of the youthful writing and games was now extended into their mature work. Charlotte acted as the 'Bells' agent and cheerfully wrote on their behalf conducting a persistent campaign to get their work accepted. A letter of 6 April 1846 shows how confidently Charlotte set about this task on her 'writers' behalf:

To Aylott & Jones
Gentlemen,
–C., E. and A. Bell are now preparing for the press a work of fiction, consisting of three distinct and unconnected tales, which may be published either together, as a work of three volumes, of the ordinary novel size, or separately as single volumes, as shall be deemed most advisable.

It is not their intention to publish these tales on their own account. They direct me to ask you whether you would be disposed to undertake the work, after having, of course, by due inspection of the MS., ascertained that its contents

William Smith Williams in later life. The reader for the publishing house of Smith Elder & Co who recognised Charlotte's promise as a writer, wrote encouragingly to her and was rewarded by having first view of Jane Eyre. *After meeting Charlotte he continued to correspond with her for the rest of her life. Their letters provide the most important insight into Charlotte's attitude to her work.*

course that company received a battered parcel bearing, as George Smith, the owner, was to recall, three or four crossed-out publishers' addresses showing that the manuscript had already been submitted elsewhere, a detail that Smith felt did nothing to prepossess him in favour of the manuscript. Again *The Professor* was rejected but the firm's reader, Mr W. S. Williams, 'said that it evinced great literary power' and Smith, Elder decided, to their lasting credit, that Williams should 'write to Currer Bell a letter of appreciative criticism declining the work, but expressing an opinion that he could produce a book which would command success'.

The letter from the perceptive Williams, alone in judging the power behind *The Professor*, was the spur that Charlotte needed. Her response was immediate and she later recorded the effect of Smith, Elder's reply:

'As a forlorn hope, he' (Currer Bell) 'tried one publishing house more. Ere long, in a much shorter space than that on which experience had taught him to calculate, there came a letter, which he opened in the dreary anticipation of finding two hard hopeless lines, intimating that "Messrs. Smith, Elder & Co were not disposed to publish the MS.", and instead, he took out of the envelope a letter of two pages. He read it trembling. It declined, indeed, to publish that tale for business reasons, but it discussed its

The title page of Jane Eyre.

JANE EYRE.

An Autobiography.

EDITED BY

CURRER BELL.

IN THREE VOLUMES.

VOL. I.

LONDON:

SMITH, ELDER, AND CO., CORNHILL.

1847.

are such as to warrant an expectation of success . . .

The true identity of the 'Bells' was to be kept a close secret. The sisters only discussed their work with each other. Charlotte's letters to Ellen carry no mention of what must have been a totally absorbing activity and there is no hint that they were trying to get work published. The dream of authorship was a private one, their industry discreet and disciplined.

As in all her affairs, Charlotte's approach to the problem of 'selling' the Bells' manuscripts was both methodical and eccentric. She obtained a list of publishers from Aylott & Jones and proceeded to send the manuscripts to one publishing house after the other, evidently without changing the wrapping papers but merely scoring out the unsuccessful addresses. By August 1846 she had succeeded in finding acceptance for Ellis Bell's *Wuthering Heights* and Acton's *Agnes Grey*, but only if those authors were prepared to bear some of the cost of production themselves. Her own work *The Professor* was rejected even on those terms. 'Currer Bell' saw his 'brothers' manuscripts accepted before any of his own, and Charlotte had set off to Manchester with her father the day yet another letter of rejection arrived.

Somewhere in the list of publishers which Charlotte compiled the name Smith, Elder & Co appeared. In due

WUTHERING HEIGHTS

A NOVEL,

BY

ELLIS BELL,

IN THREE VOLUMES.

VOL. I.

LONDON:

THOMAS CAUTLEY NEWBY, PUBLISHER,
72, MORTIMER ST., CAVENDISH Sq.

1847.

The title page of Wuthering Heights.

firm's reputation. With Currer Bell's *Jane Eyre*, he found his author and his book.

Jane Eyre's arrival at its publishers office is a romance. Williams read it and offered it to George Smith on a Saturday afternoon, Saturday was still a full working day in those days, and Smith took the manuscript home: 'After breakfast on Sunday morning I took the MS of *Jane Eyre* to my little study and began to read it. The story quickly took me captive. Before twelve o'clock my horse came to the door' (Smith had arranged to ride with a friend) 'but I could not put the book down: I scribbled two or three lines to my friend, saying I was very sorry that circumstances had arisen to prevent my meeting him, sent the note off by my groom, and went on reading the MS. Presently the servant came to tell me that luncheon was ready: I asked him to bring me a sandwich and a glass of wine and still I went on with *Jane Eyre*. Dinner came; for me the meal was a very hasty one, and before I went to bed that night I had finished reading the manuscript.

'The next day we wrote to Currer Bell accepting the book for publication.'

From the acceptance to the publication was only a matter of months. Currer Bell had first written to Smith, Elder in July 1847; by October of the same year *Jane Eyre* was launched and was a spectacular success. All literary London was alive with conjecture as to the identity of its author.

In author, reader and publisher a unique set of circumstances had come together. Charlotte had written a singular book, distinct from fashionable literary taste; she had developed her own imaginative vision and evolved her own powerful style; the novel she offered Smith was both original and polished. The peculiar individual vision was accompanied by a practised technique, the thousands of words Charlotte had poured into her juvenile writing had ensured a confidence with character, a command of words and plot that Williams had instantly recognised. Williams, who had been enticed away from one firm by the enterprising if unorthodox Smith was, moreover, just the man to discern Charlotte's quality, even in the less successful manuscript of *The Professor*. For W. S. Williams, Smith's senior, was well connected in literary circles, having known Keats, and being a friend of Thackeray and Mrs Gaskell. He was a man versed in the best literature of the day and particularly capable of responding to Charlotte's talent. Finally George Smith himself was a good businessman with an ability to know what he needed and to have the courage to seize opportunities.

The combination of talents which this trio of author, reader and publisher represented was able in due course to sustain the success of *Jane Eyre* and repeat it at least once in the next ten years with *Villette*, another novel from Currer Bell which was to be the talk of the season when it was published.

Charlotte was fortunate in her publisher. Not only had she found the house that would accept her manuscript, but she had also found a firm friend and adviser in W. S. Williams. The launching of her book was the beginning of

merits and demerits so courteously, so considerately, in a spirit so rational, with a discrimination so enlightened, that this very refusal cheered the author better than a vulgarly expressed acceptance would have done. It was added, that a work in three volumes would meet with careful attention.'

Charlotte realised at once that her almost completed *Jane Eyre* could be the very book they needed. She hastened to finish it and before long it arrived at the Cornhill offices of Messrs. Smith, Elder where its progress was the epitome of any unknown author's daydream.

George Smith, the publisher so blessed with a perceptive reader and the courage of his own convictions, was a remarkable man. He was only twenty when in 1845 he had to take over his father's business which he found 'cruelly undermined' by bad practice and poor organisation. With his mother and sisters to support he had set about making the business pay its way by sheer industry and drive. He had brought W. S. Williams in to help him and together they were determined to make a success of the firm that had earlier published Darwin's *Zoology of the Voyage of H.M.S. Beagle*. It is tempting to see that a priority for Smith was to find a runaway best-seller that would bring its author acclaim and help re-establish the

Jane Eyre

by Currer Bell

Vol. 1st

Chap. 1st

There was no possibility of taking a walk that day.
We had been wandering indeed in the leafless shrubbery
an hour in the morning, but since dinner (Mrs Reed,
when there was no company, dined early) the cold winter
wind had brought with it clouds so sombre, a rain so pen
etrating that further out-door exercise was now out of the
question.

I was glad of it; I never liked long walks – especially
on chilly afternoons; dreadful to me was the coming home
in the raw twilight with nipped fingers and toes and a heart
saddened by the chidings of Bessie, the nurse, and humbled
by the consciousness of my physical inferiority to Eliza, John
and Georgiana Reed.

The said Eliza, John and Georgiana were now clustered
round their Mamma in the drawing-room; she lay reclin...

The first page of the final manuscript of Jane Eyre.

a long correspondence with Williams and an association which was of the utmost help in her development as a writer. From his first insight into her potential from his reading of *The Professor*, Williams provided a constant stimulus through enlightened discussion which Charlotte came to value highly. As her long correspondence with Ellen chronicles her development as a young woman but tells us little of her development as an artist, so the correspondence which she now commenced with Williams provides an illuminating and detached account of a rare literary friendship. Williams she always valued for he was her first favourable critic who encouraged her right at the beginning of her career as an author. She always took his advice seriously and acted upon it.

But if Charlotte was fortunate in the publisher she found, her sisters were, sadly, less so. T. C. Newby, who had offered to produce their novels if they agreed to pay £50, was anything but straightforward with them, and, over the months that followed, underhand in his dealings with their work. Before long Charlotte was regretting her sisters' connection with Newby; the books when they did at length appear were poorly produced, being full of mistakes and hastily got together, but Anne and Emily were unwavering in their loyalty to the man who had first agreed to bring out their novels. Their books followed Charlotte's into print and were placed before the public in December 1842.

The three 'Bell' novels thus launched make an impressive collection. Emily's vigorous robust story, which was so wild that it frightened Charlotte; Anne's portrayal of the trials endured by governesses, and Charlotte's account of a young woman's battle to retain her integrity and find happiness where she loved attracted notice from all quarters. *Jane Eyre* set the pace and Currer Bell became the most talked of writer of the season. 'Jane Eyre fever' became an epidemic as more and more readers found themselves emulating the captivated George Smith and missing their meals in order to finish the story.

Thackeray's response to a copy, given in a letter to W. S. Williams, is typical of the immediacy of Charlotte's success and indicates the extent of her achievement:

Oct. 28 1847

I wish you had not sent me *Jane Eyre*. It interested me so much that I have lost (or won if you like) a whole day in reading it at the busiest period, with the printers I know waiting for copy. Who the author can be I can't guess–if a woman she knows her language better than most ladies do, or has had a 'classical' education. It is a fine book though–the man and woman capital–the style very generous and upright so to speak . . . The plot of the story is one with which I am familiar. Some of the love passages made me cry–to the astonishment of John who came in with the coals. St John the Missionary is a failure I think but a good failure. There are parts excellent, I don't know why I tell you this but that I have been exceedingly moved and pleased by *Jane Eyre*. It is a woman's writing, but whose?

Cornhill, London, during the first half of the nineteenth century. The offices of Smith Elder were situated here.

Give my respects and thanks to the author–whose novel is the first English one (the French are only romances now) that I have been able to read for many a day.

Nothing daunted, Charlotte replied that she felt 'honoured in being approved by Thackeray' but she took him to task about the plot:

The plot of *Jane Eyre* may be a hackneyed one; Mr Thackeray remarks that it is familiar to him. But having read comparatively few novels I never chanced to meet with it, and I thought it original.

Thus the full process of Charlotte's extraordinary education came to fruition. One of the most eminent of English authors was convinced of the fine education which Currer Bell displayed.

Emily's *Wuthering Heights* attracted almost as much attention as *Jane Eyre*, baffling and alarming most of its readers. An unsigned review, one of five found in Emily's writing desk after her death, is typical of the response her powerful imagination evoked;

'In *Wuthering Heights*, the reader is shocked, disgusted, almost sickened by details of cruelty, inhumanity and the most diabolical hate and vengeance, and even some passages of powerful testimony to the supreme power of love–even over demons in the human form. The women in the book are of a strange fiendish-angelic nature, tantalising and terrible, and the men are undesirable out of the book itself . . .

'. . . We strongly recommend all our readers who love novelty to get this story, for we can promise them that they never read anything like it before. It is very puzzling and very interesting . . .'

Anne's *Agnes Grey* was of all the works the most gently received:

'It is a simple tale of a governess's experiences and trials of love, born with that meekness, and met by that fortitude, that ensure a final triumph . . . It fills the mind with a lasting picture of love and happiness succeeding to scorn and affliction and teaches us to put every trust in a supreme wisdom and goodness.'

The Messrs. Bell had published, and their writing had been noticed. All that remained was that the mystery of their sex, their number, their habitation and their history should be unravelled. Society buzzed with suggestions. How many writers were there? Was Currer Bell responsible for all the works? There were, after all, striking similarities in style, content and treatment. Some guessed Yorkshire as the setting for all the works and considerable pleasure was derived from attempts to identify people and places in the stories.

George Smith claimed that, with the evidence of Currer Bell's handwriting before him, both he and Williams guessed all along, as did Thackeray, that Currer Bell was a woman. Only their obligation to observe their author's wishes restrained them from using this information.

There is a tradition in the village that the postman at Haworth was not a little curious about the mysterious gentlemen that were hidden away in the parsonage and to whom so much mail was sent.

Chapter 14

'Ocular proof'

It is generally believed that the writing of the novels and all the activity associated with publishing them was kept a secret from Branwell. There is no way of knowing for sure whether the sisters were successful in keeping their secret. Their father, much later, protested that he knew full well that they were writing but that he never interfered, believing that the opinion of an ageing clergyman could be of little value or relevance, where young women's novels were concerned. There is a charming piece of Brontë-lore associated with *Jane Eyre* which Mrs Gaskell faithfully reported:

'Now, however, when the demand for the work had assured success to *Jane Eyre*, her sisters urged Charlotte to tell their father of its publication. She accordingly went into his study one afternoon after his early dinner, carrying with her a copy of the book, and one or two reviews, taking care to include a notice adverse to it.

'She informed me that something like the following conversation took place between her and him. (I wrote down her words the day after I heard them; and I am pretty sure they are quite accurate).

' "Papa, I've been writing a book."

' "Have you, my dear?"

' "Yes, and I want you to read it."

' "I am afraid it will try my eyes too much."

' "But it is not in manuscript: it is printed."

' "My dear! you've never thought of the expense it will be! It will be almost sure to be a loss, for how can you get a book sold? No one knows you or your name."

' "But, papa, I don't think it will be a loss; no more will you, if you will just let me read you a review or two, and tell you more about it."

'So she sat down and read some of the reviews to her father; and then, giving him the copy of *Jane Eyre* that she intended for him, she left him to read it. When he came in to tea, he said,

' "Girls, do you know Charlotte has been writing a book, and it is much better than likely?" '

In time Patrick became justly proud of his daughters' books, they had clearly achieved much which he as a lifelong scribbler could appreciate.

From the date of publication there was continuous correspondence with London. Reviews were sent together with letters telling of the rapid sale of *Jane Eyre* and, as is usual with any best-selling novel, Currer Bell attracted considerable interest from fellow artists. G. H. Lewes was one who corresponded with Charlotte and discussed literary matters. As with Williams, Charlotte adopted an individual stance in her letters to Lewes. She was indebted to him for a review of *Jane Eyre* which she found lenient and was prepared to discuss with him the whole process of writing. Despite the success of *Jane Eyre*, Charlotte remained soberly modest about her talents:

12 Jan. 1848

I mean to observe your warning about being careful how I undertake new works; my stock of materials is not abundant, but very slender; and,

First Class rail travel in the nineteenth century. When Charlotte and Anne set off at short notice to visit Smith Elder's offices in London they travelled by rail from Leeds, indulging in the luxury of first class seats since they were unaccompanied. Charlotte seldom spoke of journeys in any detail, being infuriatingly silent about what must have been considerable adventures in the early days of rail travel. Only once does she hint at the very real risks involved. Once, from London, she wrote to her father to tell him that she had arrived safely 'without any damage or smash in tunnels or cuttings'.

THE RAILWAY—FIRST CLASS.

besides, neither my experience, my acquirements, nor my powers, are sufficiently varied to justify my ever becoming a frequent writer. I tell you this, because your article in *Frazer* left in me an uneasy impression that you were disposed to think better of the author of *Jane Eyre* than that individual deserved; and I would rather you had a correct than a flattering opinion of me, even though I should never see you.

If I ever *do* write another book, I think I will have nothing of what you call 'melodrama'; I think so, but I am not sure. I *think*, too, I will endeavour to follow the counsel which shines out of Miss Austen's 'mild eyes', 'to finish more and be more subdued'; but neither am I sure of that.

Charlotte was by no means confident that she was on the brink of a life of authorship. She was reluctant to promise George Smith another novel, other than a rewrite of *The Professor* which at this stage he would not accept. 'As to my next book,' she wrote to Williams, 'I suppose it will grow to maturity in time'. She protested that she could not force it as it was not every day nor every week that she could 'write anything worth reading'.

Such was the success of *Jane Eyre* that within months it was being reprinted. Delighted with the letter from Thackeray with his praise for the book, Charlotte asked that the second edition be dedicated to him, quite unaware that, like Rochester in the novel, he too had an insane wife. The book appeared with the dedication— Charlotte was horrified when she discovered her mistake—

George Smith, the director of Smith Elder & Co., who published Jane Eyre *and all Charlotte's other novels.*

Thackeray, Charlotte's hero, who infuriated her by his un-serious attitude to literature. Thackeray considered Jane Eyre *a remarkable achievement and considered Charlotte's wish to dedicate the second edition to him as the 'greatest compliment of his life'.*

and there was an instant rumour that Currer Bell was the pen-name for a young lady novelist who was really Thackeray's mistress.

Thackeray rode the storm and graciously accepted what he took as a great honour:

'The greatest compliment I have ever received in my life.'

The slight scandal over Charlotte's innocent error in choosing Thackeray for the dedication of the second edition was not the only confusion to arise over Mr Currer Bell's novel. The other scandal was caused by Newby, the tardy publisher of Ellis and Acton Bell's novels, for Newby had been so dilatory in doing anything about their books that they were only ready for their first printing at the time *Jane Eyre* was reprinting. Never slow to see an opportunity, Newby showed no scruple at pretending that his authors, or at least one of them, was also the author of that well-known best seller *Jane Eyre*. As the literary world was agog to see more of Currer Bell's work it seemed obvious to Newby that the current conjecture that all the Bells were one person should, if given a slight nudge by himself and a few 'appropriate' advertisements be turned to profitable account. If this merely confused what was already to many a conundrum, then all well and good. But Newby would not let the matter rest there. In time he even offered Harper Brothers in America the 'new work' of Currer Bell (Anne's *Tenant of Wildfell Hall*, in fact) protesting that all the Bells were in fact one and the same person.

It was at this point that Newby came to grief. Harper Brothers had already been in touch with Smith, Elder, who published the real 'Currer Bell' and news got to George Smith that something rather odd, if not unethical, was taking place. Either Currer Bell was dealing with two publishers at the same time or Newby was misinformed. George Smith wrote at once to Currer Bell c/o Charlotte Brontë at Haworth to find out the truth of the matter. His letter was to produce startling results.

As soon as Charlotte received Smith's gentle enquiry, 'was there only one Bell and were there any negotiations afoot with other publishers' she decided that she and Anne should go at once to London and present themselves at Smith, Elder's offices as proof that at least Acton and Currer Bell were separate persons. With this surprise in store, and having failed to persuade Emily to accompany them, Anne and Charlotte left for London the very day the letter arrived.

Determined to settle the confusion as far as George Smith was concerned, they walked to Keighley, just caught a train for Leeds and travelled overnight from Leeds to London. They made for the only place they knew, the Chapter Coffee House by St Pauls which their father and Branwell had used. In a state of 'queer inward excitement' they prepared for the confrontation in Cornhill.

George Smith later retold the story of their arrival at his office:

'I was at work in my room when a clerk reported that two ladies wished to see me. I was very busy and sent out to ask their names. The clerk returned to say that the ladies declined to give their names, but wished to see me on a private matter. . . . Two rather quaintly dressed little ladies, pale-faced and anxious looking, walked into my room; one of them came forward and presented me with a letter addressed, in my own handwriting to "Currer Bell, Esq.". I noticed that the letter had been opened, and said, with some sharpness, "Where did you get this from?" "From the Post Office," was the reply, "it was addressed to me. We have both come that you might have ocular proof that there are at least two of us." This then was "Currer Bell" in person. I need hardly say that I was once keenly interested, not to say excited. Mr Williams was called down and introduced, and I began to plan all sorts of attentions to our visitors.'

The 'attentions' were to put Charlotte and Anne, who, it must be remembered had not had any sleep all night, in a whirl. With the best intentions in the world Smith exhausted both of them and Charlotte, writing to Ellen, admitted that she returned from London 'weak and restless':

A more jaded wretch than I looked, it would be
difficult to conceive. I was thin when I went, but
I was meagre indeed when I returned, my face
looking grey and very old, with strange deep lines
ploughed in it—my eyes stared unnaturally.

In her anxiety to prove the separate identity of Ellis, Acton and Currer Bell, Charlotte blurted out that they were three sisters and immediately regretted her mistake, and withdrew her announcement. She had not obtained

Emily's permission to disclose *her* identity. Quickly correcting herself she begged Smith to forgive her indiscretion and later wrote appealing to him not to disclose that he knew the identity of Ellis. Thus Emily continued in her singular way to make her own decisions and to isolate herself from events.

Beyond our debt to Smith for publishing Currer Bell's work, we are beholden to him for the clearest description of Charlotte's appearance at this time:

'I must confess that my first impression of Charlotte Brontë's personal appearance was that it was interesting rather than attractive. She was very small, and had a quaint old-fashioned look. Her head seemed too large for her body. She had fine eyes, but her face was marred by the shape of the mouth and by the complexion. There was but little feminine charm about her; and of this fact she herself was uneasily and perpetually conscious. It may seem strange that the possession of genius did not lift her above the weakness of an excessive anxiety about her personal appearance. But I believe she would have given all her genius and her fame to have been beautiful. Perhaps few women ever existed more anxious to be pretty than she, or more angrily conscious of the circumstance that she was *not* pretty.'

Anne, George Smith described as a gentle, quiet and rather subdued person. Unlike Ellen Nussey he did not find her pretty but thought her appearance pleasing. He found Anne's manner 'curiously expressive of a wish for protection and encouragement, a kind of constant appeal which invited sympathy'.

The impetuous trip to London, necessary as it had seemed to Charlotte, became something of an ordeal. George Smith was determined, perhaps rather thoughtlessly, that 'Currer and Acton Bell' should be well-entertained in their brief stay in London. He organised a surprise visit to the Opera at Covent Garden and arrived resplendent in full evening dress to collect a startled Charlotte, engrossed with a 'thundering headache' and Anne, who hastily dressed for the Opera in the same old fashioned plain highnecked dresses they had worn to meet him in his office earlier that day. Smith could hardly have known that the Brontë sisters had no suitable clothes with them, or indeed in their possession, for a night at the Opera House. His two authors must have presented an odd picture together with his evening-gowned and bejewelled sisters who made up the rest of the party. The ill-attired, embarrassed, bespectacled Charlotte found Rossini's *The Barber of Seville* 'very brilliant' though she fancied that there were things she should like better! Both she and Anne were relieved when they eventually got back to Haworth where Emily waited to hear Charlotte's account of the whole affair.

Back at home the sisters could present a beguiling picture of alert bright-eyed delight at their success. They were, all of them, published writers, respected and acknowledged. If some reviews were harsh and unsympathetic there were those that weren't and at least the books were noticed, discussed and evidently selling.

But the joys of finding their work in print were only a small part of the total pattern of their lives. Whatever was happening in the literary salons of London, the daily problems of Haworth parsonage bore little resemblance to refined literary chatter. Branwell remained at home as ill, wretched and pitifully exasperating as ever.

The main staircase of the Royal Italian Opera House, Covent Garden, to which George Smith took Charlotte and Anne for a performance of Rossini's Barber of Seville. *Charlotte was amused to find her bespectacled, plainly dressed self in the midst of an audience resplendent in evening dress and describes her ascent of the staircase beneath the gaze of puzzled patrons.*

Chapter 15

The Cruel Winter

Against the heady world of literary debate and the exchange of niceties about style which was now a regular part of the Brontë daughters' life, we must not fail to set the grim domestic realities of Branwell's increasing decline and the constant torment that his illness caused the entire family. For within a year of *Jane Eyre* being published, Branwell's decline was complete.

Throughout 1847 and on into '48, Branwell increasingly ran himself into debt. It appears that sums of money came to him from time to time. Charlotte refers to him getting money from 'the old source' which is generally taken to mean Lydia Robinson. When he had money, life became less tolerable in the parsonage; at least without it he would remain sober for long periods. His debts preoccupy him in letters to Leyland, his sculptor friend from Bradford, and well they might, for the hapless Leyland was to end his days in York Debtors' prison, still owed money by Branwell amongst others. Charlotte and her father paid off his debts when they could and both she and Branwell wrote of a Sheriff's Officer 'inviting him' (Branwell) 'to pay his debts, or to take a trip to York'. 'Jail,' said Branwell, 'would finish him'; indeed it probably would have done. The fact of Branwell's drunkenness and his addiction to drugs when he could get them has become so embellished with romance that from this distance in time it is impossible to tell the truth from the tale.

We can never know whether Emily did leave a light burning in the window of a bedroom to guide him back from the Black Bull after a night drinking, or whether she crept down to unbolt the door for him after Papa had locked up. From the letters to his friends, and Charlotte's bitter comments about the misery he caused, we can judge that life in the parsonage in 1848 was a mixed cup.

Suddenly, on 24 September in that year Branwell died. He was only ill for a few days and the evidence suggests that the whole family reeled when faced by the truth about his constant abuse of his body, and the extent to which he had destroyed his constitution. The cause of his death was given as 'Marasmus' which is a 'Progressive emaciation and general wasting due to enfeebled constitution rather than any specific or ascertainable cause.'

Branwell's death stunned Charlotte and she fell ill with fever and jaundice. She claimed that it was the first death she had witnessed and she was startled, she told Ellen, by her own reactions:

> The final separation, the spectacle of his pale corpse, gave more acute, bitter pain than I could have imagined. Till the last hour comes, we never know how much we can forgive pity, regret a near relation.

In a letter to Williams of Smith, Elder she admitted her grief:

> When the struggle was over and a marble calm began to succeed the last agony, I felt, as I have never felt before, that there was peace and forgiveness for him in Heaven. All his errors—to speak plainly, all his vices—seemed nothing to me in that moment; every wrong he had done, every pain he had caused, vanished; his sufferings only were remembered; the wrench to the natural affections only was left.

With Branwell's death, and as his coffin was carried from the parsonage through the little gate of the dead opposite the tower, a whole era in the family's story came to an end. September 1848 saw the beginning of a short period in which everything that they had known and believed would be called into doubt and shaken to its foundations. In a relentless interwoven pattern sickness and death now dominated the parsonage. No sooner was Branwell laid to rest in the family vault in the chancel of the old church than Charlotte, scarcely recovered from her own sickbed, felt uneasy about her sisters. Anne was suffering with asthma and Emily had an obstinate cold and cough:

> Oct. 1848
>
> All the days of this winter have gone by darkly and heavily like a funeral train. Since September sickness has not quitted the house. It is strange it did not use to be so, but I suspect now all this

Patrick Reid "turned off," without his cap. 1848.

DRACO THE FIREDRAKE.

St John in the wilderness.

SUCDENIENSIS.

PHIDIAS

St patrick alias Lord Peter.

punch bowl.

The rescue of the ~~Talbot~~ a scene in the Talbot.

Sketches by Branwell. Towards the end of his life he more and more embellished letters and writing with morbid drawings of this kind. The Talbot was an inn in Bradford where Branwell did most of his drinking when a painter in that town.

has been coming on for years. Unused, any of us, to the possession of robust health, we have not noticed the gradual approaches of decay; we did not know its symptoms: the little cough, the small appetite, the tendency to take cold at every variation of atmosphere have been regarded as things of course. I see them in another light now.

Charlotte's sombre tone and her talk of 'the gradual approaches of decay' in these letters to Ellen was in its way prophetic. Suddenly all did seem changed in the parsonage. Their weakened constitutions did seem to leave them vulnerable and prey to all kinds of ailments.

Emily did not get any better. Her cough persisted and she began to waste away before her sisters' eyes. By November she was seriously ill but refusing to admit the truth and stubbornly refusing to let a doctor be called. For some reason the fiercely independent Emily scorned all help, and was impervious to advice. All Charlotte, Anne and Patrick could do was watch in horror as Emily declined:

She is a real stoic in illness: she neither seeks nor will accept sympathy . . . You must look on and see her do what she is unfit to do, and dare not say a word—a painful necessity for those to whom her health and existence are as precious as life in their veins. When she is ill there seems to be no sunshine in the world for me.

Charlotte clung to Emily, telling Ellen Nussey that her sister was as dear to her as life. A slow inflammation of the lungs, difficulty with breathing, pain in the chest and fever were destroying the slender Emily, and destroying her rapidly, as Charlotte recalled:

Never in all her life had she lingered over any task that lay before her, and she did not linger now. She sank rapidly. She made haste to leave us.

On 19 December Emily Brontë died, aged thirty. Until the very end she refused all assistance, struggling to dress herself, insisting on feeding the dogs, defying anyone to help her as she gasped her way up the stone staircase. All pleas with her that she needed medicine or a doctor's advice were scorned until just before she died when she submitted, said 'You can send for a doctor if you like,' and died. The morning she died Charlotte had been out searching the December moors for a sprig of heather to take to her; finding one she saw with a profound sadness her sister's indifference to the flowers she so dearly loved. A heartbroken Charlotte told the news to Ellen Nussey who, by presents, letters and visits had done all she could to cheer the numbed and bewildered family:

Dec. 23 1848

My Dear Ellen,

Emily suffers no more from pain or weakness now. She will never suffer more in this world. She is gone, after a hard, short conflict . . . Yes; there is no Emily in time or on earth now. Yesterday we put her poor, wasted, mortal frame quietly under the chancel pavement. We are very calm

A drawing by Branwell said to be of Mrs Robinson, the lady whom he unwisely loved.

"Our Lady of grief."
"Nuestra Señora de la pena."

Emily's writing box.

at present. Why should we be otherwise? The anguish of seeing her suffer is over; the spectacle of the pains of death is gone by; the funeral day is past. We feel she is at peace. No need now to trouble for the hard frost and the keen wind. Emily does not feel them.

Emily had died on the sofa of the parlour where the sisters wove their dreams and did their writing. Charlotte grieved that Emily was 'torn, panting, reluctant, though resolute, out of a happy life'. Keeper, her favourite dog, which had lain at her bedside, 'followed her funeral to the vault, lying in the pew crouched at our feet while the burial service was being read', and the story is told that he howled at her bedroom door long after she was dead.

Somehow Charlotte found strength to go on. Both Anne and her father fell ill, the latter invoking Charlotte's strength to sustain him, begging her to bear up as he would sink if she should fail him. She felt she dare not falter, 'Somebody *must* cheer the rest.' But she raged at the horror of Emily's going:

> . . . Life has become very void, and hope has proved a strange traitor; . . . she kept whispering that Emily would not, *could* not die, and where is she now? Out of my reach, out of my world — torn from me—

The tide of calamity that overtook the Brontës had not spent its full force with Emily's death. The letters telling of her funeral also bear news of Anne's illness.

> When we lost Emily I thought we had drained the very dregs of our cup of trial, but now when I hear Anne cough as Emily coughed, I tremble

lest there should be exquisite bitterness yet to taste.

Writing to W. S. Williams, Charlotte warned him that her literary character was quite effaced. Should Anne recover then perhaps she would rally and become 'Currer Bell' again. She prayed for strength not to fail her father. As Emily had refused help, Anne accepted all the advice and medicine available, being as patient and long-suffering as Emily had been stern and independent. Charlotte was impressed by both her sisters' fortitude.

Branwell's funeral card.

IN MEMORY
OF
PATRICK BRANWELL BRONTE,
WHO DIED
SEPTEMBER 24TH, 1848,
AGED THIRTY YEARS.

126

June 5ᵗʰ /49

Dear Martha

I was very much pleased
with your note and glad to hear
that all at home are getting on pretty
well. It will still be a week or ten
days before I return and you must
not tire yourself too much with the
cleaning.

My sister Anne's death could not be
otherwise than a great trouble to me —
though I have known for many weeks
that she could not get better. She
died very calmly and gently — she was
quite sensible to the last — about three
minutes before she died she said she
was very happy and believed she
was passing out of earth into heaven
. It was not her custom to talk much
about religion but she was very good.
and I am certain she is now in
a far better place than any this world

Contains:

I mean to send one of the boxes home this week, as I have more luggage than is convenient to carry about.

Give my best love to Tabby.

I am — dear Martha

Your sincere friend.

C Brontë

Success as a writer sustained Charlotte a little through the trying times which she was now passing. When she and Anne had travelled to London to reveal the identity of Currer and Acton Bell they had returned with a collection of books, presented to them by George Smith. Once begun, this practice continued. Regular boxes of carefully chosen volumes together with reviews and journals arrived at the parsonage, providing reading and ideas for discussion for all the household. The volume of poems that the Bells produced had been re-issued by Smith, Elder and Anne's second novel *The Tenant of Wildfell Hall* had also been published, so that she was able to take some interest in other affairs than the progress of her own illness. But it was difficult work. Too often the sisters sat 'in seclusion', Anne in Emily's chair, unable to concentrate enough to read or to write, and Charlotte knew that 'clouds of impending distress' lowered above them. Again it was consumption that was bearing Anne away.

A most pathetic detail of Charlotte's anxiety was her hope that better weather would help Anne. The hope that if only she could hold on until June then she would perhaps survive, is a sharp reminder of the very real threat that winter, in the spartan conditions in which the family lived, offered to their health.

As her illness increased and the doctors confirmed the family's worst fears, Anne began to pine to visit Scarborough, of which she had many happy memories from her days as a governess. In time her father agreed that she should make the journey if it would bring her happiness, despite the knowledge that any changes of air in her condition could prove disastrous.

Anne had recently been left some money by her godparents and she decided to use this to finance the excursion. By April, a step nearer the longed-for June, plans

---

Scarborough as it was at the time of Anne's last visit with Charlotte.

Anne's grave at Scarborough old church. Anne was the only member of the family to die and be buried away from Haworth.

were afoot. Ellen Nussey wanted to accompany Charlotte and Anne, but Charlotte felt the responsibility would be too great; however, in time she agreed and the tragic trio set off from Haworth on the last pilgrimage that Anne planned and undertook.

In the last stages of planning the expedition Charlotte wrote to Ellen warning her not to be shocked by Anne's appearance. Anne was more emaciated than Emily and spent much of her time in a lethargy. In May the trio set out, staying overnight in York, where Anne visited the Minster which she loved so well. They took lodgings at No 2, Cliff, Scarborough, where Anne could sit by a window and look out to sea. On Monday 28 May in the evening, Anne died aged twenty-nine:

> My poor sister is taken quietly home at last. She died on Monday. With almost her last breath she said she was happy and thanked God that death was come, and come so gently. I did not think it would be so soon.

In less than ten months a brother and two sisters had been snatched from Charlotte, her grief was total and her

The unusual brass collars worn by Emily's dog Keeper and Anne's dog Flossie.

father's fortitude quite superhuman. In order to spare him another funeral, Charlotte arranged for Anne to be buried at the old church in Scarborough and Patrick was so in control of himself that he urged her to stay away from Haworth until she had regained a little of her own health and equilibrium.

June saw Charlotte returned home. 'I call it *home* still,' she wrote to Ellen, and returned to a most pathetic welcome from Keeper and Flossie, the former Emily's, and the latter Anne's dogs. These 'poor animals' ran past Charlotte looking for her sisters:

> I am certain they thought that, as I was returned, my sisters were not far behind. But here my sisters will come no more. Keeper may visit Emily's little bedroom—as he still does day by day—and Flossie may still look wistfully round for Anne, they will never see them again—nor shall I—at least the human part of me.

But Charlotte, like her heroine Jane Eyre, was made of stern stuff. Thoughts of her father rallied her spirits and she resolved not to soothe the reality of her anguish but to face it and in doing so take strength to endure.

> Labour must be the cure, not sympathy. Labour is the only radical cure for rooted sorrow.

She would accept no soft opiate but sought to probe and heal her wound by courage. Thus she faced the ordeal of returning:

> I left papa soon and went into the dining room: I shut the door. I tried to be glad that I was home. I have always been glad before—but this time joy was not to be the sensation. I felt the house was all silent, the rooms were all empty. I remembered where the three were laid—in what narrow dark dwellings—never more to reappear on earth. So the sense of desolation and bitterness took possession of me. The agony that *was to be undergone* and *was not* to be avoided came on. I underwent it, and passed a dreary evening and night, and a mournful morrow; today, I am better.

Chapter 16

The Celebrated Author

Charlotte and her father were left numbed by the rapid illness that had carried off Branwell, Emily and Anne. They found themselves suddenly alone, together in a weird and stunning solitude. As Charlotte left her father's study, crossed the hall, entered the dining room, and closed the door behind her, she knew that she now faced her greatest challenge. She must now endure a bitter loneliness in the room that had known so many plans, so much bustle, and so much congenial companionship. All her resolution, her determination to cope, for her father's sake, and her indomitable will to 'get on' would be taxed to the limit.

> I do not know how life will pass, (she wrote to Ellen) but I certainly do feel confidence in Him who had upheld me hitherto. Solitude may be cheered, and made endurable beyond what I can believe. The great trial is when evening closes and night approaches. At that hour, we used to assemble in the dining-room; we used to talk. Now I sit by myself; necessarily I am silent. I cannot help thinking of their last days, remembering their sufferings, and what they said and did, and how they looked in mortal affliction. Perhaps all this will become less poignant in time.

After a while Charlotte had defined the principle by which she would continue, she would endure the heart-ache and make work 'her best companion'. 'Hereafter,' she wrote, 'I look for no great earthly comfort except what congenial occupation can give.' This was her 'resolution of seclusion', she would take refuge in the solitude of the parsonage, where the ticking of the clock on the stairs filled every room, and write. Thus a battle began. A battle between her memories, which continually weakened her resolve, and her will to concentrate upon her career as an author.

Charlotte was not optimistic, she knew herself to be a slow writer and she was only too aware of her father's poor health and her own anguish. But she was encouraged from all sides. George Smith and W. S. Williams gently reminded her from time to time of the continuing success of *Jane Eyre*, and saw that she knew that all literary London was waiting for another novel from Currer Bell.

By what must have been a superhuman effort Charlotte coped with her father's many collapses with bronchitis and her own illnesses and completed two more novels in the next three years. The tussle which Charlotte had with her feelings was real and prolonged. At times she touched despair. One day when both servants were ill she was at her wits' end:

> I fairly broke down for ten minutes and cried like a fool. Martha's illness was at its height, a cry from Tabby had called me into the kitchen and I found her laid on the floor, her head under the grate; she had fallen from the chair in attempting to rise. Papa had just been declaring that Martha was in imminent danger. I was myself depressed with headache and sickness. That day I hardly knew what to do, or where to turn.

But somehow she managed, protesting to W. S. Williams that she was 'not yet crushed' and finding in her writing just the refuge she sought:

> The loss of what we possess nearest and dearest to us in this world produces an effect upon the character; we search out what we have yet left that can support, and, when found, we cling to it with a hold of new-strung tenacity. The faculty of imagination lifted me when I was sinking, three months ago; its active exercise has kept my head above water since; its results cheer me now, for I feel they have enabled me to give pleasure to others. I am thankful to God, who gave me the faculty; and it is for me a part of my religion to defend this gift and to profit by its possession.

It was Charlotte's belief that her experience as a governess had helped her develop her powers of fortitude and patience. She believed that the bitter experiences she had known as a teacher had borne precious results, that her mind and her character had been strengthened, made more 'enduring for her own afflictions' and more considerate for the afflictions of others. Whether or not this was so, the outcome was a remarkable demonstration of the qualities which she described.

The three years from Anne's death to the publication of *Villette* in 1852 were the years in which her 'secret' identity was discovered and Currer Bell's fame was replaced by the world's admiration for Charlotte Brontë. But the acknowledgement that she was indeed that mysterious author was only gradual on her part. From the outset a device to hide the sex of the writer and a step to avoid notoriety, the pseudonym was for a while remarkably effective. In time, however, gossip and prying led to the opening of letters addressed to Currer Bell and local conjecture narrowed the field. For a long time Charlotte remained fiercely jealous of her anonymity and had her most serious quarrel with Ellen Nussey, her friend for eighteen years, when Ellen hinted that she had heard Charlotte had been publishing a book.

On 3 May 1848, when the second edition of *Jane Eyre* was available, Charlotte strenuously denied her authorship, in a powerful letter to Ellen;

> ... I have given *no one* a right either to affirm, or hint, in the most distant manner, that I am 'publishing' – (humbug!). Whoever has said it, if anyone has, which I doubt – is no friend of mine. I scorn the idea utterly ... If any Birstallian or Gomersallian should presume to bore you on the subject – to ask you what 'novel' Miss Brontë has been 'publishing' – you can just say ... that you are authorised by Miss Brontë to say that she repels and disowns every accusation of this kind. You may add, if you please, that if anyone has her confidence, you believe you have, and she has made no drivelling confessions to you on the subject.

By 1849, however, Charlotte was more or less resigned to recognition. She admitted her responsibility for *Jane Eyre* which had by this time 'been read all over the district'. Happily, Ellen does not seem to have harboured any ill-feelings for the stern way in which Charlotte had previously fobbed her off.

Charlotte's pessimism about her writing derived partly from the strain under which she was living and partly from a fear that she had too narrow a range of experience from which to write. When she told Thackeray that she had only read a few novels, she meant it. Her world was circumscribed and her 'society' very few people. This became one of her chief anxieties for she felt that no one would understand the complete lack of stimulus that accompanied life in Haworth. At times, in the next few years, she came almost to loathe its solitude and quiet, finding that her 'resolution of seclusion' was not altogether beneficial. It was to offset this sense of isolation that Charlotte became so ardent a letter writer. Letters were her life-line and the next few years saw her writing copiously. Steadily her circle of correspondents and acquaintances enlarged as her fame, and identity, spread.

Before Anne's death Charlotte had begun work on another novel. She had made poor progress but had chosen a theme thoughtfully and with some regard to enlarging her range. The work in hand, to which she turned for sanity in the midst of her suffering, was an antidote to the highly personal and 'domestic' nature of *Jane Eyre*. If that novel, as one critic claimed, was merely domestic, having no learning, no research, and discussing no subject of public interest, then her next would be researched, would touch upon subjects of public interest and not be 'merely domestic'. For Charlotte had sent to Leeds for all the newspaper material related to the Luddite rioting in her father's parish at Hartshead in 1812. She had been busy researching the story, adding the newspaper accounts to those of her father and all she knew from the Taylor family, of the Red House, who owned one of the mills that had been involved in the rioting. This novel, which was to be published in October 1849, was *Shirley*, and her only attempt to deal with a theme which is partly social and partly historical as well as a love story in the tradition of *Jane Eyre*.

In writing *Shirley*, Charlotte undoubtedly achieved much. She widened her canvas, dealing with some of the problems associated with the effects of progress upon industry and the implications of economic depression; she wrote with conviction of events that took place within the locality which she knew well, and, above all, she was able to soften her grief for Emily by recreating her in the part of the character after whom the book is named. Shirley Keeldar is believed to contain much that was admired in Emily. Certainly Keeper, Emily's dog, lives in *Shirley*, having been drawn with great skill and humour.

Struggling to complete the manuscript while her father was ill and at a time when she found writing difficult, Charlotte acknowledged its therapeutic nature:

> Whatever becomes of the work, the occupation of writing it has been a boon to me. It took me out of the dark and desolate reality into the unreal but happier region. The worst of it is, my eyes are grown somewhat weak and my head somewhat weary and prone to ache with close work.

She need not have worried, the work was well received by W. S. Williams at Smith & Elder and it was rapidly printed and published.

Shirley contained some of the most readily recognisable people and places of all of Charlotte's work. She rather naively thought that she would easily escape recognition in Yorkshire, 'I am so little known that I think I shall', ignoring the fact that the curates in the book were all instantly recognisable as caricatures of curates known to the whole parish. Once published, *Shirley* afforded great delight as local people searched for themselves among its characters, and very often found that they were present to the life.

As *Shirley* made its way, Charlotte's longing to see 'some of the great literary characters' combined with her publishers' kind and frequent invitations that she should come to London, tempted her out of her seclusion and she made the first of her few visits to 'the great Babylon' whose literary coteries alarmed her but whose art galleries and bookshops beckoned. Each time she visited London she stayed with George Smith and his mother, was fêted, given tours of places of interest and made to feel very important indeed. None of the social events, however, swept her off her feet. She remained critical and clear-headed throughout the considerable homage paid her and, to the delight but puzzlement of all, remarkably forth-right. When she saw Macready act she thought he was awful and said so. When she found Thackeray flippant she scolded him in no uncertain terms. The small odd little figure mortified with shyness remained mentally composed and undaunted by the bright sophistication which sur-rounded her whilst she was in London.

Charlotte was not the easiest of persons to have as a guest. George Smith tells how, despite all his mother's and sisters' efforts, she would never be quite at ease with them. 'Strangers,' he claimed, 'used to say they were afraid of her' as she was so quiet and self-absorbed. She evidently gave the impression that she was 'always engaged in observing and analysing the people she met'.

When this 'tiny, delicate, serious little lady, pale, with fair straight hair, and steady eyes' who wore mittens, met Thackeray on one of these visits to London, the novelist was struck by her honesty and observed that although she was: 'New to the London world she entered it with an independent, indomitable spirit of her own; and judged of contemporaries, and especially spied out arrogance and affectation, with extraordinary keenness of vision.' To some, Charlotte was merely the dullest and most difficult person to talk to they had ever met.

London always exhausted Charlotte. She could never understand why her headaches, which she suffered persistently in Haworth, should follow her to London and leave her feeling wretched and exhausted. From 1849 to 1853 she made four visits to London in all, each time writing home to her father with enthusiasm and in detail to enable him to share her pleasure. She wrote to him of her visits to the Zoological Gardens, of her visits to the Great Exhibition, to the theatre and to Thackeray's lectures, going to some length to include her father's interests in her visits. George Smith described one such indulgence:

'Miss Brontë and her father had a passionate admiration for the Duke of Wellington, and I took her to the Chapel Royal, St James's, which he generally attended on Sun-day, in order that she might see him. We followed him out of the Chapel, and I indulged Miss Brontë by so arranging our walk that she met him twice on his way to Apsley House.'

The Great Exhibition of 1851. 'Yesterday I went for the second time to the Crystal Palace. We remained in it about three hours, and I must say I was more struck with it on this occasion than at my first visit. It is a wonderful place—vast, strange, new, and impossible to describe. Its grandeur does not consist in one thing, but in the unique assemblage of all things . . . It may be called a bazaar or a fair but it is such a bazaar or fair as Eastern Genii might have created. It seems as if magic only could have gathered this mass of wealth from all the ends of the Earth—as if none but supernatural hands could have arranged it thus, with such a blaze or contrast of colours and marvellous power of effect.'

George Smith failed to record, if he knew, that this same chapel, years before, was the very place where Charlotte's father had been ordained priest.

PORTRAIT AND PHRENOLOGY

Smith was responsible for two further events on visits of this kind. The one is well-known and familiar, the other less so. In June 1850 he arranged for Charlotte to sit for George Richmond, whose portrait of her now hangs in the National Portrait Gallery. In the following year, using the names of Mr and Miss Fraser he took her to have her 'head read' by a well known phrenologist, T. P. Browne, M.D. who furnished his own special 'portrait' entitled: *A Phrenological Estimate of the Talents and Dispositions of a Lady.*

In having Richmond produce a portrait of 'Currer Bell', Smith was doing posterity a great service, in accompanying Charlotte to the phrenologist he was humouring her and contributing to a life-long interest which she had in the 'pseudo-science' which had such a vogue in her day. As her father would delight in her seeing their mutual hero the Duke of Wellington, so he would be interested in her phrenological exploit. For readings in phrenology and an understanding of its terms and implications had been part of the common education and interests fostered in the parsonage.

The language of phrenology with its attendant understanding of the various 'faculties' and the subtle anlysis of character through physiognomy, pervades all of Charlotte's writing, a knowledge of its technical terms is assumed in the reader.

A single extract from *The Professor* will demonstrate a common technique and the assumptions involved. Charlotte introduces the reader to a schoolgirl:

'I wonder that anyone, looking at that girl's head and countenance, would have received her under their roof. She had precisely the same shape of skull as Pope Alexander the Sixth; her organs of benevolence, veneration, conscientiousness, adhesiveness, were singularly small, those of her self-esteem, firmness, destructiveness, combativeness, preposterously large; her head sloped up in penthouse shape, was contracted about the forehead, and prominent behind; she had rather good, though large and marked features; her temperament was fibrous and bilious, her complexion pale and dark, hair and eyes black, form angular and rigid but proportionate, age fifteen.'

The London phrenologist reported that 'Miss Fraser' presented an interesting head and, perhaps as it may be expected, provided some telling phrases demonstrating various traits in her character:

'Her attachments are strong and enduring.'

'Rather than live in a state of hostility with those she could wish to love she would depart from them, although the breaking off of friendship would be to her a source of great unhappiness.'

'She is deferential to the aged and those she deems worthy of respect, and possesses much devotional feelings . . .'

'She is endowed with an exalted taste of the beautiful and ideal, and longs for perfection. If not a poet, her senti-

Macready as Macbeth. Charlotte saw the famous actor play Othello. She was not impressed, though, to be fair, it was at the very end of his career. At every step she felt that Shakespeare outstripped the actor.

ments are poetical . . .

'In its intellectual development this head is very remarkable. The forehead is at once very large and well-formed. It bears the stamp of deep thoughtfulness and comprehensive understanding. It is highly philosophical.'

'This lady does possess a fine organ of language, and can, if she has done her talents justice by exercise, express her sentiments with clearness, precision, and force – sufficiently eloquent but not verbose . . .'

Thus the dubious so-called science evaluated the bumps on the head of this writer of great talent. Soon to be discounted as a method, phrenological estimates of character are, however, frequently employed in all of Charlotte's mature novels.

From the visits to London, after which her anonymity was finally dropped, Charlotte was to have a few friendships which cheered her and provided the intellectual stimulus which she found so lacking in Haworth. Among the new acquaintances who helped her were Harriet Martineau, Sir James and Lady Kay Shuttleworth, and Elizabeth Gaskell. All of these in turn welcomed her as a guest in their homes, being honoured to prize her among their friends. From them all she drew comfort and confidence.

In all, over these few years, Charlotte was entertained in a variety of places by distinguished people. She stayed in the Lake District, visited Edinburgh and Manchester as well as continuing to stay with Ellen Nussey and Miss Wooler, her older acquaintances.

By any standards Charlotte had found a career. The money from her books (she received £1500 for the copyright of her first three novels) and a few legacies, had given her the 'competence' which she had worked so hard to find. If only her father's health held, her life was reasonably full with plenty to occupy her mind and her publishers only too willing to discuss future projects for her writing.

Haworth parsonage now had its celebrated author and soon all kinds of curious and 'interested' people began to make their way to the little Yorkshire village to try to catch a glimpse of the famous but mysterious lady.

It is to this period that Charlotte's antipathy to the parsonage belongs. The parsonage was always her home, its memories and her anguish could never finally erase her sense of belonging, although she never fully recovered the unswerving loyalty to the house which she had known while her sisters were alive. Each time she returned from an excursion she again felt the loss of her closest companions as she was absorbed into the utter silence of the house that had changed so little but had seen so much suffering.

The years when she lived with her father, punctuated as they were by her various excursions and cheered by the frequent boxes of books and letters sent by her publisher, were also a time of trial. Patrick's health frequently failed and Charlotte, herself ever delicate and the victim of toothache, headaches, colds and fevers, was often too ill to do much writing.

In 1851 Keeper, Emily's dog, died and yet another parsonage landmark was passed. Charlotte was able to write to Ellen that she had in the recent years passed many 'black milestones'; the death of the dog which she had immortalised in *Shirley* must stand as one of these:

> . . . Poor old Keeper died last Monday morning; after being ill all night, he went gently to sleep. We laid his old faithful head in the garden. Flossy is dull and misses him. There was something very sad in losing the old dog; yet I am glad he met a natural fate; people kept hinting he ought to be put away, which neither papa nor I liked to think of . . .

Home was so different from the place of childhood. Even the moors made Charlotte melancholy as every flower and valley, stream and stone wall seemed to remind her of her former happiness in the wide landscape which had been her brother and sisters' playground.

From this time she took to describing Haworth half-facetiously as a place in the wilderness, as her warning to Mrs Gaskell shows:

> When you come to Haworth, you must do it in the spirit which might sustain you in case you were setting out on a brief trip to the backwoods of America, leaving behind you, husband, children and civilisation, you must come out to barbarism, loneliness, and liberty. The change will perhaps do you good, if not too prolonged.

Her details of how to get to Haworth, sent for Mr Taylor when he travelled from London to collect the completed manuscript of *Shirley*, provide an even fuller account of the vicissitudes that Charlotte's journeys to London implied:

> He will find Haworth a strange, uncivilised little place, such as I dare say he never saw before. It is twenty miles distant from Leeds; he will have to come by rail to Keighley (there are trains every two hours I believe). He must remember that at a station called Shipley the carriages are changed, otherwise they will take him on to Skipton or Colne, or I know not where. When he reaches Keighley, he will yet have four miles to travel; a conveyance may be hired at the Devonshire Arms – there is no coach or other regular communication.

In her own way, Charlotte became a fearless user of railways, braving the threat of what she called 'damage or smash in tunnels or cuttings' in those very early days of railway travel. One incident, while returning from a stay with Miss Wooler at Hornsea, is related with some humour.

> About half-way between Hull and Hornsea, a respectable-looking woman and her little girl were admitted into the coach. The child took her place opposite me: she had not sat long before, without any warning, or the slightest complaint of nausea, sickness seized her, and the contents of her little stomach, consisting apparently of a milk breakfast, were unceremoniously deposited in my lap! Of course, I alighted from the coach in a pretty mess, but succeeded in procuring water and a towel at the station, with which I managed to make my dress and cloak once more presentable.

The Zoological Society Gardens in Regents Park. Patrick Brontë owned the society's catalogue and had a lifelong interest in its work. Charlotte wrote at length to satisfy his interest after her visit to the Gardens on 4 June 1850. 'The Secretary of the Zoological Society also sent me an honorary ticket of admission to their gardens which I wish you could see. There are animals from all parts of the world inclosed in great cages in the open air amongst trees and shrubs . . . Eagles, ostriches, a pair of great condors from the Andes, strange ducks, and waterfowl which seem very happy and comfortable . . .'

Chapter 17

A Mr Nicholls from Ireland

As the news of Charlotte's authorship was first whispered and then gossiped all around the parish of St Michael and All Angels at Haworth, so her band of local followers and admirers grew. Martha, the younger of the parsonage servants, was overwhelmed to hear that her mistress had been writing 'clever' books with a lot of the people from the parish in them, and the Haworth branch of the Mechanics Institute found itself having to allocate copies of *Shirley* on a rota system with fines for overdue returns.

One of the most admiring of Charlotte's readers was her father's curate, Arthur Bell Nicholls, the competent, diligent, capable young clergyman whom Patrick had been able to trust with considerable responsibility. He it was who had conducted most of the services while Patrick was blind, and he also had been left to keep watch on Branwell while Patrick was in Manchester for the eye operation. The story is told that on reading *Shirley*, Nicholls became so amused by the portrayal of the curates who were, after all, modelled on him and his colleagues, that he laughed aloud and stamped the floor until his landlady, in alarm, rushed to see if he had been taken ill. One of the scorned breed of curates, people whom Charlotte customarily ignored, this graduate of Trinity College, Dublin, was to prove more than merely an admirer of Charlotte's literary achievements.

One day in December 1852, just prior to the publication of Charlotte's third novel, *Villette*, Mr Nicholls amazed her by proposing. He had admired her for a long time and now he knew that he loved her desperately but was too afraid to ask her father's permission for her hand. It was as well that he hesitated, for when Charlotte told her father what had happened, the seventy-five year old man became incensed: 'the veins on his temples started up like whipcord and his eyes became suddenly blood shot'. Charlotte was quick to assure her father that Mr Nicholls should have a 'distinct refusal' the very next day. At that point she had no feelings for the curate whatever, for the proposal had come out of the blue, and her fathers' extraordinary reaction was perhaps the first incentive for her to consider Mr Nicholl's plight seriously. Patrick

Brontë's hasty wrath, he labelled the proposal 'that obnoxious subject', made Charlotte's blood boil with the sense that Nicholls had been unjustly treated. Moreover, Patrick's assumption that no one should have the effrontery to think of her as a wife, touched a nerve. It was one thing for Charlotte to give *herself* the title 'old maid' as she frequently did in letters to her friends, but it was quite another thing to be told she *was* one by her father. Charlotte had thought long and hard about marriage, she had previously had three other proposals, which she had declined, and her apparent acceptance of her spinsterhood did not imply that the loneliness it offered was altogether to her liking. In *Shirley* she had devoted an entire chapter to a compassionate study of two kinds of spinster, which suggests, along with the many references in her letters, that it was a matter that concerned her more than a little.

Patrick Brontë's reaction to Nicholls, while violent and extreme, is perhaps partly understandable. Charlotte was thirty-six, her constitution not strong and there was a real possibility that any pregnancy could prove difficult if not fatal. Such things must have troubled Patrick. With his wife and five of his children buried, he understandably feared for himself in his old age. Pathetically, on this score, he was proved right. But he must have taken other matters into account as well. Charlotte was a celebrated author with an income from her books, the £1500 she obtained for her three novels was seven times his own income, and fifteen times that of Arthur Nicholls. With a law that made all a woman's property her husband's at marriage, there was reason to pause again. Patrick suggested to Charlotte that she would be marrying beneath her status in marrying Nicholls, that the curate's lack of money was a prohibition and any marriage a degradation. To him the matter was settled. It was an impertinence for the man to dare to think of such a thing.

In the maelstrom loosed about her head, Charlotte puzzled over a problem fit for any of her novels. She had her own objections to accepting Nicholls which were the straightforward ones; that, for example, she did not love the man, that she found 'an uncongeniality in feelings, tastes, principles'. In short she found, as she had always done before, Arthur Nicholls rather a bore. That is, until he had declared his love and been so harshly treated for displaying that passion which was the very stuff of her writing and success. Here with all its problems and difficulties was a real 'love story' where no presiding artist was able to dictate the outcome and manipulate responses.

The whole matter of the curate's love for the parson's daughter was played out against a background of parish gossip. The resolute Patrick refused to see Nicholls and dealt with him by letter and with contempt. Nicholls pined, pale and unconsolable, refusing the meals offered him by his landlady in his lodgings with the Brown family at the bottom of the parsonage lane. Martha, his land-lady's daughter, the younger servant at the parsonage, would be able to traffic in all the news about the grand business in hand, while the parish watched.

Patrick was not alone in finding Nicholls impudent. John Brown, Branwell's old friend, said he would like to shoot Nicholls and the matter clearly raised hot passions on all sides. Nicholls in turn offered his resignation, he could not accept his parson's terms—never to mention the obnoxious matter to him or his daughter ever again. Charlotte was sorry for him. 'Without loving him—I don't like to think of him suffering in solitude.'

Charlotte knew the anguish of solitude. The seclusion which suited her father in his study at seventy-five, pre-sented a different prospect to a woman of thirty-eight. In her loneliness, 'necessarily silent', in the dining room of an evening, she must have thought of the curate, two years younger than she, in his pale solitude at the bottom of the lane. It was the man's grief and suffering, which Charlotte recognised only too well, that moved her first to think of Nicholls as a man who loved, rather than as a curate who should be about his church business.

In the midst of the confusion life went on. Charlotte went to London for the launching of *Villette* and Mrs Gaskell came to stay at the parsonage for a while. During Charlotte's absence Nicholls offered himself as a mission-ary in Australia, a romantic gesture which was doomed by one means or another to failure. But the application served to do one thing; the clergy that Nicholls quoted as referees were quick to elaborate his good qualities. Patrick's own reference was a generous one and clearly no one doubted the young man's ability and integrity.

By April Nicholls decided against going to Australia and courteously withdrew his application to be a missionary. As his time at Haworth drew to an end, the silence between parson and curate continued. Two scenes have been passed down, through Charlotte's letters, which show the state of the young clergyman as he contemplated leaving Miss Brontë. The one took place at a celebration of Holy Communion on Whit Sunday, 15 May, when he was conducting the service with Charlotte in the congregation:

> . . . He struggled, faltered, then lost command over himself, stood before my eyes and in the sight of all the communicants, white, shaking, voiceless. Papa was not there, thank God!

Joseph Redman spoke some words to him—he made a great effort, but could only with difficulty whisper and falter through the service. I suppose he thought this would be the last time; he goes either this week or the next . . . what had hap-pened was reported to papa either by Joseph Redman or John Brown; it excited only anger, and such expressions as 'unmanly driveller'. Compassion or relenting is no more to be looked for from Papa than sap from firewood . . .

The other describes his leavetaking. On returning the deeds of the National School to Patrick, Nicholls had hoped to see Charlotte. She had avoided him only to find him sobbing at the garden gate in a 'paroxysm of anguish'. She had to comfort him, hoping that he realised that she was not blind to his suffering. Nicholls left for the south of England but soon returned to Yorkshire to be curate of Kirksmeaton near Pontefract.

Following Nicholl's removal from Haworth things turned in his favour. The curate who replaced him was by no means as efficient or reliable, and Patrick Brontë came to realise this. Meanwhile Charlotte, perhaps for the only time in her life, knowingly deceived her father. Nicholls wrote to her, she concealed his letters and eventually not only answered them, but agreed to meet Nicholl's secretly when he came to stay with the Grant's at Oxenhope, the next village from Haworth. Nicholl's fidelity, persistence

Rev. Arthur Bell Nicholls, a photograph believed to have been taken on his wedding journey. He and Charlotte were married at Haworth on 29 June 1854.

and ability to write a persuasive letter must account for the lengths to which Miss Brontë was prepared to go. She gave Nicholls to believe that he could continue in hope, as she set about the gradual process of coaxing her father into some reversal of his former opinion. Choosing her moment, when the new curate had been particularly inept, she petitioned her father that she might write to and even see Nicholls. She won the day. After a harsh winter all seemed to be more promising. In April 1854 'Papa's consent is gained', the courtship by correspondence, a very shrewd move on Nicholl's part, had succeeded.

For the first time in her life Charlotte had offered her affection to someone who returned it in full measure. Unlike Heger, whose coolness towards her and final refusal to answer her sad pleading letters at all had caused her so much pain, Nicholls responded warmly to her slightest offers of love. He responded to her need for comfort and offered her a loving companionship in the midst of her stark solitude. When she had once 'loved unloved' she now found herself able both to offer and receive affection. Nicholl's patient persistence and his utter devotion to her, carried in his letters, did much to clear his path. With Charlotte's affection and esteem he could count on her strength as an ally in winning Patrick Brontë over to his point of view. It is small wonder that Patrick's anger gradually cooled until he finally agreed to reinstate Nicholls as curate of Haworth.

With Patrick's capitulation, arrangements went speedily ahead; Nicholl's readily agreed that once married they should live in the parsonage, and Charlotte would be able to continue to look after her father, whose health was precarious and who, at one stage, had threatened to move into lodgings if she married.

> What seemed at one time impossible is now arranged, and papa begins really to take a pleasure in the prospect.

By mid-April Charlotte was able to write to Ellen Nussey and Mrs Gaskell, telling them that her early dislike for Nicholls had grown through a respect and sympathy to a real affection and that she now found herself 'what people called engaged'. Mrs Gaskell was delighted and she seemed able to understand the love Charlotte was offered and the attraction of the 'engagement';

> He sounds vehemently in love with her. And I like his having known her dead sisters and dead brother and all she has gone through of home trials, and not being a person who has just fancied himself in love with her because he was dazzled by her genius. Mr N. never knew until long after *Shirley* was published that she wrote books.

There were many aspects of the proposed marriage that would please Charlotte. It appeared, after all, that there was a reprieve from her solitude. She had cried out that it was not that she was single that grieved her but that she was so lonely after the deaths of Branwell, Emily and Anne. She had also believed that Haworth would never again hold any comfort for her, while knowing that she could never leave it for any alternative. The life of a successful, fêted author, which she had tasted, meant little to her now, and nothing compared with her former happiness. Haworth, the parsonage itself, was where her roots lay. She knew, at thirty-eight, that she could never establish herself anywhere else and that no other life and no other place could provide the peace of mind she needed. Arthur Nicholls offered her a chance for continuation, a life that was a coherent part of all that she had endured and enjoyed before the agony of the last years. With him it would be possible to live in Haworth with the memories of the people that meant so much; with him it could be possible to think of a future. Her life could be held in a piece; her commitment to her home, her father and her brother and sisters could be preserved within the embrace of the unexpected but most welcome comfort which Arthur's companionship might bring.

Almost unbelieving, Charlotte was purposefully cool in telling of her happiness; she had too much at stake. Ever before the opening of her heart, the giving of herself, had led to bitter agonies. It is to her great credit that she was still prepared to offer herself and her love in a world that had dealt her so many cruel blows. She allowed herself no ecstatic joys but soberly looked to happiness, if all should go well. Cautiously, she wrote of her *respect* for Arthur, and that what she tasted of happiness was of the soberest order. 'I begin to hope all will end for the best. My expectations however are very subdued.'

Charlotte married Arthur Nicholls on Thursday, 29 June 1854, quietly and without many guests. Her father refused to attend the church service, remaining in the house, but was at the wedding breakfast. No one knows why he balked at the ceremony though Charlotte records that he seemed to have a superstition of the wedding service and had been avoiding taking a wedding for some time. Miss Wooler, her former teacher, friend and colleague gave her away, with Ellen Nussey and herself signing as witnesses. The honeymoon was spent visiting Nicholls home, Cuba House, at Banagher in Ireland where Charlotte found to her surprise, that she had married into a family of new relations whom she liked beyond expectation. The Nicholls family had all gathered in her honour and she found them delightful, she told Ellen:

> My dear husband, appears in a new light here in his own country. More than once I have had deep pleasure in hearing his praises on all sides. Some of the old servants and followers of the family tell me I am a most fortunate person for I have got one of the best gentlemen in the country. His aunt too speaks of him with a mixture of affection and respect.

If she had hung back in declaring her love for Arthur, hoping to grow to love him, she now seemed to realise her good fortune and hoped that she could repay 'the affectionate devotion of a truthful, honourable, unboastful man'. The more she knew Arthur the more she came to love him. He in turn was careful to be considerate and attentive:

> 27 July 1854
> My husband is not a poet or a poetical man – and one of my grand doubts before marriage was about 'congenial tastes and so on'. The first

morning we went out on the cliffs and saw the Atlantic coming in all white foam, I did not know whether I should get leave or time to take the matter in my own way. I did not want to talk – but I *did* want to look and be silent. Having hinted a petition, licence was not refused – covered with a rug to keep off the spray I was allowed to sit where I chose – and he only interrupted me when he thought I crept too near the edge of the cliff. So far he is always good in this way – and this protection which does not interfere or pretend is I believe a thousand times better than any half sort of pseudo-sympathy. I will try with God's help to be as indulgent to him wherever indulgence is needed.

The thirty-eight-year-old woman, who like her mother forty-two years earlier had ever been used to·being her own mistress, found herself more blessed in her husband than she could ever have imagined. Charlotte's happiness for a while looked secure. Her marriage seemed successful beyond expectation and her new novel, *Villette*, was repeating the success of *Jane Eyre*. Once back in Haworth the trio were quickly established, with Arthur in his own study, the former peat store at the back of the house, and Papa clearly benefiting from the reappointment of one of his best curates.

In August Charlotte could write hopefully to Miss Wooler:

... My dear father was not well when we returned from Ireland – I am, however, most thankful to say that he is better now – May God preserve him to us yet for some years! The wish for his continued life – together with a certain solicitude for his happiness and health seems – I scarcely know why – stronger in me now than before I was married. So far the understanding between Papa and Mr Nicholls seems excellent – if it only continues thus I shall be truly grateful. Papa has taken no duty since we returned – and each time I see Mr Nicholls put on gown or surplice – I feel comforted to think that this marriage has secured Papa good aid in his old age ...

But tragically, as was so often the case in the story of Charlotte's life, the new found happiness was to be brief. Charlotte, as her father feared, became pregnant, and a chill which she caught after walking on the moors in a rainstorm compounded complications of the pregnancy which made her seriously ill. From the November after her marriage in June she steadily grew weaker. Nursed with great devotion by her husband and Martha she faded. By the following February her condition was grave.

Will you be so kind as to write to Miss Wooler, and Mrs Joe Taylor, and inform them that we requested you to do so, telling them of our present condition?

Ever truly and respectfully yours, P. Brontë

She died in the early hours of the next day, Saturday, 31 March 1855. On hearing her husband praying at her bedside she roused herself to say: 'Oh, I am not going to die, am I? He will not separate us, we have been so happy.'

The cause of her death was recorded as phthisis, a wasting or consumption of the tissue. Thus Charlotte died, Currer Bell and t'parsons Charlotte, Mrs Nicholls, all were laid to rest with the other members of Patrick Brontë's family.

The old man stood alone above the vault where all he loved were now laid. He had outlived them all, and carried the greatest burden of grief.

A faintly pencilled letter of Charlotte's is eloquent witness to the comfort that her husband had been to her, from her sick bed she told Ellen Nussey that she was sure 'No kinder, better husband than mine, it seems to me, there can be in the world.'

At last she had found 'the best earthly comfort' that she ever imagined. Characteristically, it was Patrick Brontë who most fully summed up the disappointment and grief that had concluded Charlotte's brief happiness. Writing to Mrs Gaskell, he confirmed the rumour, which she had heard, that Charlotte had died:

Haworth, near Keighley
April 5 1855

My dear Madam,

I thank you for your kind sympathy. My daughter is indeed dead and the solemn truth presses upon her worthy and affectionate husband and me, with great, it may be with unusual weight. But others also have or shall have their sorrows, and we feel our own the most. The marriage that took place, seem'd to hold forth long and bright prospects of happiness, but in the inscrutable providence of God, all our hopes have ended in disappointment and our joy in the mourning. May we resign to the Will of the Most High. After three months of sickness,

as tranquil death closed the scene. But our loss we trust is her gain.

But why should I trouble you longer with our sorrows? 'The heart knoweth its own bitterness—and we ought to bear with fortitude our own grievances and not to bring others into our sufferings . . .'

Nausea overwhelmed her and her delicate constitution collapsed. Notes to her friends, written in pencil, give a harrowing picture of her condition:

Let me speak the plain truth—my sufferings are very great—my nights indescribable—sickness with scarce a reprieve—I strain until what I vomit is mixed with blood . . . As to my husband—my heart is knit to him—he is so tender, so good, helpful, patient . . .

While Charlotte was suffering, Tabitha, her old nurse, and the faithful servant of the house for over thirty years, died. Once again it looked as if death had the parsonage in its grip. Patrick Brontë contained his grief with great self control, writing in March when all hope of a recovery had gone and he realised Charlotte was going to die, he yet wrote with dignity:

Haworth, Nr. Keighley, March 30th 1855.
To Miss Nussey.
Bookroyd, Birstall, Nr. Leeds.
My Dear Madam,
We are all in great trouble, and Mr Nicholls so much so, that he is not so sufficiently strong and composed as to be able to write. I therefore devote a few moments to tell you that my dear Daughter is very ill, and apparently on the verge of the grave. If she could speak, she would no doubt dictate to us while answering your kind letter, but we are left to ourselves to give what answer we can. The Doctors have no hope of her case, and fondly as we, a long time, cherished hope, that hope is now gone, and we have only to look forward to the solemn event, with prayer to God that He will give us grace and strength sufficient unto our day.

Charlotte's funeral card.

In Memory of

CHARLOTTE NICHOLLS,

WHO DIED MARCH XXXI, MDCCCLV,

Aged 38 Years.

Chapter 18

'This is a sorrowful world'

Arthur Nicholls stayed with Patrick Brontë, caring for him in his old age until he died aged eighty-five on 7 June 1861. The lonely clergymen came to have a mutual respect for each other and in time Patrick came to regard Nicholls as his 'beloved' son-in-law.

The two men, living with their unequal memories of Charlotte, soon came to realise that the woman they both cherished and had buried was becoming the subject of a legend. Before long they found themselves having to contend with more and more visitors who made their way to the small town perched on the edge of the moors. Patrick wrote to Mrs Gaskell:

> From different parts of this variegated world, we have, in this place, daily many strangers who from various motives pay a visit to the Church and neighbourhood, and would, if we let them, pay a gossiping visit to us, in our proper persons.

Together with the many strangers went as many different versions of the story of Charlotte's life, until it became clear that public curiosity was weaving legends and its own tales about the whole family. Led by Ellen Nussey, friends prevailed upon Patrick to put a stop to all the conjecture by letting someone write an authoritative account of Charlotte's life. In due course he agreed and Mrs Gaskell, a person he believed to be quite close to Charlotte, was commissioned to undertake the writing.

After extensive research Mrs Gaskell produced her *Life of Charlotte Brontë* which is a masterpiece of biography. First published in 1857, the success of this book combined with that of the Brontës' own works ensured that the flow of visitors increased steadily. Having buried *their* Charlotte, Patrick Brontë and Arthur Nicholls now realised that she belonged to history. Their personal sorrow was reflected in the world's sadness; as their memories faded, so Haworth became increasingly a place of pilgrimage.

At Patrick's death Nicholls sold up the parsonage and returned to Ireland. By 1862 the Brontës were all gone from the house and the village that had known them for over forty years.

Of them all, Patrick must remain the most enigmatic figure. Setting off from Ireland years before, he had made his way and conducted his ministry in the church. Blow after blow had fallen on his shoulders and his faith had been sorely tried. Throughout it all, through the loss of his wife and the deaths of all his children he still retained vast resources of compassion.

As the parson, he was asked to write to a woman of the village who was away when her two year old daughter Jane died of scarlet fever. This he did in the following way:

> Eliza,
> This is a sorrowful world, and I write to you on a sorrowful subject. You have already been inform'd that little Jane was in the scarlet fever; after some time it was hoped she was recovering and that the danger was past. However, she rather suddenly got worse, and yesterday, and

Patrick's spectacles, like so many other of the Brontë effects highly prized souvenirs, regardless of Mrs Oliphant's protest that 'one line of their writing is worth a whole heap of their cast-off clothing'.

this morning, things took an unfavourable turn, and, she got worse and worse till at last she seem'd to sleep away, till she closed her eyes, on time, and opened them in eternity, I doubt not in an eternity of glory and bliss. Thus she had made an exchange infinitely for the better. This will, as it ought to do, give you trouble for a time, but on reflection, after a while, under all the circumstances of the case, you will perceive that for her, for you and many others, it is a merciful dispensation, and that the best use you can make of it is for yourself to live the remainder of your days a holy life, to be wise and good, avoiding temptation to evil, so that you may be prepared for death, come, where, how, and when it will.

Everything has been done for little Jane that could be done. She has been duly attended to by Mr Ingham, Betty Lambert, and your kind mother and Tabitha; Martha also has sometimes seen her so that there is nothing to regret, left behind. You will of course come home as soon as you conveniently can.

Yours truly
P. Brontë

That was written in 1859. Charlotte, the last of his children, had been dead for four years; he was eighty-two years old, and alone. But he was still sensitive to the suffering of others and the letter is a fitting tribute to his dignity and the humanity which he brought to his position as a parson, and showed throughout his life as a husband and father.

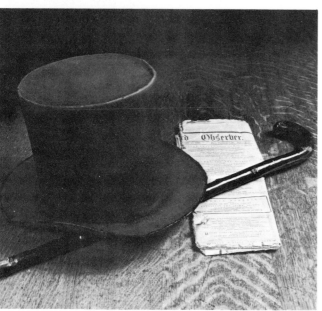

Above: A letter written to a mother telling her of the death of her child, typical of the many responsibilities that a nineteenth-century clergyman of Patrick's kind would shoulder. The remarkable thing is the poise and composure of a father who had lost his wife and six children. The letter is compassionate, kindly and sorrowful, hardly that of a harsh Victorian recluse. Patrick was eighty-two and almost blind when he wrote this letter.

Left: Patrick Brontë's top hat and stick, and the newspaper of the day that he died.

Top and above: A photograph purporting to be of Haworth old church at the time of the Brontës. In fact the picture is faked, to depict the tower as it was in Patrick's time. The smaller picture shows the original photograph, taken after Patrick's death, when Wade had planted trees in the churchyard and raised the tower by a further storey to install a clock. Such 'arrangement' of detail pervades almost every aspect of Brontëana, making the search for fact a complex and difficult task.

Above: The Rev. Wade, who succeeded Patrick and so deplored the literary pilgrims that troubled his housekeeper that he earnt himself the name The Envious Wade. He it was who demolished the old church, seen by many to be an act of vandalism, and enlarged the parsonage, refusing to live in a 'pigsty'.

Acknowledgments

The illustrations supplied by the Brontë Parsonage Museum are reproduced by permission of the Brontë Society; that on p. 52 top by courtesy of the Master and Fellows of St John's College, Cambridge; on p. 89 top by courtesy of Keighley Public Library; on p. 132 by permission of Sir Nevil Macready; on p. 15 and 85 by permission of *Punch*.

Sources of Colour Illustrations:
Barnaby's Picture Library, London, 53;
Brontë Parsonage Museum, Haworth, 49 bottom, 52 bottom, 55, 57 top, 57 bottom, 60 left, 60 right, 61, 64 top, 97 top, 97 bottom right, 104 bottom, 105;
J. Allan Cash, London, 64 bottom;
Davidson, W. F., front cover;
Hamlyn Group Picture Library – John Webb, 104 top;
National Gallery of Canada, Ottawa, 49 top;
National Portrait Gallery, London, 100, 101, 109, 112;
Walter Scott Ltd, Bradford 108.

Sources of Black and White illustrations:
Aerofilms Ltd., 31;
British Museum, London, 69, 95, 113, 117;
Brontë Parsonage Museum, Haworth 7, 8 bottom, 9 left, 9 right, 10, 11 top, 11 bottom, 12, 13 top, 16, 20, 11, 22, 25, 27, 28, 29, 32, 36, 37, 40, 41, 42, 43, 44, 48, 55, 58 top, 58 bottom, 59 top, 59 bottom, 62, 63, 70, 71, 73, 74, 75 top, 79 top, 79 bottom, 80, 84 top left, 84 top right, 84 bottom, 87, 89 bottom, 92 top, 96, 98, 99, 102 top, 106, 107, 111, 115 bottom, 116, 120, 125 top, 125 bottom, 126, 127 top, 129 bottom, 135, 138, 139 bottom, 140 top, 140 bottom, 141 bottom right;
Davidson, W. F., title page;
Fogg Art Museum, Cambridge, Massachussetts, 47 top;
Ronald Grant, Clare, Suffolk, 45;
Guildhall Library, London, 82, 118;
Hamlyn Group Picture Library, 30, 46 centre, 47 centre, 47 bottom, 77, 94, 115 top, 137 – John Webb, 33 top, 33 bottom, 50, 81 – Eric de Maré, 76 top;
N. K. Howarth, Keighley, 102 bottom;
Leeds City Art Galleries, 68;
Leeds City Libraries, Boyne Collection, 24, 51 bottom;
London Museum, 131;
Mansell Collection, London, 8 top, 13 bottom, 14, 18, 19, 51 top, 91 bottom, 122;
National Monuments Record, London, 35;
National Portrait Gallery, London 67 left, 67 right, 75 bottom, 83;
René Péchère, Brussels, 92 bottom, 93;
Radio Times Hulton Picture Library, London, 76 bottom, 91 top, 119, 121, 133;
Royal Academy, London, 78;
Royal Shakespeare Theatre Picture Gallery, Stratford-upon-Avon, 132;
Scarborough Art Gallery, 127 bottom;
Walter Scott, Bradford, 128 top, 141 top;
G. Bernard Wood, Bradford-on-Avon, 88, 103;
York Minster Library, 34, 139 top;
Yorkshire Post, 72.

Index